Going Away to Think

Going Away to Think

ENGAGEMENT, RETREAT, AND
ECOCRITICAL RESPONSIBILITY

Scott Slovic

UNIVERSITY OF NEVADA PRESS
RENO & LAS VEGAS

University of Nevada Press, Reno, Nevada 89557 USA
Copyright © 2008 by University of Nevada Press
All rights reserved
Manufactured in the United States of America
Design by Kathleen Szawiola

Library of Congress Cataloging-in-Publication Data
Slovic, Scott, 1960–
Going away to think : engagement, retreat, and
ecocritical responsibility / Scott Slovic.
   p. cm.
Includes bibliographical references and index.
ISBN 978-0-87417-756-5 (pbk. : alk. paper)
1. American literature—History and criticism. ·
2. Ecocriticism. 3. Nature in literature. I. Title.
PS169.E25558 2008
810.9´36—dc22   2008014521

The paper used in this book is a recycled stock made
from 100 percent post-consumer waste materials,
and meets the requirements of American National
Standard for Information Sciences—Permanence of
Paper for Printed Library Materials, ANSI/NISO
Z39.48-1992 (R2002). Binding materials were
selected for strength and durability.

FIRST PRINTING
17 16 15 14 13 12 11 10 09 08
5 · 4 3 2 1

To Susie, to Jacinto—favorite travel companions

To the international community of ecocritics and
environmental writers—for inspiration, friendship, and
providing so many opportunities to "go away to think"

Contents

Contents

Preface

I suppose it's a cliché for those who resist the political status quo to recall these lines from William Butler Yeats's 1920 poem "The Second Coming": "The best lack all conviction, while the worst / Are full of passionate intensity." I find myself routinely fretting about Yeats's insight into human nature when I hear the headlines: Congress voicing disapproval and then voting to provide more money for war, the Environmental Protection Agency blocking a state's efforts to achieve higher emissions standards for automobiles, presidential candidates pandering to religious fundamentalists, suicide bombers blasting their way onto the front pages while tree-sitters mutely look down on college campuses. Could it be true that corruption is everywhere? That those who seek something other than money or power are meek and silent, conciliatory? The essays that follow emerge from the belief that people should put their hearts and minds on the line. Academics and artists spend a lot of time on the high road, turning clever phrases and crafting soothing images. Meanwhile Yeats's monstrous hybrid beast—think Halliburton, think Coca-Cola—lurches toward global domination.

But what form should the "passionate intensity" of resistance take? From the vivid obliqueness of Barry Lopez's short stories in *Resistance* to the wry humor of Michael Moore's documentaries, our generation knows staunch examples of political disapproval. Writers and public speakers sometimes adopt quieter strategies as well: literary essays, academic lectures, correspondence with faceless corporations (and corporate representatives who decline to use full names). What follows are the efforts of a scholar and teacher to come to terms with—and at times to *confront*—the state of the world.

Several of the following pieces have appeared in other collections or in literary journals, some were presented as lectures in academic or public forums, and others have never been printed or spoken. I am grateful to various editors and publishers (see acknowledgments at the end of the book) for permission to reuse this material here. The work that has appeared elsewhere takes on a new and different meaning, I feel, by being placed together in a single volume, showing the wide range of interests and concerns of a single scholar. Critics and artists don't typically wish to be described as narrow minded and predictable, as "Johnny one-notes," an epithet harshly applied by some readers to John Muir, the icon of American environmental writing and activism. At the same time, it seems inevitable that there will emerge certain patterns, certain motifs, in any thinker's work—and such patterns are points of coherence and order, pathways of mindfulness. To be honest, I sometimes feel when I undertake a new project as if there's something random and erratic about the multiple directions of my work, since much of what I do happens at the request of groups that have asked me to speak or publications offering an assignment on one topic or another. But it's become clear over the years that these invitations have tended to come because I'm known to have certain kinds of interests. When grouped together in a collection like this one, particular patterns—such as the alternation or convergence of social engagement and retreat and the unending quest to ascertain the responsibilities of an ecocritic—rather forcefully emerge.

The book begins and ends with two narratives of retreat—"Going Away to Think, and "Out of Time"—and "Even Better than the Real Thing" acts as a de facto postscript. As a full-time university teacher, I seize opportunities for research and reflection whenever I can. Often this occurs during brief breaks between or during semesters. The essential bookends of this collection are essays written during consecutive spring breaks in 2004 and 2005. In 2004 the opportunity to participate in an Earthwatch research program on mangrove ecology in La Manzanilla, Mexico, became the title essay of this collection. Another opportunity to "go away and think" arose in 2005, when I served as the third writer-in-residence to spend a week walking and watching in the damp forests on the western slope of the Oregon Cascades, near the town of Blue River. Thanks to the vision of Charles Goodrich, Kathleen Dean Moore, Fred Swanson, and others associated with the National Science Foundation's Long-term Ecological Research Project at the H. J. Andrews Experimental Forest and Oregon State University's Spring Creek Project, it is now possible for occasional writers to add our "experiential data" to the technical data on tree decomposition and other forest processes that have been accumulating since the research station was established half a century ago. I wrote the eleven brief essays that constitute "Out of Time" during my solitary week at the Andrews— a week during which I tried to suspend myself from clock-time.

I am, in truth, a rather quiet and nonconfrontational person, hardly a firebrand. And yet for some reason, I find myself called upon to issue perspectives on some of the most conflagrational issues of our time—impending wars, ecological crises, and scientific gambles. In March 2003, just as U.S. forces were poised to invade Iraq, I spoke at a gathering in the Reno City Council chambers. Amid the flag-waving and army-bashing offered by other speakers, I felt it important to speak out in favor of *dialogue* itself, of bringing together citizens of divergent perspectives, especially in an era of intimidation and increasingly restricted freedoms in the name of "homeland security." A year later, asked by a local peace group to address a vigil on the subject of violence in the Middle East, I tried, from a Jewish American perspective, to express my empathy with and frustration toward both participants in the Palestinian *intifada* and citizens of Israel grappling with an ongoing series of suicide bombings, calling for an end to intransigence on both sides.

Sometimes "intransigence" occurs even when fellow activists and intellectuals gather together, and an example of that is the January 2000 symposium in Mexico City, where journalist Bill McKibben and I were drafted by Homero and Betty Aridjis to compose a "manifesto" on behalf of the two dozen scientists and writers who'd come from around the world to discuss our thoughts about the state of the global environment at the turn of the new millennium. Despite the consensus that we were facing an assortment of environmental and social crises at that moment in history, we could not agree on our priorities among these crises, and thus the effort to speak with a unified voice failed. The document included in this collection, however, offers an example of how Bill McKibben and I felt about the perspectives offered during what may well have been the first environmental conference of the current millennium. Because of the relevance of this manifesto to the environmental motifs of this collection, I have decided to include it here, along with my contextualizing remarks about the difficulty of achieving unanimity even among like-minded scholars and writers.

Teachers and literary critics quickly become accustomed to "preaching to the choir," lecturing to fellow devotees of beautiful writing and often to people who share our politics, more or less. In January 2005 I was asked for the first time to address an actual choir (as well as a congregation) at the Unitarian Universalist Fellowship of Northern Nevada, reading a "sermon" on "The Story of Climate Change." This spiritual community had just decided to devote the next two years to learning about and responding to "global warming" as an important social issue, and my task was to explain, in a fifteen-minute talk, some of the ways in which *language* was an important dimension of this issue. I've included in this book an enlarged version of the sermon, sketching out some of the basic facets of this topic.

When I was on sabbatical in Australia in 2002, Great Basin National Park ranger Roberta Moore contacted me about contributing to *Wild Nevada*, a collection of testimonial statements on Nevada wilderness in the tradition of Stephen Trimble and Terry Tempest Williams's *Testimony* (1995) on behalf of wilderness in southern Utah and Hank Lentfer and Carolyn Servid's *Arctic Refuge: A Circle of Testimony* (2001) in defense of the Arctic National Wildlife Refuge. Although Nevada is a land of ample "big wilderness," it is also, ironically, a state in which most people live in thoroughly urban settings—and what nourishes many urban Nevadans is the proximity of (and for the time being, *access to*) undeveloped desert and mountain areas. My essay on "Gated Mountains" for *Wild Nevada* was an opportunity to express concern about urban sprawl and the shutting off of trail access in the contemporary West and the "gating" of Yucca Mountain in southern Nevada as an ill-advised solution to the nation's nuclear-waste dilemma. Since the book's appearance in 2005, many local people—

ranging from college students to officials from the Truckee Meadows Regional Planning Agency—have contacted me to say that this piece gives voice to their own worries about the future of our community.

Another unexpected opportunity to speak out arose when I was asked in May 2005 by *Orion* magazine to respond with a short essay—in about a week—to recent publicity about stem-cell research at the University of Nevada, Reno, my home institution, and particularly to the phenomenon of bioengineered "chimeras," mixed-species organisms. Here at UNR, researchers are currently implanting human cells into sheep in the hope of growing organs that can later be transplanted into humans. With this issue, my respect for science and my uneasiness with seed patenting and the murky health effects of GM products collided; rather than voicing a single-minded perspective on this topic, I tried to speak a word for *ambivalence*. I also tried to imagine how public qualms about the chimeric mixing of species represented a curious extension of longtime uncertainties about ethnic mixing, a subject frequently treated in literature and film. Often, in complex social or environmental contexts, ambivalence—rather than foolish, narrow-minded, unwavering certainty—is the responsible perspective. The relatively nondogmatic nature of literary expression, and critical analysis, lends itself to the forceful articulation of uncertainty.

"Even Better than the Real Thing" is a small example of "practice what you preach." As I explain in the essay itself, during a lecture and research trip to India in 2006, I encountered activists working to halt the destructive privatization of water resources in that country and in developing nations throughout the world, and I came home to the United States determined to do whatever I could to help publicize this issue. I began by writing a letter to the CEO of Coca-Cola, and I've included my brief and inconclusive correspondence with that giant company in this essay. I also try to include mention of the water privatization practices of Coca-Cola, PepsiCo, and other multinational soft-drink and bottled-water companies in many of the guest lectures I give around the world. A number of us who teach writing at the university level use letters to public or corporate officials as writing assignments for college students. In using whatever skills I have as a writer and public speaker to help address what

I consider to be an important social and environmental issue, I'm trying to demonstrate the socially engaged use of language that I hope to encourage my students to practice.

It's not as though I conduct my life of travel and literary activism without good examples for such work. I've often stated that my greatest examples of literary style and social commitment are the writers whose work I teach and study, such as the dozen contemporary writers who've contributed to Milkweed Editions' Credo Series, which I have edited since 1999. Several of the essays here, like the Credo portraits, employ the technique of combining personal stories and broader philosophical and literary commentary that I began calling "narrative scholarship" in the 1994 essay "Ecocriticism: Storytelling, Values, Communication, Contact." In particular, such pieces as "'Be Prepared for the Worst': Love, Anticipated Loss, and Environmental Valuation" and "Oh, Lovely Slab: Robinson Jeffers, Stone Work, and the Locus of the Real" are experiments in this hybrid mode of communication.

Finally, I have included here several samples of my more broadly "theoretical" and informative essays about ecocriticism and environmental literature: the essay "Seeking the Language of Solid Ground: Reflections on Ecocriticism and Narrative," which further considers the importance of narrative language within ecocritical analysis; an essay on the rhetoric of protecting wild places with a particular focus on Montana writer Rick Bass; a lecture on the state of the field presented several months following the September 11, 2001, terrorist attacks and revised for inclusion in this book; an appreciation of the forceful ethical pronouncements in Randy Malamud's 2003 ecocritical study, *Poetic Animals and Animal Souls;* a preliminary consideration of how story and image, so essential in environmental literature, could help us respond to calls for a more powerful and effective kind of language in environmental law and policy; and an essay on the use of story to overcome the deadening effects of numerical discourse about environmental topics. "Ecocriticism: Storytelling, Values, Communication, Contact" lays out some of the strategic and ethical dimensions of ecocriticism in a way that may be helpful to newcomers to the field, trying to appreciate how the tensions between "engagement" and "retreat" may somehow explain the phenomenon I've called "ecocritical responsibility" in the book's title. The focus on authenticity and rhetorical efficacy in Rick Bass's energetic efforts to protect wilderness in Montana's Yaak Valley anticipates the discussion of environmental literature's perennial quest for "the real," which arises later in this collection in the context of Robinson Jeffers's writing about stone. I first lectured on "Ecocriticism on and After September 11" to an audience at Hiroshima University in Japan, where it was necessary not only to explain how American culture had changed (and not changed) in the wake of the attacks, but also to offer rather basic background about the motivations and concerns of ecocriticism—I've added some discussion of David Gessner's "The Punctured Pastoral" and Susan Hanson's "Homeland Security: Safe at Home in the World" to this essay. I tend to seize opportunities to grapple with new issues and force myself to read more widely, and this is how I came to write about Randy Malamud's impressive book on poetic treatments of animals.

In October 2003 I was pleased to be one of the few literary critics to join a group of environmental writers at the first Watermark Nature Writers' Muster several hours north of Sydney, Australia, on the wind-struck, sun-shimmering coast of New South Wales. I presented the talk "There's Something about Your Voice I Cannot Hear" in several brief installments at that gathering, trying to explain how ecocriticism might fit into the picture with environmental literature and public policy. I've lectured numerous times in the past decade—in Mexico, Finland, Australia, China, Malaysia, and throughout the United States—on the subject of "numbers and nerves," and my study of "a discourse of environmental sensitivity in a world of data" explains, in part, how innovative approaches to explaining vast, slow, uncertain environmental phenomena constitute a major contribution of so-called "environmental literature" to contemporary society.

Academics are reputed to stand in campus lecture halls, dryly explaining topics of timeless significance. "Relevance" is a dirty word, a trivializing inclination. But in ecocriticism and related fields relevance is the Holy Grail—an intensifier of meaning, a trigger of passion. The work presented in this volume comes from my conviction that ecocritical responsibility requires both social engagement and reflective retreat.

Going Away to Think

1 Savoring, Saving, and the Practice of Ecocritical Responsibility

Driving along the cracked and narrow highways of southern Mexico years ago, I saw a corporate slogan on a peeling billboard that has stuck with me ever since. "La vida tiene sabor" read the Coca-Cola sign. Life has flavor. Life has vigor and energy—life *is* vigor and energy. How strange, I thought, that we require slogans and billboards to remind us of what should be evident with every breath.

During that drive on the Mexican backroads and in the ensuing months, I realized that my own life as a writer, literary critic, and teacher is largely guided by the twin motivations of savoring life's intense moments and seeking to "save" communities, places, and other phenomena that seem to require spokespeople. On the one hand, it may appear foolishly hedonistic to concern oneself with the richness of experience—and foolishly trite to articulate this concern. On the other hand, it may well seem desperately naive to imagine that one might "save" anything in this world, even oneself. Yet life, human and nonhuman alike, consists of a constellation of urges and drives, some conscious and many not. We tend to do what "feels right," often not caring what others think about our actions. However, competing with this live-for-the-moment obliviousness, many of us also feel a compulsion to live in responsive, responsible ways—to "do the right thing." Where does this come from? Good breeding? Good reading? Perhaps this idea of living with a sense of urgent appropriateness is what Henry

David Thoreau means when he asserts in *Walden,* "Let us spend one day as deliberately as Nature" (97). Does nature ever do the wrong thing? Does nature ever look back and second guess itself?

As activist and author Rebecca Solnit states, "A game of checkers ends. The weather never does. That's why you can't save anything. Saving is the wrong word, one invoked over and over again, for almost every cause. . . . Saving suggests a laying up where neither moth nor rust doth corrupt; it imagines an extraction from the dangerous, unstable, ever-changing process called life on earth" (*Hope* 59). Despite the fact that the word "saving" has been inflated to imply permanence and absoluteness, suspension above the ephemeral and contingent nature of life on earth, it is very human to want to make a positive contribution to the world, whether for a moment or for a generation. Solnit's criticism of the word "save" has a lot to do with her sense of what it takes to motivate activists to take to the streets—and the woods and courtrooms—day after day. If you think you're supposed to achieve permanent victories and yet you recognize that you've only managed a series of modest, tenuous, short-lived successes, you could easily become demoralized. Species can be protected from year to year, but not removed entirely from the possibility of extinction. Air and water can be made cleaner through legislation and lifestyle changes, but never removed entirely from the threat of future degradation—never "saved" once and for all. Nonetheless, with the understanding that all "saves" are contingent and temporary, the urge to help and protect is a forceful one.

Today, I gaze through my study window at a trio of baby robins, alternately hidden in the depths of their straw nest and then flinging their open mouths skyward to receive pieces of life-giving nourishment from their mother and father—both parents flitting back and forth between the nest and the nearby lawn. There seems to be no calculation in this reach for food, for life, nothing more than an intrinsic urge. I associate this urge with the photocopy on my office door of a William Blake etching that shows a human child climbing a ladder from earth to moon, hands outstretched, exclaiming, "I want, I want."

■   ■   ■   "I want, I want." Not to feel any desire at all is to be classified as listless, catatonic, "clinically depressed." A good many people in our society fall into this category these days, while even more display a greedy excess of self-serving desire. We live in an age and in a society that seem hell-bent on "pleasure now," regardless of the implications of our wishes and behaviors for other people today, other organisms, other places, or our own children and grandchildren.

What I want myself is to find some way to balance the urge to *savor* and the urge to *save*, the impulse to enjoy life and the commitment to do some good in the world. Looking back on years of writing and lecturing in the field of ecological literary studies—or "ecocriticism"—it becomes clear to me that much of my own work wavers between these two poles of "responsibility" . . . the responsibility (shared by every living organism) to be fully present in *this life* and the responsibility (of a privileged, empowered human citizen) to be involved with the transgressions and the opportunities of my community. My writing demonstrates a vacillation between various forms of engagement and retreat, all in pursuit of "responsibility," in quest of meaningful *responses* to the world as I experience it and gather information about it.

There's nothing stunningly new about this quest—this is, in a sense, the quintessential pattern of artistic and scholarly life. I see models for my own processes of action and thought wherever I turn, but especially in such fields as environmental literature and literary criticism, where I've devoted my attention for more than two decades now. The notion of "ecocritical responsibility," as I've phrased it in my title, underlies virtually all of the work that happens under the rubric of "ecocriticism" or "environmental criticism." As Lawrence Buell puts it in *The Future of Environmental Criticism*:

Criticism worthy of the name arises from commitments deeper than professionalism. Environmental criticism, even when constrained by academic protocols, is usually energized by environmental concern. Often it is openly polemical. This is entirely understandable in the case of an issue widely recognized as grave, yet not so widely believed to require immediate action. (97)

And Michael P. Cohen even more explicitly invokes the rubric of "engagement" to describe the political aspect of ecocriticism, stating, "by definition, ecological literary criticism must be engaged. It wants to know but also wants to do. . . .

Ecocriticism needs to inform personal and political actions, in the same way that feminist criticism was able to do only a few decades ago" ("Blues" 27). The modern thinking person, daily confronted with new information about natural and social disasters, is confronted as well with incessant ethical decisions: how to consume goods and services, how to travel from home to the office, how to communicate concerns to public officials, how to allocate money to a dizzying array of worthy causes. To be a literary scholar operating with an acute awareness of social and environmental concerns means bearing the constant burden (and opportunity) of considering the gravity of the world's predicaments, while *acting* through the diffuse, delayed processes of teaching and writing, often for relatively small audiences of students and colleagues, most of whom are already in agreement. My graduate students these days are growing restless, sensing that this is feel-good scholarship—salve for the scholar's soul, and meanwhile the world is burning. And yet . . . without the salve and without the explanations, where will the frontline activists turn when they wonder why they're doing what they're doing? To each according to his or her needs, from each according to his or her abilities. My wife hands me the new issue of *Yoga International* to see an article on the latest biofuel research in India, and as I page through the magazine, my eyes catch a quotation by the writer E. B. White: "I arise in the morning torn between a desire to improve (or save) the world and a desire to enjoy (or savor) the world. This makes it hard to plan the day" (15). I say, "Plan to do both."

I recall what White wrote in "A Slight Sound at Evening," his meditation on the life and work of Henry David Thoreau a century after the initial publication of *Walden* in 1854:

Henry went forth to battle when he took to the woods, and *Walden* is the report of a man torn by two powerful and opposing drives—the desire to enjoy the world (and not be derailed by a mosquito wing) and the urge to set the world straight. One cannot join these two successfully, but sometimes, in rare cases, something good or even great results from the attempt of the tormented spirit to reconcile them. (*Essays* 238)

I can point to example after example of contemporary writers around the world—from Rick Bass to Arundhati Roy—who have evolved an urgent aesthetic from the sibling urges to enjoy the world and also to set it straight. What I'm trying to suggest in the following essays is the actual *complementarity* of these urges. Yes, there are only so many hours in a day, so many days in a life. But I believe that social commitment deepens the intensity of writers' joyful pauses—and reflective pauses deepen the value of writers' social interventions. Why must the two be "reconciled"? Why must the cycling between engagement and retreat result in "torment"? I would modify White's eloquent summary of the writer's dilemma by saying, for myself: I arise in the morning eager to savor and to save, hoping to draw upon each impulse in support of the other.

Especially when the world is burning, we need places to turn for solace and inspiration. Like many people, I often turn to books, such as Terry Tempest Williams's *An Unspoken Hunger* and Robert Hass's *Twentieth Century Pleasures,* both of which have long inspired me and have served, perhaps *obliquely,* as models for my work. In the title essay from *An Unspoken Hunger,* Williams writes:

We smother the avocado with salsa, hot chiles at noon in the desert. We look at each other and smile, eating avocados with sharp silver blades, risking the blood of our tongues repeatedly. (79)

Those lines imply the inextricability of appetite, community, and danger. The speaker and her companion enjoy a noontime meal of avocados and salsa, eaten from the blade of a knife, a smile offered between mouthfuls. What's risked is the blood of their *tongues,* their organs of articulation, of language. Throughout the eighteen brief essays in Williams's book, we encounter the alternation of passionate sensation and emotionally risky social committedness, ranging from the title piece to "A Patriot's Journal," a response to the 1991 Gulf War. My own essays in this book and elsewhere are also, without exception, derived from varying combinations of excitement and beauty and danger and fear. Sometimes these conditions are fully evident in the content of the narratives, such as a nighttime crocodile survey in the mangrove lagoon of La Manzanilla or a solitary hike among tilting Douglas fir "widowmakers" in Oregon's Andrews Experimental Forest. Other times the risk associated with my work—the thrill—is more cerebral, more subtle, as in the case of a speech about the invasion of Iraq by U.S. forces in 2003 (not collected here), delivered to a roomful of pro-war and anti-war activists in a hall ringed with uniformed policemen and police dogs. Life has flavor, and life has risk—the paradigm revealed in *An Unspoken Hunger,* the combination of pleasure and danger, operates delicately in the work I try to do as an ecocritic.

Former U.S. poet laureate Robert Hass's beautiful collection of critical essays, *Twentieth Century Pleasures,* also hovers in the back of my mind as I strive to engage myself with the world itself and with the world's troubling "issues," and as I strive to *disengage* myself, to *retreat,* in order to gain perspective on myself and my work. Hass concludes his essay "Listening and Making," devoted to the magic of poetic art, with a reflection on the horrific and exquisite extremes of human invention:

I have it in mind that, during the Vietnam War, one of the inventions of American technology was a small antipersonnel bomb that contained sharp fragments of plastic which, having torn through the flesh and lodged in the body, could not be found by an x-ray. Often I just think about the fact that some person created it. At other times I have thought about the fact that the bomb works on people just the way the rhythms of poetry do. And it seems to me then that there really are technes on the side of life and technes on the side of death. Durable and life-giving human inventions—tragedy, restaurants that stay open late at night, holding hands, the edible artichoke—were probably half discovered and half invented from the materials the world makes available, but I think that they were also the result of an active and attentive capacity for creation that humans have—and that a poetry that makes fresh and resilient forms extends the possibilities of being alive. (132–33)

Appreciating the human condition requires coming to terms, in Hass's words, with "technes on the side of life and technes on the side of death." Human inventions, or *technes,* are not in and of themselves intrinsically good or bad. We are an inventive, imaginative species—this is our nature. But we can *apply* our minds and our physical energy in sustaining or destructive ways. It has always seemed to me that most of what we call "ecocriticism," a branch of literary scholarship that was named in 1978 by critic William Rueckert and that became an energetic movement in the United States and internationally during the 1980s and '90s, tries to be "on the side of life." Both the scholarship and the poetry and prose it examines have sought, as Hass puts it, to make "fresh and resilient forms" in order to extend "the possibilities of being alive." Hass's essay collection weaves together personal images and stories with profiles of admired poets and theoretical commentary on the genre of poetry. Likewise, my goal in this book is to combine narratives of engagement and retreat; pronouncements on social issues ranging from urban sprawl in the American West to stem-cell research, to global commerce; commentaries on the work of major environmental writers and literary scholars; and more theoretical treatments of the connections between ecocriticism, environmental literature, and public policy and the use of narrative discourse in environmental writing as a way of overcoming the emotionally numbing effects of statistical data.

■ ■ ■   I mentioned above that my essay on biotech chimeras led me to contemplate the widely shared ambivalence toward the *mixing* of unalike things in my culture. For whatever reason, I have actually seldom felt this ambivalence in my own life, instead heartily appreciating every opportunity to interact with different kinds of people, learn new languages, see new landscapes, eat new foods. As an academic administrator (head for the better part of a decade of UNR's Center for Environmental Arts and Humanities), I delighted in organizing forums for interdisciplinary discussions of scholarly and practical topics, bringing together biologists and photographers, anthropologists and geographers. Much of my own research has resulted from collaborations with social scientists, natural scientists, journalists, and full-time creative writers. Assembling this collection, however, brings home the fact of my own *hybrid* nature—my love for narrative prose as well as analytical commentary about other writers' work, and my sense of how important it is for the life of the mind both to pull back and ask big questions and to charge in and grapple with pressing issues of the day.

Life has flavor, and life has risks. My sense of delight in experiencing new places and beautiful words should be amply clear in the following essays. The sense of risk may be less visible, but it's implicit in the process of writing (and speaking publicly) about various emotionally charged issues and even in writing detailed profiles of writers (the Credo portraits) for inclusion in the writers' own books, trying to strike an appropriate balance between appreciation and analytical discussion.

To those who regard literary scholarship as a delicate and useless enterprise for aesthetes and the socially disengaged, I hope to argue otherwise. Literature is a lens through which we're able to sharpen our understanding of the world's vital problems—and literary criticism the mechanism for articulating what we come to understand. The "literary critic" is not quarantined in the realm of textual analysis, restricted from striking out to take stands on public issues and tell stories about life. As the critic James S. Hans put it in *The Value(s) of Literature,* "literature does not exist in its own discrete space, so to limit our discussions of it to its 'literariness' is to denude it of its crucial links to the other systems that combine to articulate our sense of values" (5). Along these lines, nature writer and philosopher Kathleen Dean Moore recalls in *Riverwalking* her encounter as a beginning graduate student with a professor who admonished her: "There is one thing you will need to learn. And that is that philosophy is not about life. Philosophy is about ideas. Life and ideas are not the same." Years later, Moore wrote:

I never doubted him. Shame I felt in full measure. Stupidity. But never doubt. The possibility never entered my mind that a philosophy professor might be wrong about philosophy, or about life—or that I might have had the power to make a different set of definitions. (140–41)

My own view of life and language takes its "set of definitions" from the writers I read and admire—from Moore herself, from Barry Lopez, David Mas Masumoto, Simon J. Ortiz, and dozens like them. From their serious and entertaining immersion in both the abstract realm of ideas and politics and the visceral realm of experience. The following essays are an extended series of meditations on and demonstrations of engagement, retreat, and ecocritical responsibility, built upon the premise that life, language, and ideas inevitably intersect.

Biologist Edward O. Wilson used the term "biophilia" to describe the affinity for life he ascribes to all beings; Abraham Maslow cast this in a psychological context, writing about "peak experiences" as "both the sign and the goal of self-actualization" (Marshall, *Peak Experiences* 164); Henry David Thoreau "wanted to live deep and suck out all the marrow of life" (*Walden* 91). For me, all of these ideas, biophilia and peak experience and living deep, are subsumed within the twin impulses of life-savoring and life-saving. They are the compulsions this book displays and explores through stories of reading and travel.

When he addressed the large crowd at the opening plenary session of the June 2007 conference of the Association for the Study of Literature and Environment in Spartanburg, South Carolina, Bill McKibben placed strong emphasis on the emotions that propel him through his life of writing and activism: fear, guilt, sadness, and resolve. I suspect that many in the audience that evening nodded their heads, as I did, at this familiar catalog of moods. This essay collection, too, draws upon these very feelings in fluctuating combinations. When any of us "go away to think," when we climb into our cars or board an airplane, we're likely to be silencing the guilty inner voices reminding us about the implications of "burning dinosaurs" in order to move ourselves from place to place. But . . . but this guilt develops into resolve if, as McKibben argued in his lecture, we try to "make our travel count for something."

Whether we travel through the sky in planes or travel mentally through texts, I agree that we should seek to make our efforts *count,* make them mean something more than a tag of self-identifying graffiti: "I was here." When others encounter the stories of engagement and retreat in this book, I hope they'll be inspired to recommit themselves to the issues, places, people, and writings that matter most to *them.* I hope they'll seek to live up to their own visions of responsive and responsible citizenship.

2 | ## Going Away to Think

I find myself constantly impressed with how quickly the sensational world compresses itself into sameness and mundanity, how easily our species etches routine tedium into the structure of every day. Whatever it takes, I think to myself . . . whatever it takes to revivify experience, to bring my mind to life, may well be worth the cost.

Like many people in the world, academics and artists chief among them, I delight in the life of the mind. In my love-hate relationship with the office, I find myself often seduced by the lure of my book-filled lair, knowing deeply the spell that occurs when I enter Frandsen Humanities Room 038, hit the light switch, and then turn on the gleaming white dome of the eMac. It is quite possible to lose entire days staring into the screen of the machine, absorbed in words and ideas, translating life and life's intuitions into text. Even for a scholar fondly devoted to the world beyond the words, the temptation to perch in a semidarkened room staring for many hours at a computer is often overwhelming, seemingly unavoidable. And yet sometimes it seems not to be enough.

■ ■ ■   I write these words in March 2004, sitting on the porch of my rustic casita in La Manzanilla, Jalisco, Mexico, where I am participating in an Earthwatch program coordinated by my Ph.D. student Jerry Keir, director of the Great Basin Institute. Half a dozen volunteers and university students and a similar number of Guadalajara-based ecologists have come together for the week to discuss "Mexican Mangroves and Wildlife" and to conduct bird and crocodile censuses and studies. I squint into the sun as I write·these words, savoring the humid sea breeze. Families walk past on the beach, one hundred feet away. Dogs wrestle for control of flotsam and jetsam. I watch an elderly man bodysurf amid jellyfish and stingrays, oblivious of the painful presence of the creatures that have been washing ashore all day. The sun lowers beyond the tropical sea as afternoon passes into evening, and my squint tightens. The dazzling sun corresponds to my properly bedazzled mind. "You are not in Reno anymore," I tell myself.

In truth, even this extraordinary scene would become ordinary if I lived here all the time, as many do. In fact, Jerry Keir points out the fact that the tropics seem to induce such torpor among residents that he anticipates difficulty in accomplishing his conservation objectives. Neither the locals nor the ex-patriots can be roused easily to activism on behalf of mangrove swamps, threatened crocs, or endangered sea turtles.

But torpor has not yet addled me, reduced me to a condition of unawareness. My flight touched down in Manzanillo just twenty-four hours ago, and when I arrived here at the beachside camp, it was so dark that all remained mysterious until morning. I had no inkling of the glinting Tenacatita Bay, the palm-lined beaches, or the pelicans and terns diving for fish until dawn, when I left the thatched-roof hut and trotted to the surf for my morning run. For me, as an academic, this sort of experience—arriving in a new place at dusk and waking to an astonishing world of unfamiliar beauty—is one of the ultimate pleasures. The question is how does this contribute to "thought," to work? And are these merely the self-satisfied musings of a privileged traveler?

■ ■ ■   A large, black frigate bird, with its noticeably arced wings and V-shaped tail, flies overhead. There are many of these birds here, circling high above the fracas of the pelicans and gulls. Ornithologist Al Gubanich, who has accompanied me to this week's program, tells me that the frigate birds scavenge and steal to make their living, benefiting from the industry of other birds. I sometimes wonder if academics do much the same thing, hovering over the sweep of reality, allowing others to struggle through life, and then descending to pick up the pieces and offer hazy explanations. The frigate birds of the species.

Several months ago, while speaking at a gathering of nature writers in Australia, I found myself referring to literary critics as the "third wheel" of the literary world: those who provide context and commentary for "texts," while others experience the world directly and render that experience in rich and riveting words. I believe the contextualizing perspective of the scholar is important, and yet it doesn't quite seem enough. I love the telescoping process of engagement and retreat, conscious living and detached contemplation. The attractions of this rhythm—coming close, going away—may be what induce me to do both personal essays and formal, analytical "scholarly writing," sometimes combining the two in so-called "narrative scholarship." Perhaps this rhythm parallels the process of "going away to think" and then coming home to see the familiar anew.

My reflexive comparison of academics and frigate birds is only half sincere. I do think some kinds of academic work are exploitative and self-serving. But I also recognize the idealism and selflessness—the taste for beauty, elegance, and justice—that can drive intellectual work. I take to heart the title of historian Richard White's well-known essay, "Are You an Environmentalist or Do You Work for a Living?" (171). Sometimes I rephrase it in my mind: "Are You a Literary Critic or Do You Work for a Living, Do You Contribute Meaningfully to Society?" I do actually believe environmentalists—and literary critics—"work for a living." I suspect Richard White—despite his forceful complaint against self-righteousness, privilege, and arrogance—would agree. And yet I appreciate the warning not to become complacent and self-satisfied, oblivious of the toil and suffering of others, of different ways of knowing and expressing. When I see the elegant frigate birds floating free of the mob below, I find myself wondering how the flock of literary critics serves the rest of its species and, indeed, serves the planet. Travel can shake us free from accepted routine and enable us to use metaphor as a tool of self-examination and critique.

■ ■ ■ Name one activity your mother would have forbidden you to do. Had it occurred to her, it probably would have been the following. Walk down a dusty, lightless road in rural Mexico next to a mangrove swamp filled with crocodiles. Hop aboard a small metal boat with a local biologist and three friends. And then launch out into the steamy darkness, headlamps on, searching for red beads in the blackness—the signs of floating dinosaurs.

Last night my colleague Al Gubanich and I joined Paulino Campos and his colleague Rudolfo of the conservation group Bosque Tropical on a nighttime crocodile survey in the white mangrove swamp of La Manzanilla. We clambered over a small wire fence to reach the skiff, shoved off from the fecal-smelling bank into the brackish water, and paddled our way into the middle of the first lagoon. Here and there we saw red dots, like cigarette ends. At about eight-thirty on a cool, March evening, this was not an ideal night for crocodile viewing—but even to be out on a dark body of water in pitch black night with a single animal of this kind would defy the fiercest warning of one's mother.

We maintained a calm chatter as we drifted further into the swamp, staying in the center of the water to achieve the best possible view of each bank. Eventually, Paulino, who'd begun the trip in the rear with an oar in hand, traded places with Rudolfo and used a headlamp to spot "crocs" hiding in the shoreline mangroves. Again and again, he exclaimed—"There's a croc! I see another"—his practiced eyes noticing life where the rest of us observed only empty space. We marveled at the discernment of experienced eyes in contrast to our novitiate blindness.

Eventually, near the site where local people are contemplating the development of a crocodile farm, Paulino caught sight of a small croc near the bank, leaned forward from the front of the boat, and grabbed the eight-month-old animal in his bare hands as easily as I might have snagged a water lily. We spent twenty minutes measuring and examining the hapless animal. I was struck by the softness of the saurian skin—the half-meter juvenile looked as if it was wearing a suit of armor, and yet it felt like soft leather. It became motionless, passive, under our attention. Paulino handed the small croc to each of the passengers in turn and snapped digital pictures of us posing with it and pretending to release it into the saline soup of the lagoon. He said this is what he does even when he captures large crocs on the shore—animals reaching up to two and a half meters in length. He invites local people and tourists to come and touch the animals and pose for pictures with them. This helps them to understand the crocs and to value them rather than thinking of them as hostile, mysterious monsters lurking in the hidden depths of the mangroves. It's clear that, in his own way, as a conservation biologist, Paulino has thought carefully about the rhetoric of environmental education.

We spent two hours in the boat, pushing ever further into the tightening vice of the mangroves, fighting our way through the jigsaw puzzle of branches. Sometimes the glint our headlights caught was only the reflection of a spider dangling in its web. I wondered what other living creatures were awake and moving in the darkness—snakes, insects, wild cats, birds. Occasionally the clanking of our oars on the metal boat startled roosting herons, who squawked and flapped loudly aloft, unhappy to be rousted from their night's rest.

We made our way back to the beach where we had begun our evening journey, pleased to have held a small croc and come slightly closer to appreciating its intimidating otherness. Al and I clambered out of the boat, while our Mexican companions stayed aboard to return it to its hiding place. We walked back to the camp with our headlamps off, a little less afraid of the dark.

There's something about the process of coming face-to-face with the exotic, the scary, or the bewildering—of "normalizing the new," so to speak—that emboldens me to breathe in experience more deeply. Floating among the mangrove crocs at night has helped me to open my mind and senses more widely to the experience of La Manzanilla. I suppose my goal is to carry home some of this renewed openness at the end of the week, a state of mind I can direct toward my everyday work and surroundings.

■ ■ ■ This morning I took a brief walk along the beach before breakfast. A hundred yards from camp, I found a plump red fish lying on the sand. Three days ago, I suspect I would have gingerly kicked it with my sandal, reluctant to infect myself with whatever disease resulted in its beaching. Today I pick it up and marvel at its red skin and its redder-then-red eye. It is a jewel of life, present on the beach as if by magic. Soon it will feed the ever-hungry shorebirds—willets, night herons, turkey vultures. Sometimes it takes an encounter with living jewels on faraway beaches to respark our inquisitiveness about gems and germs of meaning in our ordinary neighborhoods. This reawakening to the daily meanings of our lives, hidden in texts and present in the physical world, is a big part of why I travel. Through my life as a writer and teacher, I wish to pick up and examine the brilliant red fish of reality.

■ ■ ■ "You stay home," admonishes poet Wendell Berry. "I am at home. Don't come with me" (199). This, of course, is the quandary, the anxiety, of the place-conscious scholar. Should we wish to sustain our species on this planet, we must learn to live more lightly—to use fewer resources and trample less aggressively on this surprisingly delicate globe. Chances are this will be a very difficult lesson for us. We seem programmed to accomplish whatever is in our power, and we have a devil-may-care attitude about the consequences. If we can do something today, we'll do it—tomorrow will take care of itself. Or so we seem to think. This mañana attitude is not limited to any particular culture—it's certainly as true of the mainstream view of conservation in the United States as it is anywhere else.

In his brief poem "Stay Home," Berry pricks my conscience and leads me to consider the virtues of my traveling life and the possible virtues of a more sedentary, home-rooted life. I choose to take the poem as a prompt and point of departure for such meditations, not as an absolute statement of prohibition—a literal condemnation of movement and exploration. I suspect the work was written precisely with people like me in mind—and with *himself* in mind, for Berry, too, is a traveling writer and public speaker. The point is not to push everyone into a sudden immobility, but to nudge those of us who travel frequently to do so more mindfully, with more awareness of the costs of such a life to ourselves and to the planet.

Environmental activists and scholars sometimes joke that a "bioregionalist" is someone who travels around the country urging other people to stay home. This may not be far from the truth. But most bioregionalists understand that we can all benefit from more engagement and attentiveness to our home places and from the revivifying experience of movement across the earth.

■ ■ ■   The bathroom in my beachside casita is walled from the sleeping area by vertical rows of slender bamboo poles nailed side by side. There is plenty of room between each pole to peer through the wall into the bedroom and through the front door beyond that, out to the beach and the ever-pounding surf. Standing in the bathroom a few minutes ago, I found myself looking past the upright screen of my laptop to the rows of waves beyond, new waves pouring themselves onto the beach every six or seven seconds, on and on and on. The process is so routine and yet so variable. No two waves are quite alike, and yet the process has occurred uncountable times. Perhaps there is nothing more beautiful in all the world than the simple action of waves falling upon sandy beaches. Perhaps, as well, there is nothing more routine.

I think to myself that the ultimate lesson of this particular journey to tropical Mexico may not be how to savor the exotic. That is a lesson that needs no teaching—a lesson as automatic as breathing. No—the lesson here was present in the waves I heard breaking immediately upon arrival at this dark beachside camp and witnessed each day when I awakened to run along the surf and dodge jellyfish and spiny puffers. The lesson of the routinely pounding surf—the utter everydayness of the motion. Water and sand doing what they must do in relation to gravity, wind, and rock. Is this not what we, too, ultimately seek? To know what we must do and then to do it?

■ ■ ■   Let me see if I can recall my travels of the past year—spring break at Zion National Park in southern Utah, a late-March trip to speak at an international symposium on environmental literature in Okinawa, a talk to the senior class of St. Bonaventure University in upstate New York in April, ten days in New England in early June to participate in the biennial meeting of the Association for the Study of Literature and Environment, a week in Mississippi in July for the thirtieth annual Faulkner and Yoknapatawpha Conference, and ten days on Australia's eastern coast in October for the Watermark Nature Writers' Muster, followed immediately by two days of lectures and meetings at Iowa State University, plus various family trips to Seattle and Washington, DC, mixed in with the work-related wanderings. Each of these journeys has been delightful and inspiring in different ways. The drain of falling behind with my teaching, writing, and editing responsibilities at home is outweighed by the pleasures of interacting with new and old friends and absorbing various landscapes.

I draw my title for this cluster of informal meditations from Gary Paul Nabhan's 2002 book, *Coming Home to Eat: The Pleasures and Politics of Local Foods*. Although the bulk of his book focuses on the experiment in local eating that he conducted in Tucson, Arizona, in the late 1990s, he actually begins his discussion by telling the story of his trip to see family members in Lebanon and the experience of eating local delicacies with distant relatives in the Bekaa Valley. Traveling to experience other people's local places and cultures and ideas triggered Nabhan's own experiment in local living.

Much the same thing tends to occur as I respond to each of my own journeys. Place is a central component in my academic life, and place, for me, is built from the tension between going away and coming home. I've found that my own working life is fundamentally shaped by my habit of traveling to visit new landscapes and talk with literary and scientific colleagues in order to gain perspective on the meaning of my life at home. My teaching and writing at home are rooted in the specific physical environments of office, house, and nearby mountain trails, and the experience of these places provides a kind of ballast or core of meaning that helps me to appreciate and understand the implications of my travels.

▩ ▩ ▩ When I travel, I try to wake up each morning and go running. This week, Earthwatch participant Bob Lewis, a semiretired dentist from Seattle, said, "You can take the boy out of Oregon, but you can't take Oregon out of the boy" when he saw me return from an early morning run. These runs are one of the key features of my traveling regimen. I ran competitively for many years in junior high, high school, and part of college, but now I run simply for fitness and for geography. I experience places most vividly while oxygen deprived, moving steadily through neighborhoods and along trails and beaches. One of the frustrating aspects of being at home is the tendency to become so compulsive about rushing to the office each morning and staying late "to get things done" that meaningful exercise drops by the wayside. And yet using my body helps me to be at home in this body—and being at home in my body enables me to exist more fully in place and to think about the implications of placedness in literature.

I wake up each morning while traveling and explore the neighborhood, ranging from Naha's winding alleyways in Okinawa to the cornfields skirting Ames, Iowa, to the man-made and natural debris washed up on La Manzanilla's three-mile beach. Not only does this running help to sharpen my attention for the rest of the day, but it gives me a view of the layout of the place—a view unavailable from most meeting rooms. I pay close attention to the shape of the land, the direction of the wind, the feel of the air, the types of trees and birds I see and hear. I feel as if I begin to belong to each place as I pass through it, breathing steadily and knowing it with the strain of my leg muscles.

I once told an interviewer that many of the ecocritics I know are "muscular scholars," people who enjoy using their bodies on mountains and hiking trails as well as their minds in offices and classrooms. I realize that academics in general are often quite interested in physical fitness, understanding that their mental abilities are linked to the health of their bodies. Growing up, I spent quite a bit of time in the summer running with my father and his colleagues at the University of Oregon, and I have clear memories of the psychologists and biologists and literary scholars gathering in the locker room before noontime runs. But it seems to me that ecocritics are particularly given to this sort of activity, and that our actual work is enhanced and deepened by getting outside and testing our strength and frailty against the physical features of the landscape. From the beginning, as the community of ecocritics began to gather under the auspices of the Association for the Study of Literature and Environment and similar organizations, there has been a tendency to make field trips—and often significant hikes and climbs and river trips—an integral part of our academic culture. I recall, for instance, several days of hectic meetings at Boston University during ASLE's fifth biennial conference in 2003, followed by a climb of Mount Monadnock in New Hampshire with more than a dozen colleagues on the last day of the academic meeting, intellectuals continuing their conversations while huffing up the trail in a chilly June rain.

■ ■ ■   I lay awake most of last night listening to the explosive smack of waves on the nearby beach, frustrated by the disruption of my rest. At home the sounds of night are almost indiscernible, even when the windows are open during the warmer months. Sometimes we hear doves cooing outside the bedroom window. Here on the beach at La Manzanilla there is a steady rhythm of shushing water withdrawing into the sea followed by the thwack of a new wave, shush then thwack, shush then thwack. Paulino Campos tells me he loves the sound of the crashing waves here, but to me they are a disruption, even sometimes an annoyance. This is in so many ways a beautiful place—a good place to rest and put my life and work into broader perspective. And yet at the same time there are inconveniences and annoyances—the sleepless nights caused by the thunderous waves outside the casita, the mosquito and sand flea bites, the inability to control my own diet as at home. Travel has its benefits and its banes—not to mention this would be to distort the truth. But even the frustrations can, and perhaps *should*, be savored—even pain, fatigue, and aggravation are interesting dimensions of life.

"La vida tiene sabor," says the Coca-Cola billboard we passed en route to Barra de Navidad yesterday afternoon for a few hours of shopping and lounging in the jellyfish-free surf. I savor those words as we drive, quickly forgetting that they come from a corporate advertising campaign. Life has flavor, life has flavor. The words lose their consumer context, and it occurs to me that this is absolutely true—life has, indeed, many flavors. And this is what I try to remember in everything I do, even during the sometimes numbing process of reading freshman papers and discussing familiar pieces of writing with jaded students. Life has flavor, I suggest to my students. Life has flavor, I remind myself.

In the process of traveling to distant beaches to lie awake to the whip-crack of dropping waves and the nasal hum of mosquitoes, I am saying to myself, "La vida tiene sabor."

■ ■ ■   Life has flavor, and life has risk. One of the risks is complacency and tedium. As I meditate on the sound of the waves, I remember the sea life I find washed ashore each morning, particularly the striking spiny puffer fish, so different from the shells on the Oregon beaches and the stinking alewives on Lake Michigan's shores I've known since childhood. Each morning while running here in La Manzanilla, I've wrenched my back by dodging tattered fish carcasses and still-breathing puffers. Multicolored, covered with inch-long white spines, with striking white bony beaks, these fish of tropical reefs are clearly out of their element lying on the beach. Soon they will be food for insects and birds. After five days of observing them, I take a moment to look them up in a field guide to "reef life" and learn that they are "black-blotched porcupine fish" (*Diodon liturosus*). They are meant to inhabit coastal reefs in the tropical Indo-Pacific. To be honest, I do not know why they've ended their lives on the beach at La Manzanilla. But it occurs to me that they've somehow allowed themselves to drift free from the reefs of home and become complacent in the relatively calm waters of Tenacatita Bay—and then suddenly their benign environment thrashes them violently onto the sandy beach, where they wash, stunned, to their sunny doom.

Our species, too, is prone to complacency, perhaps even more so than most other organisms. We insulate ourselves from risk—Americans are particularly eager to achieve security, to have insurance protecting us from loss of property, loss of health, loss of life. Here in Mexico, the unavailability of true security is all too plain. Floating through the crocodile estuary, I watch schools of tiny fish leap momentarily ahead of the boat, knowing that they will soon feed baby crocs and multitudes of long-beaked fishing birds—herons, egrets, kingfishers, stilts—perched in the nearby trees. Sitting yesterday beneath the cloth umbrella at Barra de Navidad, I reflected upon the many hawkers wandering from one cluster of tourists to the next, selling trinkets, multicolored baskets, and even donuts and cakes. We marveled at the man with the broad basket of chocolate-covered donuts, eager to unload calories to bikini-clad vacationers. A weathered, dark-skinned woman, seemingly beyond her sixties, lugged heavy buckets of arroz con leche and ceviche to prospective customers—no one was buying. "That's a hard way to make a living," someone from our group muttered. "Imagine feeding your family like that," said another. On a day with no sales, one would have no income. There is no security.

But back to the example of the porcupine fish—imagine the significance of a benign environment suddenly turned lethal. This is, perhaps, the core message of environmental literature, science, education, and activism. Many people today can see the future coming. They know what's happening to the planet and to specific, local places. And they wish to get the word out. Sometimes these writers and educators sound like Jeremiah, seeming to issue exaggerated warnings of unrealized catastrophes. More often, their fate is that of Cassandra—a classical story I learned from Alan AtKisson's recent book, *Believing Cassandra*: they can see the future, but they are fated not to be heard, not to be believed.

The evening before leaving on this trip to Costa Alegre, Mexico's "Happy Coast," I was hosting visiting author Bill McKibben in Reno. His talk was titled "Global Warming, Genetic Engineering and Other Questions of Human Scale" and drew some of its core ideas from his beautiful book *The Comforting Whirlwind*. He began his lecture with a brief Bible lesson, summarizing the Book of Job, in which God admonishes Job to remember his small place in the scheme of the universe, for after all only God can determine the tides of the sea and other fundamental natural processes. Bill then rehearsed, as he's done hundreds of times in the past decade, the facts and figures of global climate change, convincingly demonstrating the fundamental changes occurring in our planet's atmosphere and down on earth as well, chiefly the result of our releasing so much carbon into the air through the use of fossil fuels. Next, Bill explained the field of "germ-line" genetic engineering, a process by which contemporary scientists have been able to mold (without a great deal of control) the minute genetic codes of life. He concluded his lecture by suggesting that, unlike Job, we can now reply to God that we, too, are able to affect the large and small dimensions of nature. We have that power. And yet the consequences of wielding this power may well be to create a planetary environment deeply inhospitable to our own continued existence. It seems, for instance, entirely likely that in the coming decades, there will be a profound shortage of water for drinking and agriculture, and desalination of seawater will not be able to compensate for this shortage. As Bill McKibben stated the other evening, these ideas make him sad and worried, and he travels to give lectures in order to make his listeners "sad," too. This elicited a nervous laugh from the full auditorium at the Nevada Museum of Art. Why would a speaker wish to make his audience sad? Could this really be so?

After other questioners were unable to summon an explicit prognostication about the future of life on earth from the speaker, a final questioner struck home by reminding McKibben of his ten-year-old daughter. "What sort of life to you expect for her?" the man asked from the audience. "I'm afraid her life will be very difficult," was the answer. "We are approaching an ecological bottleneck, and it's unclear who will make it through—which species will make it through."

■ ■ ■   A boy wades into the surf before me, shirtless and in gray shorts, carrying a circular net folded over his left forearm that he casts into the sea with a quick motion of his right hand. He can see glints of silver in the water that indicate a school of fish. He casts his net, crouches to help it sink into the water just beyond the surf, and waits for the fish to become entangled. Then he gathers a dozen wriggling fish into the folds of the net and wades ashore to his waiting friend, who carries a red plastic grocery bag, laden with their catch. This, too, is a ready metaphor, a literal casting of one's net into the sea of reality, hoping for a worthwhile take. I continue to watch as the young fisherman scans the surface of the bay in search of more fish, much as the flock of pelicans circles down the coast, also seeking nourishment. And here I sit, perched at my yellow wooden table on the porch of a simple casita, shielded from the rising sun by the thatched roof of palm fronds. I scan the view, I watch the neighboring encampment to the left, and I listen to my friends and Earthwatch colleagues under the *palapa* (the wall-less, thatched-roof structure) to my right. I am reminded of my constant daily search for ideas and words, the substance of my own life.

■ ■ ■   Before me, the sea is placid here on the Happy Coast. The fishing boy has moved on in search of richer waters. There are no tourists. The water has become glassy and reflects the sky's wispy clouds. And then suddenly the next wave crashes ashore, and somewhere along the curves of Tenacatita Bay, porcupine fish and jellies are cast from the benign environment of the bay onto the hostile sand.

I come to this place for a change of scenery, yes, and also for an enlivened perspective on the familiar scenery of home. No matter where I travel on this planet, I can never forget where I normally dwell, the other places I visit, and the fact that the place I inhabit at any given moment is connected fundamentally to the places I've passed through before. My senses are sharpened, my view is broadened, my consciousness deepened.

I have gone away from home to think, and now I am ready to return home, still thinking. There will be no crashing waves, no gasping porcupine fish, as I gaze from the windows of home at the snowy foothills of the Sierra. But the waves will pound ashore in my memory, motivating my continued efforts as teacher and writer, until my next journey.

■   ■   ■   Always the push and pull of home and away—I reflect on the pull of home as I fly back from Manzanillo to Los Angeles and then to Reno. The last few days of this Earthwatch trip have been filled with learning and adventure, and now it's time to return to the eastern slopes of the Sierra, to the quiet mountain nights with no surf pounding nearby, to the dining-room table where I work at home (tomorrow will be a day of grading student papers), and to the office lined with thousands of books and networked via phone, fax, and e-mail to the rest of the world. Despite the fact that I have been almost wholly "off-line" during this week on Costa Alegre (apart from one call home to let Susie know all was going well), I have felt in many ways more deeply engaged with the concrete details of place than I do in my hurried, abstract life of the mind at home. Yesterday's itinerary began with a six-kilometer kayaking trip on the Río Cuixmala, including a pineapple and trail-mix snack enjoyed on a pristine Pacific beach near the Cuixmala Biosphere Reserve. After loading the eight kayaks back on his trailer, Dave Collins from Immersion Adventures drove a bumpy, dusty back road to the village of Talacatita, where our bunch of students, professors, trail crew leaders, and retiree volunteers donned fins, masks, and snorkels and spent an hour bobbing in the sea, observing fluorescent tropical fish near the fringing coral reef. While birding from the kayaks, walking along the beach at the mouth of Río Cuixmala, and gazing downward at the reef life, our only task—my only task—was to be as fully present in these places as possible. To pay attention. To practice the mindful condition I so often speak and write about in my classrooms and my office. Without such an opportunity to *live* the mental processes I think about abstractly, these processes would eventually cease to happen—and I would cease to believe in them. I fear my work itself would grind to a frustrated halt.

Indeed, following yesterday's trip to Cuixmala and Tanacatita, it was finally my turn to offer a formal presentation to the Earthwatch group. At four P.M., tanned and sweaty after the day's activity, full from the beachside Mexican seafood I'd eaten at our late lunch, I lectured on "Art and Activism: Literature and Environmentalism in the United States and Mexico." I expected the group to fall asleep and feared that my own voice would be drowned out by the pounding surf near the wall-less, thatch-roofed *palapa* at our La Manzanilla camp. But just the opposite occurred. I introduced my three premises—that words are powerful, that there is a physical world surrounding us of ultimate importance and meaning, and that words are not merely mental toys but also tools of activism. I read and commented on Ofelia Zepeda's "It Is Going to Rain" (emphasizing the idea that poetry emerges from ordinary experience and values attentiveness) and John Daniel's "Ourselves" (showing how careful, intensified use of language elevates the ordinary into the magical, deepening our appreciation, combating complacency). Then I asked crocodile biologist Paulino Campos to read Octavio Paz's "Viento, Agua, Piedra" ("Wind, Water, Stone"), University of Guadalajara undergraduate Diana to read Homero Aridjis's "Ballena Gris" ("Grey Whale"), and ornithologist Sara Huerta to read Aridjis's "Poema de Amor en la Ciudad de Mexico" ("Love Poem in Mexico City"). We talked about Paz's use of poetry as a medium for contemplating profound, timeless concepts of nature's interconnectedness and Aridjis's activist use of poetry to combat air pollution in Mexico City, destruction of gray whale calving waters in the Vizcaino Biosphere Reserve near Baja California, and the logging in Michoacan that threatens monarch butterfly wintering areas. Despite a day of physical exertion and parching sun, the group was alert and lively. Seventy-seven-year-old Oyvind Frock, one of the Earthwatch volunteers, raised his hand at the end of the session and read a poem he had written during the lecture about the week's experiences in La Manzanilla. The discussion of nature and language and science and Mexico's future was energetic and emotional over dinner.

As my friends made their way one by one to their tents and I prepared to return to the casita and climb under the mosquito netting, I felt the push and pull of travel and home with new intensity. I regretted the fact that I would be leaving the group the following day to return to my office and classroom, following a morning of birding in Barranca el Choncho, an afternoon adventure capturing and measuring crocodiles, and a sweaty dash to the Manzanillo airport. And yet I realized, too, that I could—that I needed to—take away from La Manzanilla a commitment to reengage myself with the specificities of Reno. Naturalist Ann Zwinger once wrote that traveling by plane offers her a splendid sense of isolation for writing, and especially *editing,* a sense of being enclosed in a "blessedly impersonal aluminum tube" hurtling through space, undistracted by the daily realities of home ("What's a Nice Girl" 288). I know what Ann means and share this feeling of momentary freedom. And yet as I glanced away from my laptop to appreciate the metabird's-eye view of the Sea of Cortés en route to Los Angeles, I understood that this freedom is an illusion. The opportunity to "go away to think" is an extraordinary privilege. It is a gift, and with this gift come inevitable responsibilities.

This sense of my work as something more than a way to "pay the bills"—as a way of contributing positively to society and to the planet—preoccupies me every day. Life and work, self-interest and altruism—I have trouble recognizing any distinctions among these processes and attitudes. When I go away to think, I do so with an appetite for joy and an earnest hope to do work that others may find helpful.

■ ■ ■ Sunday morning, back home in Reno, Nevada. After a run through the neighborhood hills, I pour a cup of coffee and walk down to our rustic backyard with the dogs. A week ago, I would have restlessly toured the yard, looking for projects to do. Today, I look for a plastic chair and find one resembling the shape of those at the La Manzanilla beach camp. I then find a spot in the sun and take a seat for ten minutes, gazing at the mountains, listening intently to birdsong. I recognize the coo of the mourning doves, the bubbly cackle of the California quail. I hear chatter from many small birds and feel an urge to grab my field guides from the house and identify birds I've always been content to categorize lazily as what birders call "LBJs" (little brown jobbies).

With my "habit of attention" (as Thoreau put it in his journal) sharpened among the beaches, mangrove estuaries, and arid hillsides of Jalisco, I settle back into home (Thoreau 1906, 351). And then I come inside, boot up the computer, and return to work.

3 | Ecocriticism

In 1993–94, I spent eleven months in Japan, serving as a kind of temporary "nature writing guru" among scholars and students who had never heard of "ecocriticism"[1] or "nature writing." After months of traveling and lecturing, after countless introductory spiels on "literature and environment" (my lecturing voice invaded my dreams at night) and the distribution of examples of nature writing in both Japanese and English, there came to be a budding new movement in this field on those islands of mountains, rice fields, temples, skyscrapers, and haiku. In my introductory talks on nature writing and environmentally conscious literary scholarship, this is how I generally defined "ecocriticism": "the term means either the study of nature writing by way of *any* scholarly approach or, conversely, the scrutiny of ecological implications and human-nature relationships in *any* literary text, even texts that seem (at first glance) oblivious of the nonhuman world. This new enthusiasm for the study of 'literature and environment' in the United States is not only a reaction to the impressive aesthetic achievement of American nature writing, but an indication of contemporary society's growing consciousness of the importance and fragility of the nonhuman world." That's my general description of this field, but there are several other basic ideas/strategies that, I think, are essential for ecocritics to keep in mind, essential to the vitality and meaningfulness of what we're doing.

STORYTELLING

Ecocritics should tell stories, should use narrative as a constant or intermittent strategy for literary analysis. The purpose is not to compete with the literature itself, but simply to illuminate and appreciate the context of reading—that is, to embrace the literary text as language that somehow contributes to our lives "out in the world." We must not reduce our scholarship to an arid, hyperintellectual game, devoid of smells and tastes, devoid of actual experience. Encounter the world and literature together, then report about the conjunctions, the intersecting patterns. Analyze and explain literature through storytelling—or tell your own stories and then, subsequently, show how contact with the world shapes your responses to texts. See John Elder's *Imagining the Earth* (1985) and Kent Ryden's *Mapping the Invisible Landscape* (1993) for examples of intermittent "narrative scholarship." I've experimented with it at the end of *Seeking Awareness in American Nature Writing* (1992).[2]

VALUES

For several years I've pondered a bold claim that Glen Love made in "Revaluing Nature: Toward an Ecological Literary Criticism." I often begin my courses with this thought, transforming Love's assertion into a question: could it be that "the most important function of literature today is to redirect human consciousness to a full consideration of its place in a threatened natural world" (213)? This seems to throw "scholarly poise and neutrality" out the window. But it occurs to me more and more these days that literature is, indeed, much more than an intellectual toy, created for the pleasure of clever, but "irresponsible," critics who resist taking stances on what's happening in the world. Literary scholarship and literature itself are, on the most fundamental level, associated with human values and attitudes. We should, as critics and teachers of literature, consider how literary expression challenges and directs readers to decide what in the world is meaningful/important to them. We can't afford to shy away from the issue of values—this is the proper domain of literary studies (and such fields as philosophy and religious studies), and it's one reason why the humanities should be a crucial part of university programs in environmental studies.

COMMUNICATION

Try not to waste words and paper. If you have something to say, say it clearly and directly—communicate. So much literary scholarship is unreadable garbage, apparently not intended for a real audience. I think ecocritics, of all people, ought to challenge themselves to use language with clarity and elegance. Those of us who study nature writing have some of the world's best models (writing that communicates) in front of us day after day.

CONTACT

In the summer of 1994, two Japanese nature-writing scholars arranged for me to visit eighty-four-year-old farmer/philosopher Masanobu Fukuoka, the author of *The One-Straw Revolution: An Introduction to Natural Farming*, in the mountains outside of Matsuyama on the southern island of Shikoku. After spending a few hours walking around Fukuoka-san's junglelike orchards, we went to have tea in a primitive hut. While drinking the tea, we listened to Fukuoka-san talk about farming and nature. Then I asked him something I had been wondering during our entire visit. Did he think it might be possible for academia to contribute anything to our understanding of nature and the relationship between nature and culture? (What did he think about these three literature professors who had come to visit him?) Fukuoka-san seemed to look right past me, and then he said (in Japanese), "Listen to the bird sing." I thought he simply hadn't heard my question or that he found it unimportant. But everyone stopped talking and, sure enough, there was a nightingale (*uguisu* in Japanese) calling outside the hut. Then Fukuoka-san's assistant leaned over to me and whispered, "He means, it is possible if you have a simple mind." In other words, those of us who work at universities might be able to contribute to society's understanding of nature if we remember to pay attention to nature itself, if we don't lose ourselves in lectures, theories, texts, laboratories. A powerful admonition: ecocritics (and our colleagues in other environmental disciplines) need contact not just with literature and not just with each other, but with the physical world.

NOTES

1. Lawrence Buell has proposed in *The Future of Environmental Criticism: Environmental Crisis and Literary Imagination* (2005) that such terms as "environmental criticism" and "literary-environmental studies" might be more accurate in describing the "concourse of discrepant practices" that constitutes the field (10). He also distinguishes between "first-wave" and "second-wave" ecocriticism, and his own *The Environmental Imagination: Thoreau, Nature Writing, and the Formation of American Culture* (1995) would fall into the former category, while his *Writing for an Endangered World: Literature, Culture and Environment in the United States and Beyond* (2001) would fit into the latter, which is characterized by "a growing diversification of critical method and a broadening of focus from an original concentration on such genres as nature writing, nature poetry, and wilderness fiction toward engagement with a broader range of landscapes and genres and a greater internal debate over environmental commitment that has taken the movement in a more sociocentric direction" (*Future* 138). See my discussion of "environmental justice ecocriticism" in chapter 8, "Ecocriticism on and after 9/11," for further focus on this "sociocentric direction."

2. Splendid examples of narrative scholarship abound as I compile this collection of essays in 2007. John Elder followed his preliminary narrative experiments in *Imagining the Earth: Poetry and the Vision of Nature* (1996) with the learned and compelling narratives of *Reading the Mountains of Home* (1998) and *Pilgrimage to Vallombrosa: From Vermont to Italy in the Footsteps of George Perkins Marsh* (2006). Since I first wrote this brief position paper on ecocriticism, Ian Marshall has published two important monographs, *Story Line: Exploring the Literature of the Appalachian Trail* (1998) and *Peak Experiences: Walking Meditations on Literature, Nature, and Need* (2003), and John Tallmadge has elegantly woven personal stories together with larger reflections on the academic profession and the literature of place in *Meeting the Tree of Life: A Teacher's Path* (1997) and *The Cincinnati Arch: Learning from Nature in the City* (2004). My former student, Corey Lee Lewis, has applied the strategies of narrative scholarship to his work on place-based teaching and scholarship in *Reading the Trail: Exploring the Literature and Natural History of the California Crest* (2005).

4 | Seeking the Language of Solid Ground

REFLECTIONS ON ECOCRITICISM AND NARRATIVE

Seldom does the fallen climber survive to tell his or her own tale.

Years ago, overburdened by a backpack full of books and distracted by my professional role as textual critic, I ignored my place in the physical world, stepped off a mountain wall, and nearly lost my life and my voice as a scholar. Ecocritics, in forgetting the worldly context of their reading, of their thinking, do so at the peril of their own language. Language without context, without grounding in the world, means next to nothing.

At the end of July 1995, a group of eight traveled to the Shirakami Mountains in northwestern Honshu, a United Nations World Heritage Site, to do a story on wilderness protection in Japan for *Audubon* magazine.[1] Three of us—nature writer Rick Bass, photographer Mike Yamashita, and I—had come from the United States for this excursion. Translator and nature writer Bruce Allen, editor Nobuhiro Sato, and environmental journalist Shigeyuki Okajima joined us in Tokyo for the flight north to Aomori. Our guides were Makoto Nebuka, a prolific outdoor writer and the principal defender of the Shirakami wilderness, and one of his mountain-man friends, known to us only as "Narita-san." We were an all-male group. Hisako Tanaka, an editor for the popular Japanese nature magazine called *Shinra,* had flown up separately from Tokyo just to interview Rick during the limo ride to the trailhead; she hiked with us for an hour on a paved path to see a few picturesque waterfalls, but when the rest of us left the trail and began dragging ourselves on hands and knees up a sheer, overgrown ridge, she smiled and waved good-bye.

We hadn't expected such rugged conditions. For three days in the virgin beech forests of Shirakami, we worked our way up rivers in special hiking shoes called "chicatabi" with rubber cushions and metal spikes on the bottom, climbed small waterfalls, and crawled up steep mountainsides with scraggly trees and bamboolike sasa grass, interwoven with poison ivy, as handholds. These forests were trail-less, except for occasional deer paths. I found myself preoccupied with the other writers on the trip and the efforts of Mike, the photographer, to document the place and the people while struggling to keep up with Nebuka-san's steady pace. The expedition was like a hall of mirrors—everyone watching, interviewing, taking photographs or videos, keeping a notebook. I was fascinated with Rick's ability to take notes on a pocket-sized pad even while wobbling across rivers or while pausing on a taxing slope. Occasionally, he would say something aloud like, "So many images of light. Sunlight, bright-colored frogs, light on water, light through leaves" or "The strands of the story break apart and reweave themselves—first bears, then the Shirakami Preserve, and now Nebuka-san himself is emerging as the center." My own notebook reflects Rick's comments more than the place itself.

At the end of our second day in the mountains, after ten hours of grueling travel, our guides became disoriented just as it began to get dark; we clambered and fought our way downhill through a dense thicket of sasa grass, following an apparent animal trail, until we found ourselves looking over the dribbling lip of a narrow waterfall—two hundred feet down. We paused there for another half hour—Rick took notes and I took notes about his note taking, and photographs—as our guides deliberated. The guides figured we could inch our way across the top of the waterfall and along the sheer slope to one side, then climb down to a possible campsite. Back and forth they crawled, scouting out the route. I continued watching Rick and bantering with the others. Then it was my turn to go. I was the second person to follow the guides, trying to secure myself by holding slender sasa stalks and using my spiked shoes to grip the grassy lip on the side of the waterfall. Mike, the *Audubon* photographer, was right behind me. Just as I stepped out from the ledge where all of us had been resting, Shigeyuki Okajima, the Everest climber and environmental journalist, shouted, "Watch out, Scott! It's slippy, very slippy!" Smiling at Shige's Japanese English, I stepped out, felt the earth give way beneath my feet, and realized I was clinging to a tiny, bending tree trunk, hanging over the edge of the nearly vertical cliff. Without a pack, I might have been able to pull myself up to safety, but I had sixty pounds strapped to my back, much of it useless paper. I felt myself sliding down toward the end of the tree. I hadn't even glanced down to see how big the drop-off was. I looked toward Shige, who was now shouting, "No, no, no!" And then I was suddenly sliding rapidly down the grassy upper portion of the cliff, arms outstretched and hands digging into the dirt, seeking any possible handhold. I slid faster and faster, not knowing what lay beneath me and when I might sail out from the wall and into some kind of final, fatal drop through empty space. Suddenly, the noise changed and I felt my boots and legs scraping across jagged rocks, my shirt sleeves ripping—and then silence and dizziness. A moment later, Mike came tumbling sideways down the same section of cliff that I had descended, pulled down by the weight of his camera equipment, grunting and moaning as he splashed into two feet of water, just inches away from me. Soon the water turned red, absorbing the blood from a cut somewhere beneath my jeans.

We had fallen eighty feet and landed on a ten-foot ledge in the middle of the narrow waterfall, barely missing the final, vertical portion of the fall. Up above, Rick and the other members of the party were sure one of us had been killed. When they realized we were able to stand on our own, Rick shouted down, "Lean back, lean back. If you faint, you'll fall forward and drown." For an hour we stood on that ledge. "We're really fucked now," Mike moaned. Finally, one of our guides, the nimble, muscular Narita-san, emerged and stood with us on the ledge, having clambered up from the bottom of the cliff. After verifying that we had miraculously avoided serious injury, he fixed a rope to the rock wall and belayed us down through the rest of the waterfall. This process took another hour. Then Narita climbed up to the other hikers, roped them all up, and found a detour for them around the waterfall. When our entire party of eight was reunited at the base of the cliff, the others seemed to treat Mike and me as if we were ghosts, not quite believing that we had stepped off the side of the mountain and lived.

During the rest of our two-week stay in Japan, I watched Rick, Mike, and Nebuka-san take photographs of clear-cutting and road building just outside the World Heritage Site; I listened to Rick interview a bear biologist at the Historical Museum of Hokkaido; I accompanied him to the Peace Memorial Park in Hiroshima and to the orange shrine in the Inland Sea at Miyajima; and we gave several presentations together—first my contextualizing comments and then his reading of fiction or essays. At times during this trip, I felt demoralized about my role as "literary scholar" tagging along with an "actual nature writer." The phrase that kept coming to mind was "third wheel." I was the third wheel during our travels, and perhaps ecocritics are the "third wheels of the environmental writing community." Rick had genuine work to accomplish—*literature* to write. And Bruce Allen played a crucial role as translator. Meanwhile, I stood back and watched Rick watch the world. Nobody seemed to mind my presence, but nobody quite understood it, either.

I remembered a discussion I had had a year earlier with Terry Tempest Williams. "So what exactly do you do as an ecocritic?" she asked. "What do you do?" It doesn't seem quite right to tell writers, keen to communicate as most of them are, "Well, I help people understand your work." Writers like Rick Bass and Terry Tempest Williams can communicate quite well on their own, of course, without the help of literary scholars. So what is our role then? Again and again, I come back to the ideas of contextualization and synthesis. Ecocritics, to do something genuinely meaningful—something more than propping up their own careers by producing endless unread and unreadable commentaries about perfectly lucid and even eloquent literary texts—must offer readers a broader, deeper, and perhaps more explicit explanation of how and what environmental literature communicates than the writers do themselves, immersed as they are in their own specific narratives. Crucial to this ecocritical process of pulling things (ideas, texts, authors) together and putting them in perspective is our awareness of who and where we are. Our awareness, literally, of where we stand in the world and why we're writing. Storytelling, combined with clear exposition, produces the most engaging and trenchant scholarly discourse. Nature writers themselves realize this, as a quick look at the work of Wendell Berry, John Daniel, Barry Lopez, David Mas Masumoto, Gary Paul Nabhan, Robert Michael Pyle, Sharman Apt Russell, Scott Russell Sanders, Ann Zwinger, and many others will show. Ecocritics should take a hint. Ecocriticism without narrative is like stepping off the face of a mountain—it's the disoriented language of free fall.

In the previous chapter, I related my story of visiting the elderly farmer and theorist of alternative agriculture and environmental ethics, Masanobu Fukuoka, on his jungle farm back in 1994. When he urged me, cryptically, to listen to the *uguisu*, the nightingale singing outside the hut where we sipped our tea, I felt he was confirming my own belief in the importance of attending to our actual lives, our existence in the physical world, as we move through the world and also when we retreat to our offices and work our way through memories and texts and speculations. I find myself extending this powerful admonition, offered over tea in the steamy summer mountains of Shikoku, to the language that literary scholars, and especially those of us who call ourselves "ecocritics," use to illuminate and contextualize the literature we study. To the extent that our scholarship emerges from our experiences in and concern for the physical world of nature and the complexities of our social interactions, we must seek an appropriately grounded language. The language of stories, charged with emotion and sensation, may be our best bet.

NOTE

1. Although funded by *Audubon*, Rick Bass's commissioned article never appeared in the magazine. Instead, the essay "Into the Shirakamis" was published in the journal *ISLE: Interdisciplinary Studies in Literature and Environment* 5.2 (Summer 1998): 69–96.

5

"Be Prepared for the Worst"

LOVE, ANTICIPATED LOSS, AND
ENVIRONMENTAL VALUATION

2000

"I live for autumn," wrote John Nichols in 1982 in *The Last Beautiful Days of Autumn*. "All year long I have reveries of those cool beautiful days to come, and memories of Octobers past. It is the most alive, the most heartbreakingly real season in my bones" (3). "I write as though there were no sorrow like my sorrow," wrote Harriet Beecher Stowe in a letter to her husband in 1849 (qtd. in Graulich 168).

"Be prepared for the worst." "I live for autumn." The same paradox operates in each of these expressions. What does it mean to exist in a state of readiness—to be prepared—for something, a decline or an absence, not yet experienced? How do we ever know the true delicacy of existence, the frailty of a life hanging on from breath to breath, the subtle beat of a heart just born and now dying?

SEPTEMBER 8, 1994

"Be prepared for the worst." I am never prepared for the worst. What I want is to hold and love and experience. To make a family and then to exist as part of it. When did the making occur? In the dark sometime—ages ago, months ago—hugging and thrusting. It all seems so vague now. Then, after sufficient gestation, this: the stain of water, the late-night drive, the waiting in the surgical prep room with the brown ball of fertility exposed. We hold hands until she is taken away for the emptying, the delivery—and then, here it is, here he is: shock of black hair, skin wrinkled and red, sprawled in the nursery for requisite measuring. I, the comaker, am finally invited to meet the new life. The pediatrician, in his white coat, pokes and stretches, wobbles the legs like a bicycle mechanic spinning new tires, and records his numbers. There is no warmth, no love, in his touch. And I cannot yet bring myself to hold this new life, so present to me.

1997

"Be prepared for the worst." I keep on my shelf a book called *Regret*. That's it—simply *Regret*. "Regret has very little respect for rule books, etiquette manuals, lists of commandments, or economic models," writes Janet Landman. "Like other emotions (as well as other psychological processes in general)," she continues,

regret depends less on universal, objective assessments than on personal values and norms. Anything that one cares about or that conflicts with one's values or falls below one's standards may produce regret. Inasmuch as norms and values lack universality, it would be foolish to attempt to formulate universal propositions as to what is a "proper" occasion for regret. . . . The only certainty is that one of the incorrigible costs of caring about something . . . is vulnerability to the experience of regret. (168)

Just think of it that way—that the cost of caring is vulnerability to regret, vulnerability to wishing things otherwise. Whatever we love, then, according to our individual attractions and concerns, makes us susceptible to doubts and second guesses. We're caught in a web of private dubiety. If I do this, am I sacrificing my opportunity to do that? I love to hike and I love to study, so when I hit the trail I find myself wondering what I might be reading or writing back in my office, and when I'm inside at the computer I dream of the mountains. When Jacinto, my ten-year-old son, is skateboarding in front of our house, I imagine he's dreaming about the great shows he could be watching on TV or the funny designs he could be making in his hair, now blue and black. What action today might forestall the loss of something dearly loved tomorrow?

But the other side of regret may be that when we imagine it, anticipate it, in the wake of a future decision, its mere probability inspires us to care. Hold onto this idea. "Anticipated regret"—nostalgia for what was or could have been. I'm talking about nostalgia experienced, paradoxically, before actual loss.

There's another book on my shelf called *Yearning for Yesterday: A Sociology of Nostalgia*. Fred Davis reminds us that "*Nostalgia* is from the Greek *nostos*, to return home, and *algia*, a painful condition—thus, a painful yearning to return home" (1). "That art thrives on nostalgia and that, simultaneously, it does much to shape the form and provide the substance of our nostalgic experience is, perhaps, as evident as it is difficult to explain," he writes. Furthermore, he elaborates:

But that all of the arts . . . are forever rummaging through the apparently lost beauties of the past would seem incontestable. We need only reflect on the character of our aesthetic experience, on how often the poem, the story, the song, the picture "reminds us of" or "captures exactly" the way we felt then or "makes us feel sad for some lovely time and place we shall never see again." So frequently and uniformly does nostalgic sentiment seem to infuse our aesthetic experience that we can rightly begin to suspect that nostalgia is not only a feeling or mood that is somehow magically evoked by the art object but also a distinctive modality in its own right, a kind of code or patterning of symbolic elements, which by some obscure mimetic isomorphism comes, much as in language itself, to serve as a substitute for the feeling or mood it aims to arouse. (73)

Davis argues that an audience will respond to certain nostalgic patterns in music, art, and literature even when there is no "immediate or 'real' reason" for this feeling because we have, by living in a particular culture, "through long associative exposure assimilated the aesthetic code that evokes the emotion" (82). Store this idea, too: the ubiquity of nostalgic elements in art, particularly in environmental literature of the past century and increasingly in the years approaching the millennium.

■ ■ ▓ "Be prepared for the worst." I am trying to put my finger on the vaguest of emotions—complacency, numbness, shock. The heart wrung dry, passion turned inside out, experience not yet imagined or simply beyond the mind's reach. "Yah, yah, we've heard it all before and nothing ever happens." I awaken in the darkness on a cold fall night and walk stiffly to the living room to meditate with a piece of paper. My feet shuffle across the wooden floor. I give myself some dim light and then sit cross-legged on the couch, surrounded by evidence of life: skateboarding magazines, a school backpack, boxer shorts, a brown paper bag with "Jacinto lunch" written on the side in my handwriting and a wad of pink, chewed gum stuck on the inside. There's a laminated drawing that the ten-year-old has made: a floating Martin Luther King Jr. head nearly touching a fragmentary rainbow—bands of red, blue, yellow, orange—and several cartoonish, Chagall-like birds—white with orange beaks—floating beside, above, and below the human figure. A brown hand with a peace sign tattooed on it reaches up from the bottom of the page toward the suspended civil rights leader. Signs of life—a vast, encompassing "still life" that includes me and my sleeplessness. The house seems to breathe when the heater comes on—minutes' long sighs. Then nothing. The faint sounds of nighttime traffic on distant streets, the restless creaking of furniture and door jambs. I can hear Jacinto breathing in another room now and then, and Analinda rustles the sheets in the other room, missing something. When I can't hear them, I take it for granted that they're there, alive, dreaming.

■ ■ ■   "Be prepared for the worst." What is the "worst"? How can we imagine this? I've been to Hiroshima, seen the empty, eerie Peace Memorial Park, walked the halls and galleries of the museum to cringe at dioramas that display hanging shreds of skin and flaming buildings. One hundred thousand souls erased in a flash of light, an entire planet enshrouded for half a century now in the possibility of nuclear apocalypse. But does this register in my mind? In the minds of my neighbors? Every day?

I have also been to an even darker place, the basement sanctum of a distant children's hospital, a windowless realm of whispers and shadows. "You must come soon. He isn't doing very well," Analinda's voice had trembled on the phone. So I went to the hospital—paid attention to daily traffic, thought about student papers, fretted over the disruption of my schedule. There sat Analinda in a dark storage room, her breasts still dripping milk that month-old Pablo would never drink. Fifty feet away, in a windowed room of quarantine, the innocent lay naked again, strapped to a white bed, covered with tape and tubes, eyes heavy lidded with fear and drugs. I didn't know it at the time, but a machine already breathed for him. Young Dr. Anglin took my arm and brought me to a room within view of Pablo's distress. A series of x-rays showed tiny lungs increasingly white with spreading infection. "We're doing all we can," the doctor said. "But be prepared for the worst."

■ ■ ■ "Be prepared for the worst." Every morning now I look out the window and see a new sky, clouds reshaping themselves over Mount Rose, the pink promise of another brilliant day. Subtle sounds outside my vision imply the continuation of life. I take to the streets in running shoes, then soon to the rocky trails of Keystone Canyon, and every aching step, every flex of my body, assures me that I am still here, three years after everything—after one small black-haired, machine-breathing organism—vanished. But sometimes, like tonight, while Analinda and Jacinto sleep, while the house alternately purrs and creaks, I come to sit by myself and reflect on the moment when innocence stopped breathing: 5:20 A.M., October 18, 1994. I recall the hours before that moment. Analinda's phone call: "Scott, you've got to come now. He's dying. Come now to say good-bye." I recall my call to a friend: "Sharon, please come stay with Jacinto. Pablo's dying and I need to go." The predawn drive to Austin, the breathless walk to the bowels of pediatric intensive care, the nurse increasing the medication—"So he will feel nothing"—and the monitors going flat. The nurse methodically, delicately removes the tape and tubes, then swaddles tiny Pablo as if the infant is truly newborn, hands him to sitting Analinda. She and I are too numb to cry or to know if we are in fact crying. "Touch your son," Analinda says. "Touch him and say good-bye." "I can't," I reply. As if in a dream, we hand the body to the nurse and walk unsteadily through a room of silent, unstaring doctors and nurses toward the still-dark parking garage, where all we can do is hug and breathe.

■ ■ ■ "Be prepared for the worst" is a phrase that I speak to you, when in fact I am thinking of myself and what it has meant in my own life to steel my emotions and hold my breath in anticipation of what I do not want but cannot avoid. *Expecting* the worst is not the same as *accepting* the worst. There is an air of inevitability to the words "be prepared for the worst," and this sense of unavoidable failure inspires in us an ardent—perhaps childlike—desire for another chance, for an alternative future.

But what is it that leads human beings to think first of *themselves,* then of others, of broad abstractions? In his introductory essay on "Grief and a Headhunter's Rage," from *Culture and Truth: The Remaking of Social Analysis,* the anthropologist and cultural theorist Renato Rosaldo talks about his fieldwork among the Ilongot headhunters in the Philippines during the 1960s and 1970s, incorporating an account of his own experience with grief and rage following the accidental death of his wife, Michelle Rosaldo, in 1981, when she fell off a sixty-five-foot cliff into a rushing river while doing field research. Later in the chapter, Rosaldo reflects on his use of this story:

> My use of personal experience serves as a vehicle for making the quality and intensity of the rage in Ilongot grief more readily accessible to readers than certain more detached modes of composition. At the same time, by invoking personal experience as an analytical category one risks easy dismissal. Unsympathetic readers could reduce this introduction to an act of mourning or a mere report on my discovery of the anger possible in bereavement. Frankly, this introduction is both and more. An act of mourning, a personal report, and a critical analysis of anthropological method, it simultaneously encompasses a number of distinguishable processes, no one of which cancels out the others. (11)

Likewise, my own readers may wonder about the motives and techniques of my report of loss and bereavement. To tell the story of my infant son's death three years ago requires me to think directly about something that I would otherwise sublimate and repress—something I've so far tried to ignore while going on with life, but which in fact is turning and turning in my subconscious mind, waiting for expression. I can articulate the experience of Pablo's death for myself and for a public audience in a way that I cannot begin to discuss with Analinda and Jacinto, my wife and son. The three of us shared Pablo's death together—"You mean I won't be a big brother anymore?" cried seven-year-old Jacinto on the steps of the Ronald McDonald house when we told him about the seriousness of Pablo's condition, the night before he died—and yet we have never been able to share our subsequent grief, fearing perhaps that open grieving would prevent us from daily functioning, would result in such a collapse into sadness that we could never recover. So when I tell the story of Pablo's dying, I am, in part, trying to explore what has in my life been the ultimate experience of lost hope, lost innocence, in order to understand the poignancy of warning and the subsequent confirmation of the anticipated event. "How do we experience pain?" I am asking myself. And how does pain transform into numbness? And, once numbed, can we be restored to feeling? And what are the implications of post-traumatic numbness for the language of environmental warning? A cascade of questions. What follows is an extended discussion of the rhetoric of environmental warning, considering why warning is such a pervasive mode of contemporary writing about nature and attempting to explain why such warnings are so difficult to heed.

2000

"Be prepared for the worst." Is the "worst" the end of something or the *feeling* of loss after something ends or disappears? Or is it *complacency*—the lack of feeling or engagement, the suffering painlessness of enervation—that is the worst that can happen to us? I think of Hemingway's short story, "The End of Something," published in the mid-1920s, a post–World War I story in which Nick Adams and his girl—Marjorie—break up. The cause of the breakup is numbness and the result is more numbness. What is the *something* that ends? Love, innocence, a relationship between two people? The word "something"—so vague—says it all.

1997

"Be prepared . . ." for what? When? The warning often comes too late. We are doomed to look for concrete, specific causes and effects. Thus our love for literature, the philosophy of the anecdotal and imagistic. And yet, as Bill McKibben explains in *The Age of Missing Information*, our devotion to new high-speed information technologies dooms us to miss much of what occurs in the world: "[T]he worst disasters," he writes, "move much more slowly, and thereby sneak past the cameras. Consider . . . the decay of the global environment and the wicked, miserable poverty that traps so much of the country and the planet. . . . [T]hey happen on time scales that defy television's relentless dailiness" (156–57).

In the daylight, the circle of my attention widens, from self to community to world. The private nightmare of my family's loss three years ago, which sometimes returns acutely to me at night, washes into the numb generality of daily experience when the sun is out. But the memory lingers, the memory of Pablo's death and of last night's meditation—and this haunting memory takes on metaphorical significance as I reflect on David Quammen's recent warning that we, as human beings, tend to think about death too concretely and specifically, to regard the phenomenon of extinction as we would the death of an individual organism. In *The Song of the Dodo,* Quammen tells the story of the last credible eyewitness report of the rare dodo bird on the island of Mauritius by the Dutchman Volquard Iversen in the year 1662. But he then follows this narrative with a critique of the anecdotal approach to extinction, to environmental loss:

The vividness of the Iversen episode is somewhat misleading. The crux of the matter of extinction—the extinction of Raphus cucullatus or any species—is not who or what kills the last individual. That final death reflects only a proximate cause. The ultimate cause, or causes, may be quite different. By the time the death of its last individual becomes imminent, a species has already lost too many battles in the war for survival. It has been swept into a vortex of compounded woes. Its evolutionary adaptability is largely gone. Ecologically, it has become moribund. Sheer chance, among other factors, is working against it. The toilet of its destiny has been flushed. (274)

Response to an abstract threat—to the language of warning or to a vaguely perceived physical threat in the world—this is the issue that most concerns me in this essay. Beyond the veil of extinction literature, so abundant in these waning days of the millennium, is the idea that we ourselves, *Homo sapiens*, are the ultimate dodos—the arrogant, self-destructive, sapient dodos careening toward oblivion, unable or unwilling to change our culture in order to stave off our own extinction and yet full of remorse at the loss of individual members of our kind and indifferent to the dire prognostications of our sages.

What is it in human nature that makes it so difficult for us to heed a warning? How can we "be prepared for the worst" when most of us, most of the time, ignore threats that are too abstract or too slow and widespread to be perceived by the individual human observer? As Donald Worster reminds us in *Nature's Economy*, Thomas Malthus formulated "his tragic ratios" in the late eighteenth century to show that "population must eventually overrun the supply of food, bringing intense competition for wages to meet rising prices, and finally misery and starvation to those 'unhappy persons who, in the great lottery of life, have drawn a blank'" (150). Vast patterns, recognized in population statistics, food production data, and economic and employment figures—not to mention Malthus's inherent pessimism and caution with regard to providential ecological views—enabled the author to formulate the *Essay on the Principle of Population,* an essay that Charles Darwin could read for amusement and appreciation but that would surely fall on deaf ears among the general public. Nearly two centuries later, Paul Ehrlich issued his own essay on population—*The Population Bomb: Population Control or Race to Oblivion?*—with data and warnings and advice much more specific to our time, arguing that the current trend of rampant population growth will likely continue "to its logical conclusion: mass starvation. The rich are going to get richer," he explained in 1968:

but the more numerous poor are going to get poorer. Of these poor, a minimum of three and one-half million will starve to death this year, mostly children. But this is a mere handful compared to the numbers that will be starving in a decade or so. And it is too late to take action to save many of those people. (17)

Mass starvation, too late to help. It is the nature of warnings to have a delayed effect on massive problems. It is also the nature of human beings, as Ehrlich mentioned in a talk he gave in Reno in October 1997, "not to take dictation well," not to heed admonishments and commands. Thirty years after the first publication of *The Population Bomb*, we live in a world in which many of the book's population predictions have come true. Ehrlich anticipated a global human population of 5.65 billion in 1995; the actual population was

5.7 billion. Ehrlich predicted an overpopulated world beset by gangsters and war and environmental degradation. What he did not predict, though, was the "brownlash" phenomenon of the 1980s and 1990s, the so-called Wise Use Movement and the rash of books like Ronald Bailey's *Eco-Scam: The False Prophets of Ecological Apocalypse* (1993) and Gregg Easterbrook's *A Moment on the Earth: The Coming Age of Environmental Optimism* (1995).

Paul and Anne Ehrlich responded to this widespread effort to pooh-pooh environmental warnings such as theirs by publishing *Betrayal of Science and Reason: How Anti-Environmental Rhetoric Threatens Our Future.* "The time has come," they state in the introduction,

to write a book about efforts being made to minimize the seriousness of environmental problems. We call these attempts the "brownlash" because they help to fuel a backlash against "green" policies. The brownlash has been generated by a diverse group of individuals and organizations, doubtless often with differing motives and backgrounds. We classify them as brownlashers by what they say, not by who they are. With strong and appealing messages, they have successfully sowed seeds of doubt among journalists, policy makers, and the public at large about the reality and importance of such phenomena as overpopulation, global climate change, ozone depletion, and losses of biodiversity. In writing this book, we try to set the record straight with respect to environmental science and its proper interpretation. By exposing and refuting the misinformation disseminated by the brownlash, we hope to return to higher ground the crucial dialogue on how to sustain society's essential environmental services. (1–2)

It's well and good to "set the record straight," to use the latest data and analytical models in proposing new approaches for agriculture and environmental science, and to expose the dangers of new "fables" about population and climate and toxic waste. But, the Ehrlichs ask in the title of one of the chapters of their 1996 book, "How Can Good Science Become Good Policy?" "One especially unpalatable consequence of the brownlash's attempts to disseminate erroneous information," they write,

is the undue influence its rhetoric has on public policy. Brownlashers try to convince not only policy makers but also the public at large that their view is the right one—a moderate, scientifically justified position on environmental matters. But we have seen that much of the propaganda is seriously at variance with informed scientific opinion on many critical issues.

How can decision makers and the general public be made more aware of the actual findings of environmental science, and thus of the increasingly grave threats posed by environmental deterioration? (203)

The chapter from *Betrayal of Science and Reason* proceeds to urge environmental scientists to devote their energy to public education, not merely to technical research. And there is a list of thirteen topics—from discussion of "how the scale of the human enterprise critically affects the environment" to consideration of "risk assessment: how to deal with uncertainty"—that the Ehrlichs themselves routinely include in university courses and public lectures (206). But how can the mere presentation of such information overcome the massive unmindfulness of the public and the seeds of skepticism sown recently by the brownlash movement? People do not want to be afraid of what's coming, to be made aware of the dire circumstances of the present. And our minds have developed various strategies to slough off fearful information. More potent perhaps than fear as a means of triggering concern and caring is the emotion of regret, the sense that we've squandered something important or that such squandering is imminent. Yet even regret wrestles with a childlike desire for complacency and peace of mind, and our impulse as a species is to abandon healthy concern at the slightest invitation, even if such an invitation comes without evidence, without substantiation.

1999

Can you feel it slipping yet? The lyric intensity of one family's story? A single baby dies; a single family is torn apart and must learn to live under a cloud of lost innocence. A single scholar—a human being—turns to narrative in order to voice his revelation of what it means to lose something dear. But the narrative changes into something broader, more encompassing—an effort to stabilize the self by perceiving and hooking into a larger pattern. I want you, reader, to accept my tale of Pablo's death as credible and real. This experience happened, just as surely as you can clasp your lover's hand or tousle the hair of your own sweet child. And yet I find myself compelled to explain the feeling of loss, perhaps even to "explain it away."

Can you feel the lyric intensity of the narrative voice slipping into the white noise of equivocation and explanation, of "academic discourse"? "I write as though there were no sorrow like my sorrow," wrote Harriet Beecher Stowe to her husband in 1849, following the death of her baby boy, Charley. On the contrary, I write as though every sorrow were like my sorrow, as if the entire planet's potential—inevitable—sorrow were somehow indicated in my emotional response to Pablo's death. In her survey of women's tales of loss, Melody Graulich, from whom I've taken the Stowe passage, notes the great frequency of "lost child" narratives in American women's literature, from Charlotte Perkins Gilman to Amy Tan; the scholar, embedding her own variation on this theme within her commentary on "mourning literature," is "reminded that a literary tradition is a mighty comforting thing" (169). I, too, find comfort in the process of locating myself, my family, and our story in the context of the universal experience of loss. What I find disquieting, in fact, is how easy it is to take comfort in context, in abstraction, in the apparent immutability of a big pattern. My purpose in this exploration is not to soothe, but to worry. Numbness, I sense, is everywhere, accessible—and it is as inviting as sleep.

2000

"Be prepared for the worst." Commentators such as Edith Efron would disparage such a statement as "apocalypticism" and would accuse the speaker of being an alarmist crank. In her 1984 book, *The Apocalyptics: How Environmental Politics Controls What We Know about Cancer,* Efron exhorts the public not to accept the warnings of such "leading apocalyptic scientists" as Rachel Carson, Paul Ehrlich, Barry Commoner, René Dubos, and George Wald. Don't be prepared for the worst, she argues, don't take a cautious view toward human selfishness and consumptiveness, but be ready to do battle with scientific ideologues who allow their moral visions to interfere with empirical truth. Rachel Carson, complains Efron, "was imbued with a profoundly ecological perspective and bore a deep animus against modern technology.... The bulk of [*Silent Spring*] was a passionate denunciation of the life-destroying evils of modern industrial technology" (33).

Ehrlich is characterized as a purveyor of "ecological totalitarianism" whose books "played a powerful role in feeding the apocalyptic fever which was building in the country. He almost single-handedly launched the 'Zero Population Growth' movement and convinced many in the upper middle class that it was immoral to have children. 'Man,' above all, was Ehrlich's enemy" (35).

We find ourselves—the laypeople—faced with claims and counterclaims. Whom shall we believe? Who is free of ideology? Where can we turn for the empirical foundation of our evolving environmental values? Edith Efron concludes her book with a call for honest, right-minded, nonapocalyptic scientists and journalists to come forward:

Just as the public grasped the apocalyptic abstraction that "chemicals" were evil and that "nature" was benign, so will it grasp that the scientists who hid nature and pitted them against their own economic system are not to be trusted. A bomb has been dropped on the Carsonian religious-political parable which is the only meaning Americans have ever been given for "environmental cancer. . . ." While the Biologist State was concocting a pseudo-science and regulating industry on the basis of a fairy tale, while it was manipulating theory and data the way a cardsharp shuffles cards, while it was suffocating American minds with myth . . . *where were the critical scientists who knew that this was happening . . . and where was the watchdog press?* (423)

So much venom, so much self-righteousness, on many sides of the environmental discussion. The layperson—including the literary artist—has nowhere to turn for neutral science, for there is no such thing. We must begin to study, then, how environmental values—how values in general—are received and constructed, so as to better account for this process in considering the conflicting arguments presented by the inevitable defenders and critics who will participate in any debate. In both private decision making and the formulation of public policy, we struggle today, in an age of relativism and social constructivism, to locate guideposts of "truth." Furthermore, although the news reports indicate that we live in an increasingly violent and volatile society, many of us no longer understand what it means to be in danger. Danger has, for the most part, become a muted, abstract phenomenon, likely to reveal itself only as a vague economic irritant or as a sudden, unexpected physical threat—a flooding river, an avalanche, a sidewalk mugging. We are losing our ability to process warnings of all kinds, including environmental warnings, driven as we are into becoming ideologically intransigent interpreters of science and complacent recipients of doomsday messages.

Even clever restatements of Rachel Carson's "Fable for Tomorrow" and Paul Ehrlich's vision of a war-torn, resource-scarce world fall upon deaf ears. Think of the Cherokee/Appalachian writer Marilou Awiakta's poem called "Mother Nature Sends a Pink Slip," from her 1993 collection *Selu: Seeking the Corn-Mother's Wisdom:*

To: Homo Sapiens
Re: Termination

My business is producing life.
The bottom line is
you are not cost-effective workers.
Over the millennia, I have repeatedly
clarified my management goals and objectives.
Your failure to comply is well documented.
It stems from your inability to be
a team player:
    • you interact badly with co-workers
    • contaminate the workplace
    • sabotage the machinery
    • hold up production
    • consume profits
In short, you are a disloyal species.

Within the last decade
I have given you three warnings:
    • made the workplace too hot for you
    • shaken up your home office
    • utilized plague to cut back personnel
Your failure to take appropriate action
has locked these warnings into
the Phase-Out Mode, which will result
in termination.   No appeal. (88)

The poem acknowledges the failure of warnings—such pronounced "natural disasters" as global warming, major earthquakes, and virus epidemics such as AIDS and Ebola—to instill humanity with a more cautious, respectful attitude toward their place—our place—in the world. So what might the impact of a mere poem be? Chastisement seems not to work, as ample evidence shows. Information, even from the most authoritative sources, seems to be a lightning rod for skepticism. Even scientific discussions, even academic debates, now function like courtroom melodrama: witness, counterwitness, character assassination, kowtowing to research funding agencies. In Awiakta's case, at least in the poem presented above, ironic humor—with Mother Nature using standard corporate language—is the rhetorical strategy of choice. But many environmental writers these days seem able to do little more than seek to establish their own moral certainty, as if preparing ultimately to voice a last-minute collective "I told you so" if their subtle—and not so subtle—apocalyptic statements become physically manifest decades from now. Or perhaps, more optimistically (as in Awiakta's poem), such warnings offer more than moral admonishments. They serve as practical maps, showing combinations of values-formation strategies and conservative, sustainable behaviors and employing new vocabularies of warning in order to pierce minds paralyzed by don't-worry-be-happy rhetoric and ears numbed by too many shrill predictions. No one wants, ultimately, to be lost and disoriented, so we pretend that we are at home and at peace, that we are morally centered—we relax in our era of mind-made everything, knowing that nothing is real.

■ ■ ■ Do you feel it slipping away yet, the lyrical intensity of the narrative voice? What do you feel at this very moment?

Readers of literature, beware: what follows is the emotional vacuum of policy and economics. This is the language that holds sway in the halls of power. Provocative poems and engaging narratives seldom occupy the minds of those who decide how to dispose of natural resources, who determine what to protect. If you want to understand how the rule makers think, why they do what they do, try a sample of their language.

Try to hold onto your emotional sharpness as you enter the discourse of steady-state economics and Contingent Valuation. Try to be a human being in this atmosphere. Think about what it is that you love.

■ ■ ■ "Be prepared for the worst." The worst thing of all may be to be lost and not to know it. In contemplating the vast and ubiquitous abstraction of death, John Daniel once wrote, "My mind, like my hands, is best suited to the grasping of smaller things, things that happen close in front of me, things I can see and turn slowly in memory and see again, in imagination's second light" ("Some Mortal Speculations" 199). Although I blithely use the abstract language of the academic world, I resonate emotionally to the soundness of Daniel's confession. My mind, too—like *all* human minds, I suspect—is better suited to small, concrete specifics than to the management of large, systemic patterns. Literary artists work, of course, in the realm of vivid particulars, and readers of literature relish the particular, while maneuvering to extrapolate more general patterns of the imagination, patterns of the social and natural realms, patterns of the individual mind. Environmental writers such as Marilou Awiakta, Rick Bass, T. Coraghessan Boyle, William Kittredge, Barry Lopez, Scott Russell Sanders, and Terry Tempest Williams operate routinely in the mode of the evocative parable, not simply dictating moral reform, but guiding audiences afflicted with moral relativism and clichéd, knee-jerk, moral polarization to rethink their fundamental values, their needs and fears and desires. We live in a time of rapidly shifting physical conditions and yet, tragically, our ability to reshape worldviews and ethical schemes to match the physical and social changes has atrophied. As Robert Ornstein and Paul Ehrlich suggest in their 1989 volume *New World New Mind: Moving Toward Conscious Evolution,*

We don't perceive the world as it is, because our nervous system evolved to select only a small extract of reality and to ignore the rest. We never experience *exactly* the same situation twice, so it would be uneconomical to take in every occurrence. Instead of conveying everything about the world, our nervous system is "impressed" only by *dramatic changes.* (3)

The phenomenon of *valuation*—the actual process of forging values—is perhaps the most important aspect of our relationship to the natural world that environmental literature can help us to understand. What's more, this literature actually functions as a sort of cultural antenna, sensitizing us to significant changes in our physical surroundings that most of us—due to the normal, hurried obliviousness of daily life—would otherwise ignore.

Think of such narratives of values transformation as Barry Lopez's story "The Negro in the Kitchen," from *Field Notes,* or Terry Tempest Williams's parable of the transformation from obedience to social resistance in *Refuge.* Such tales are valuable not only for their specific narrative strategies, but for their suggestions about how the process of values formation occurs as a result of experience, whether real or imagined. Think of Scott Russell Sanders's speculative novel, *Terrarium,* which helps us to appreciate the act of historical projection as a means of imagining—and constructively questioning—the trajectory of technological progress. Or Rick Bass's *Winter* and *The Book of Yaak,* meditations on the private and political relationship between self and place, studies of the process by which alienation becomes love. William Kittredge's work, increasingly, recants not only the old mythology of the American West as an agricultural paradise, but the traditional notion of environmental adversaries—taken as a whole, his body of work exhibits a mind in steady flux, pressing continually to revise identity and recast values, seeking to locate the self within changing social and environmental realities.

■　■　■　So, let me say it again. "Be prepared for the worst." Better, worse, best, worst. By using such words, we presuppose that the speaker and his or her listener possess an active, shared system of values and perhaps, on a deeper level, an understanding of the evaluative process—something known among economists, psychologists, and policy types as "valuation." But there is little consensus among the experts on how environmental values are or should be framed or formed. Economists such as Herman Daly argue emphatically that economic value is linked to moral value. In his classic essay, "The Steady-State Economy: Toward a Political Economy of Biophysical Equilibrium and Moral Growth," however, Daly is forced to call into question the very possibility of using actual societal values as a guide in developing environmental policy. "Is it realistic in our secular, 'pluralistic' society to expect any kind of moral consensus?" he asks:

Where is this moral consensus to come from? Not from a spineless relativism or from the hallucinatory psychic epiphenomena that seem to haunt complex systems. Let us state it directly in the strongest terms. Ultimately, the possibility of moral consensus presupposes a dogmatic belief in objective value. If values are subjective, or thought to be merely cultural artifacts, then there is nothing objective to which appeal can be made or around which a consensus might be formed. . . . Only real objective values can command consensus in a sophisticated self-analytical society. We have no guarantee that objective value can be clarified, nor that, once clarified, it would be accorded the consensus it merits. But without faith in the existence of an objective hierarchy of value and in our ability at least vaguely to perceive it, we must resign ourselves to being driven by technological determinism into an unchosen, and perhaps unbearable, future. On what grounds is technical determinism to be resisted? Just as physical research must be based on dogmatic faith that nature is orderly, so research into policy questions must presuppose the reality of an ordered hierarchy of value. If *better* or *worse* are meaningless terms, then all policy is nonsense. (357–58)

Daly proposes the following "revised utilitarian rule" to govern technological development and the use of natural resources: "All present people take priority over future numbers, but the existence of more future people takes priority over the trivial wants of the present." The goal of this rule is to "maximize life, . . . to economize the long-run capacity of the earth to support life at a sufficient level of individual wealth" (361). Edith Efron would run shrieking from the room upon hearing this insanely antigrowth, antimachine values statement. But she need not fear. In reality most environmental policy decisions today are still in the hands of resource harvesters and processors, consulting economists, and politically sensitized policy wonks. There is no consensus on a shared moral foundation, nor is there consensus on methodologies for values elicitation.

Even among specialists in environmental valuation, there is profound disagreement. Witness the current brouhaha over the methodology known as Contingent Valuation (or CV), the favored strategy among contemporary natural-resource economists, which "posits a hypothetical market for an unpriced good and asks individuals to state the dollar value they place on a proposed change in its quantity, quality, or access" (Gregory et al. 177). Psychologists involved in the debate over CV argue that while "there is a need for monetary assessments of environmental damages and that an evaluation approach based on an individual's expressed preferences is appropriate for this purpose, . . . the measures of monetary value used in current CV methods are flawed because they impose unrealistic cognitive demands upon respondents" (178). In other words, human beings do not know how to attach monetary value to goods that have no real market. Who is going to buy Prince William Sound or Yucca Mountain? Which one of us is thinking about making a bid on the Tongass National Forest? Sure, we could pull enormous dollar figures out of thin air, but there is no way for us to gauge the actual value of these places, even if we were brazen enough to believe that we had a moral right to affix monetary value to extraordinary parts of the world. Critics of the CV methodology argue increasingly that "improved methods for valuing non-market natural resources can be found by paying closer attention to the multidimensional nature of environmental values and to the constructive nature of human preferences" (ibid.). This is where environmental literature fits into the scheme.

From 1995 to 2004, I collaborated with anthropologist Terre Satterfield on a National Science Foundation–sponsored study which posits that nature writers sense and articulate society's long-held and emerging environmental values and prod readers to reexamine biases and beliefs no longer in congruence with physical and social reality. Satterfield's research proposal asserts that "nature writers are lay ethicists who more than any other group have manifested and articulated nonmonetary, non-utilitarian expressions of values. Most nature writers have spent considerable reflective time considering the essence of environmental values and the narrative expression of those values" (C-8). What remain to be explored, however, are the specific rhetorical strategies that writers use to express their perceptions of environmental values and the processes by which this literature can contribute to the discourse of law and policy. "If the language among the people changes," says Charles Wilkinson in The Eagle Bird, "the language in the law books will change. One task is to add new kinds of words to balance out a vocabulary now dominated by board feet and cost-benefit analyses. The other task is to enrich existing words" (15–16). This is precisely the aim of environmental writers: to cut through the gray bureaucratic language of the courtroom, the corporate boardroom, and the federal office building and transfuse it with love and grief, with life. But to do so in a way that doesn't merely open old wounds and reinforce old prejudices.

■ ■ ■ "Be prepared for the worst." Imagine, if you will, a time sooner or later when what you cherish this moment will be no more. What do you love? Think about it now. And now, one breath later, believe that it is gone. You can flail and grope and plead for the preservation of your favorite forest, for the life of your husband or your wife or your lover or your child. Or you can accommodate yourself to change. Prepare yourself for loss or prepare yourself to fight. Or prepare yourself for loss in order to stimulate yourself to fight. These are the potent messages that have become ubiquitous in postindustrial writing about human culture and the natural world. Aldo Leopold issued the following statement in the Round River section appended to *A Sand County Almanac* in 1953:

One of the penalties of an ecological education is that one lives alone in a world of wounds. Much of the damage inflicted on land is quite invisible to laymen. An ecologist must either harden his shell and make believe that the consequences of science are none of his business, or he must be the doctor who sees the marks of death in a community that believes itself well and does not want to be told otherwise. (197)

Paul and Anne Ehrlich used the phrase "a world of wounds" as the working title of a recent book, thinking specifically about the role of scientific ecologists in contemporary society and urging this community of scholars to be politically active. However, I believe Leopold meant to use "ecologist" in a more inclusive sense, chastening all people sensitive to the deterioration of the planet and the endangerment of humans and other species to defy the rhetorical abyss of warning discourse and tell society what it does not want to hear.

■ ■ ■ "Be prepared for the worst" is the phrase we despise and the phrase we relish. The sweet sadness of future remorse is one of the defining emotions of beauty. We know it's coming—loss and its emotional attachment—and yet we imagine ourselves to be innocent, inculpable. Perhaps we even imagine ourselves to be impervious to the effects of loss, as if this life and this world exist in the game world of the imagination. We experience human loss in our personal lives, and we experience the annual reminder of autumn, but there is a disconcerting impulse among artists and audiences to aestheticize loss and to forget its correspondences in the physical world. This process creates an illusion of permanence that exists in poignant tension with back-of-the-mind awareness of dead infants and poisoned rivers. One might refer to this tendency as the museum-making impulse of nostalgic art.

Renato Rosaldo coins the term "imperialist nostalgia" in *Culture and Truth* in order to describe the phenomenon of "mourning for what one has destroyed." This notion applies to a variety of nostalgic (and destructive) relationships, from the cultural to the environmental. "Imperialist nostalgia revolves around a paradox," writes Rosaldo:

A person kills somebody, and then mourns the victim. In more attenuated form, someone deliberately alters a form of life, and then regrets that things have not remained as they were prior to the intervention. At one more remove, people destroy their environment, and then they worship nature. In any of its versions, imperialist nostalgia uses a pose of "innocent yearning" both to capture people's imaginations and to conceal its complicity with often brutal domination. (69–70)

In acknowledging the use of the discourse of warning—and in particular the rhetoric of nostalgia—as a trope in environmental literature, it is important to remember the potential dangers of displacing responsibility from the self to anonymous culprits (the "they did it" excuse) and transforming moral outrage into passive aesthetic pleasure (the "isn't it sad and beautiful" dismissal). And yet, with this caveat in mind, we can nonetheless appreciate the potent emotional tug of nostalgia as one of the most vigorous and useful strategies in the literature of social reform. In recent years, the nostalgic trope has, in fact, undergone a subtle transformation that may help to prevent some of the escapist deflections evident in imperialist nostalgia. For an example of this change, we have only to compare, in brief, two particular examples of nostalgic environmental writing, John Nichols's *The Last Beautiful Days of Autumn* (1982) and Rick Bass's *The Book of Yaak* (1996).

Eighteen years ago, Nichols published his photographic and essayistic paean to autumn in northern New Mexico, a rhapsodic volume sharpened by the elegiac title and subject matter and by the author's penchant for playful, inflated prose. The subject matter of this work is not merely autumn, but "the *last beautiful* days of autumn"—the rich, intense conclusion of a season of decline. By both implication and direct discussion, the book also addresses the midlife issue of personal mortality. "Sometimes I wonder: how will I die?" Nichols states in his epilogue, and then he proceeds to consider the possibilities and at the same time to celebrate the sensual life—outdoor nature and indoor sex—as if sensuality and mortality are crucially intertwined. Certainly, the *language* of the physical life and that of loss are inextricable. One of the important questions for contemporary environmental writers, though, is how to use the discourse of loss without *merely* allowing nostalgic language, as Fred Davis puts it, "to serve as a substitute for the feeling or mood it aims to arouse" (73). Nichols's book opens with the following paragraph:

I live for autumn. All year long I have reveries of those cool beautiful days to come, and memories of Octobers past. It is the most alive, the most heartbreakingly real season in my bones. I love the chilly winds and dying leaves and the first snow flurries that sweep intermittently down this lean valley. I adore the harvest smells around me, of ripe and rotting fruit, of the last alfalfa cutting. Nervous horses with their heads raised, flared nostrils tautly sniffing arctic odors, make me feel like singing. And I long for the gorgeous death of that high-country season when the mountains pulse with a pellucid varnish of winter whiteness, and the spears of a million bare aspens—only moments ago bursting with resplendent foliage—create a soft gray smirrh across jagged hillsides. (3)

Despite the vague political implications here—implications that are amplified in Nichols's other books of nature writing such as *If Mountains Die* (1979), *On the Mesa* (1986), *The Sky's the Limit* (1990), and *Keep It Simple* (1994)—this passage and most of *Last Beautiful Days* operates as a personal, nostalgic reverie involving the seasonal changes of nature. Issues of environmental and cultural preservation haunt the background of the narrative, but Nichols's principal aim seems to be the creation of a verbal and photographic analogue to the experience of an autumn in Taos. I'm not sure if Renato Rosaldo would criticize this book as an imperialist celebration of an occupied landscape by a Euro-American author, but he would likely observe that activism and responsibility-taking are hidden in the pastel language of nostalgia.

By contrast, Bass's *The Book of Yaak*, with its genre-challenging combination of personal reverie and activist plea, seems to display a promising rhetorical compromise between the traditional use of nostalgic/warning language and the cutting-edge language of contemporary social analysis, language that strives to accommodate the speaker's share in the forces of destruction. "Nostalgia at play with domination" is what Rosaldo calls this paradoxical discourse (87). It is instructive, in conclusion, to present the opening section of *The Book of Yaak*, so as to contrast it with Nichols's introduction:

I shiver, as I write this.

I'm shivering because it's winter in my windowless unheated rat-shed of a writing cabin.

I'm shivering because I'm so nakedly, openly, revealing the earned secrets of my valley—places and things I know, which the valley—the Yaak—has entrusted to me.

There is a place, a sanctuary you go to, in writing fiction, or, I suppose, poetry, that is in another world. You are not in control—and upon emerging from it, the writing of and the inhabiting of that place, you feel new energy, new understanding. You've touched mystery.

It's magic. There's no other word for it—no way known to explain it.

That's what I like to chase, or move toward: that feeling, that place. It does try to escape.

This book is not like that. It's a sourcebook, a handbook, a weapon of the heart. To a literary writer, it's a sin, to ask something of the reader, rather than to give; and to know the end, to know your agenda, from the very start, rather than discovering it along the way, or at the end itself.

My valley is on fire—my valley is burning. It has been on fire for over twenty years. These essays—these please to act to save it—it's all I know how to do. I don't know if a book can help protect a valley, and the people who live in that valley. I know that a book can harm these things—that in our acquisitive culture, now that big business has us where they want us—having advertised into us the notion that we want things and lots of them, and that we want the Best, the most Unique, the Ten Least Known—that a revelation of this valley's wild faint secrets could draw acquisitive sorts—those who come to the valley to take something, rather than give.

It is not a place to come to.

It is a place to save—a place to exercise our strength and compassion—that last little bit that the advertisers have not yet been able to breed, or condition, out of us. . . . (xiii–xiv)

There are many moments of lyrical, private reverie in *The Book of Yaak*, passages where Bass celebrates "the blood-rhythms of wilderness which remain in us"

(13) and "the rare things, the delicious things" of his valley (58). But unlike the resigned tone, the air of inevitability, that permeates *The Last Beautiful Days of Autumn,* Bass's *The Book of Yaak*—like many of his recent magazine articles and like the recent essay/story *Fiber*—both explores the artist-activist dilemma and functions as a hybrid, fragilely balanced combination of art and plea. The most prominent idea in this work, apart from the unmistakable message that logging and development are threatening the Yaak and other remote places in the American West, is the notion of the artist's sacrifice, his decision to suspend storytelling in passionate pursuit of a political end. And yet, far from the polarizing effect of politicized language that Edith Efron detects in environmental discourse, Bass pursues the dream of a changing place that will nevertheless retain its essential character, its wildness. "Fact has replaced poetry," he admits on the final page of the book:

and—despite my knowing better—desire has been allowed to become so taut as to become brittle, and even to snap—risking the result of numbness. . . .

I'm not afraid of failing at a short story—at a work of fiction. But I am afraid of failing the valley; and I am afraid of failing my neighbors, my friends and my community.

I believe the simplest and yet most inflammatory belief of all: that we can have wilderness and logging both in the Yaak Valley. (188)

The very artfulness of literature becomes endangered when the writer presses the outer boundary of nostalgia, screeching along the border of language where the story of potential loss becomes a plea. What Bass is imagining in *The Book of Yaak,* what he's hoping for, is an aesthetic trade: words for place, artistic beauty for wild beauty. An exchange that might, eventually, inspire a political reorganization that will enable art and action, wilderness and logging, to coexist. Human experience must, in its entirety, encompass both life and death, emergence and loss, and for this reason the mood and language of nostalgia are central to the artist's efforts to convey the poignancy of experience. But as we face the environmental predicaments of a new millennium, a millennium surely to be marked by ever-deepening crisis and despair and emotional numbness, the primary challenge for literary artists and for interpreters of literature may be to understand the evolving discourse of warning and nostalgia, of love and loss.

Enough of this. Enough of this gray, academic chatter. You've surely lost the narrative thread by now, and I find myself drifting into the solace of abstraction, using the sidestep of analogy and generalization to ease the lingering pain of loss. The pain of Pablo's death—the pain I felt at the moment he stopped breathing—becomes muted as I distract myself by thinking of the gradual, almost imperceptible pain we all feel as we consider the slow rot of the planet. "Academic chatter." This is what Analinda would call my effort to compare Pablo's story with the phenomenon of environmental loss, my linking of a personal story with a discussion of the language of environmental valuation. She and I never talk about Pablo, and these days we seldom talk with each other about larger matters, either. Pablo's ashes rest in a blue plastic envelope within an orange, covered bowl; we have never removed the ceramic container from its cardboard box since our move to Nevada four years ago. The box, marked only by a small, red heart drawn by Analinda at the time of our move, sits unnoticed on a shelf in the downstairs storage room.

I push my feelings into an extended, metaphorical discussion of the loss we all share. Analinda, I fear, moves ever deeper into the hollow depths of a despair she can neither recognize nor overcome—she becomes a sleepwalker, a bearer of sadness—she becomes the loss she once experienced, and even if she wishes to shed this sadness, she doubts the power of words to perform such magic. I wonder, in turn, if I place too much faith in words. Or if, from her perspective, I am the one who is inactive, disengaged, silently despairing. I wonder if we all have different ways of recognizing and responding to the losses we experience during our lives.

What I know most fearfully is this: we, Analinda and I together, must do what we can to prevent Jacinto from living his entire life beneath—or within—the unarticulated sadness of this loss. As I work through the final passage of this essay in my head, I find myself driving through the mountains north of Reno with him, talking. It is a warm day, and the windows of our car are down—we are bathed in the smell of sage.

"Jacinto," I begin, out of the blue. "There is something I'd like to talk to you about. It's related to something I'm writing. Do you ever think of Pablo? How does the memory of Pablo make you feel?"

"When I think of Pablo," he says, "I feel sad."

"Do you think about Pablo very much?"

"All the time."

"What do you remember about him?"

"I remember how good it felt to hold him in my arms. I remember how cute he was. I remember the feel of his soft skin, his hair."

"Do you remember the last time you were with him, the last time you saw him or touched him?"

Jacinto pauses. "No. I remember him in general, but I can't think of the last time I was with him. . . . But this talking about him, it makes him clearer in my mind."

NOTE

Jacinto is now twenty-one years old, trying to figure out how to make his way in the world. Analinda and I are no longer married. Pablo's ashes remain in a bowl, in a box, at Analinda's house, awaiting a ceremonial release we do not know how to perform.

6

Authenticity, Occupancy, and Credibility

RICK BASS AND THE RHETORIC OF PROTECTING PLACE

In the early 1980s, the state of Nevada switched to a new license plate on motor vehicles: it's white with blue lettering and faint local images of bighorn sheep, craggy mountains, and Joshua trees. The funny thing is how residents of the state who own the previous simple blue license plate with white letters have, almost universally, kept those old plates, switching them from car to car as they update their personal transportation. There's something intriguing about this desire to demonstrate longevity, to state proudly through one's license plate, "I'm a longtimer, not a Johnny-come-lately." It's strange to think that people who've lived in that place for little more than a decade can presume to be longtime residents.

I notice a similar tendency whenever I'm with a group of strangers, such as a new group of students at the beginning of the semester, and self-introductions are made; invariably, a few people will announce, "I'm Tom so-and-so, or I'm Linda such-and-such, and I'm a native Nevadan." It's as if nativeness—or the next best thing: long residency—is a special badge of honor in a state that had almost no stable Euro-American population a century ago (Las Vegas, with well over a million residents now, had a population of approximately forty in 1900) and where you're more likely to pass ghost towns, depopulated remnants of various mining booms and busts, than bustling, living communities when you drive the six hundred miles or so from the northern end of the state to the southern. So you'll have to forgive me for being so interested in this issue of occupancy and authenticity, this question of belonging. I've lived in Reno for thirteen years now. A newcomer in Nevada is in good company, but we know we're outsiders. This is an interesting dimension of western environmental writing, too. My goal here is to probe this literary and cultural issue, first in a general way and then by examining the work of Rick Bass, one of the major contemporary environmental writers of the American West. In Bass's case, what particularly interests me is the process by which the author comes to occupy a new place, gropes verbally and imaginatively and experientially toward a genuine—or "authentic"—relationship with his new home, and ultimately strives for a credible rhetorical stance as he speaks and writes in protection of this adopted home. Hence the tripartite title of this essay: occupancy, authenticity, credibility. Bass's processes of becoming an authentic, credible inhabitant and spokesperson for his part of the American West represents a process recognizable in the lives and work of various contemporary "immigrant western writers," such as Barbara Kingsolver (originally from Kentucky, but now long associated with Tucson, Arizona), John Daniel (from Washington, DC, but now known for writing about his adopted state, Oregon), and Mary Sojourner (raised in New York State, now residing in Flagstaff), to name only a few examples.

Many contemporary American environmental writers have come recently to think of themselves not merely as "nature writers" (with "nature" coding for "nonhuman"), but rather as "community writers," artists who regard their work as an act of exploring and reforming *relationships* in the broadest sense of that word, encompassing both the human and the nonhuman. For writers in the American West, however, *community* is a vexed and complicated concept.

Unlike authors such as Robert Finch on Cape Cod or Scott Russell Sanders, who lives in Bloomington, Indiana, western writers find themselves particularly compelled to come to terms with mobility and transience and new residency in order to explain their roles as people speaking for and about such communities as the Yaak Valley in Montana and Finn Rock, Oregon. Charles Wilkinson, in *The Eagle Bird: Mapping a New West* (1992), points out that "Communities in the West have less cohesiveness than any region in the country. Our towns lack the stability and sense of community found, for example, in villages in New England

and the Midwest. To quote Patricia Nelson Limerick [. . .], 'Indians, Hispanics, Asians, blacks, Anglos, business people, workers, politicians, bureaucrats, natives, and newcomers, we share the same region and its history, but we wait to be introduced'" (135–36). Yet Wilkinson, after several pages of documenting the tendency toward community fragmentation and violent social conflict in the West, shifts into a more optimistic assertion as his chapter, called "Toward an Ethic of Place," continues:

Still, we can ameliorate these problems. We deserve and can achieve more stable, tight-knit communities, communities bound together by the common love of this miraculous land, of this region the likes of which exists nowhere else on earth. We can do much better.

We need to develop an ethic of place. It is premised on a sense of place, the recognition that our species thrives on the subtle, intangible, but soul-deep mix of landscape, smells, sounds, history, neighbors, and friends that constitute a place, a homeland. An ethic of place respects equally the people of a region and the land, animals, vegetation, water, and air. It recognizes that westerners revere their physical surroundings and that they need and deserve a stable, productive economy that is accessible to those with modest incomes. An ethic of place ought to be a shared community value and ought to manifest itself in a dogged determination to treat the environment and its people as equals, to recognize both as sacred, and to insure that all members of the community not just search for but insist upon solutions to fulfill that ethic. (138–39)

I quote at length because I find it intriguing that a law professor, in a book devoted to regional environmental law and policy, should argue so forcefully, so eloquently, for precisely the "ethic of place" that so many literary artists in the West are also seeking to articulate and advocate. Most readers of this book could, I'm sure, name a number of favorite western writers who routinely—and in some cases *incessantly*—devote themselves to evoking the "soul-deep mix of landscape, smells, sounds, history, neighbors, and friends" that Wilkinson mentions as the defining features of "place." Perhaps the reason western writers have been so stalwart in recent decades as supporters of the process of rethinking our relationship to the land is that many of these writers are themselves, in relative terms, newcomers to the places they write about—and the recentness of their arrival contributes both to the vigor of their engagement with fresh landscapes and, sometimes, to the palpable sense of insecurity they express when they find themselves speaking in defense of these new homelands. But in spite of this newcomer's innocence and uneasiness, there is a striking attitude of responsibility and commitment—the zealous devotion of converts—in the way dozens of western environmental writers depict and explore and fight for the places they inhabit and visit.

This zeal—this intensity—has inspired many of these writers to seek new, surprising audiences for their work. Indeed, the earlier domains of literary expression have exploded in recent years as various writers—Terry Tempest Williams, Robert Michael Pyle, David Quammen, Gary Nabhan, Rick Bass, Barry Lopez, and Gary Snyder, for example—have pushed their preoccupations with natural history and environmental conservation, sometimes aggressively apropos and sometimes arcane, into such unlikely fora as the pages of *House Beautiful* and the halls of Congress. The goal of this work is nothing short of revolution—a revolution in how Americans consider what it means to inhabit the planet, to occupy this globe in an authentic, meaningful, ethical way. And a revolution in what we regard as the proper place of literary language. Somehow, the naive idealism and the passionate excitement of the newcomer—an idealism and excitement that emerge even among western writers, like Terry Tempest Williams, who come from old western families—have inspired these authors to target the most impenetrable minds and pages and buildings for their words and ideas. A few years ago, I received from Terry a package of journal articles and a note that read, "Here is an example of how our work is infiltrating law reviews and legal briefs regarding public policy." To me, this implies a new form of "literary occupancy"—a nascent inhabitation of legal discourse by the literary arts. More on this later. A few weeks after Terry's packet arrived, David Quammen, the Bozeman, Montana, science journalist, included the following statement to me in a long e-mail message:

[A]mong the firmest of my professional convictions is that a writer who wants to influence how humans interact with landscape and nature should strive to reach as large an audience as possible and NOT preach to the converted. That means, for me, flavoring my work with entertainment-value, wrapping my convictions subversively within packages that might amuse and engage a large unconverted audience, and placing my work whenever possible in publications that reach the great unwashed.

I see a pervasive uncertainty in western environmental writing regarding sense of place and attachment to place and I see a parallel uncertainty about the "place" of literature in our culture, about the potential social ramifications of environmental literature. What is "authentic" literature? Where does literary expression properly belong, and where does our society need story and image to defy discourse conventions? How do regional conflations and uncertainties emerge in the stories and essays of one of the West's most prolific contemporary writers, Rick Bass? How do issues of occupancy and authenticity pertain to his efforts to protect wild places?

Readers may sense in western literature a certain defensiveness or an eager disclaiming of indigenousness. Bass, for instance, begins his first Yaak Valley book, *Winter: Notes from Montana* (1991), by scrambling to authenticate his prior contact with a Yaak-like place: "I'd been in the mountains before" reads the opening line of this book about his first winter in northwestern Montana (1). Barry Lopez, for his part, opens a 1995 essay entitled "Occupancy" by stating, "Sandra and I arrived in the spring of 1970," both confessing that he is not native to the McKenzie River Valley in Oregon, where he resides, and suggesting that by western standards, he and his wife had been around awhile. Alison Hawthorne Deming, in her 1994 essay collection *Temporary Homelands,* explicitly avoids any claims to long-term residency, instead making a virtue of transience; "I wanted to write an honest book about my relationship with nature," she states,

not to offer theories or prescriptions for what that relationship ought to be. . . . I wanted to understand the places, events, and ideas in my own experience that seem most significant in shaping that relationship, and to explore the quality of reflection that certain loved places seem to induce. This book, finally, is about one thing—reconstructing an intimacy with nature. We live in a time of radical loss—loss of space, places, tribes, and species. Loss of a sense of belonging in and to a place. Loss of continuity and coherence." (xiii–xiv)

At the outset of his 1998 book *About This Life,* Lopez urges a young writer "to learn another language, to live with people other than her own, to separate herself from the familiar. Then, when she returns, she will be better able to understand why she loves the familiar, and will give us a fresh sense of how fortunate we are to share these things" (14). In a sense Lopez is offering the advice that he would give to a younger version of himself, a blueprint for someone aspiring to become "a writer who travels." This transient sensibility not only reinforces one's attachment to the familiar, as he states, but constantly breaks the crusts of social conformity, the ruts of complacency, against which environmental writers, particularly in the West, are prone to militate. Travel itself is a way not only to gain new adventures and collect experience, but to ritualize loss and disorientation, to force one's mind to create new maps of meaning. The mind thus destabilized and invigorated tends to see through established structures and patterns, even upon returning home.

Let me backtrack a bit and talk about the words "occupancy" and "authenticity." "Occupancy," suggests the old dictionary in my office, implies not just physical presence in a particular place or building, but *ownership*—even legal possession—of an object or a dwelling. "Authenticity," on the other hand, implies reliability, genuineness, and validity. Much of the contemporary environmental writing in the West aims, in part, to validate the author as spokesperson for a particular place or community, often straining to overcome the historical fact of the author's newness and relative lack of legal or financial commitment to the place or community. Even more interesting, though, is the moral paradox that many of these writers encounter when they seek to assert their engagement with particular places while—more or less—avoiding the ethical faux pas, from the stereotypical "green" perspective, of land ownership and resource extraction (see John Hanson Mitchell's *Trespassing: An Inquiry into the Private Ownership of Land*). Despite the fact that many western writers, sooner or later, come to purchase plots of land and build houses—as Bass and his family have done in the Yaak, as Lopez has done alongside Oregon's McKenzie River, and as Gary Snyder has done on the western slope of the Sierra Nevada—this is often done in the spirit of creating "temporary homelands," to borrow Alison Deming's locution. These writers don't view themselves as possessors and controllers of the places where they live, but rather as coinhabitants just passing through. Either that, or as Snyder put it in a 1996 *Jim Lehrer News Hour* interview, the goal of such "occupancy" is to live an ecologically responsible life, a life devoted to the preservation of land and community, that one would maintain if one expected to be present for the next ten thousand years.

One of the great, brief articulations of the moral dubiousness of "ownership" and occupancy in recent western environmental writing appears in the title essay of William Kittredge's 1987 collection *Owning It All:*

The teaching mythology we grew up with in the American West is a pastoral story of agricultural ownership. The story begins with a vast innocent continent, natural and almost magically alive, capable of inspiring us to reverence and awe, and yet savage, a wilderness. A good rural people come from the East, and they take the land from its native inhabitants, and tame it for agricultural purposes, bringing civilization: a notion of how to live embodied in law. The story is as old as invading armies, and at heart it is a racist, sexist, imperialist mythology of conquest; a rationale for violence—against other people and against nature. (62–63)

So what's the point of criticizing this mythology of agricultural ownership or any of the other western mythologies that have guided not only Kittredge's generation, which came of age in the 1930s and 1940s, but younger generations of westerners as well? What is the goal of a book like *Owning It All?*

Kittredge extends his criticism of the prevailing, traditional land ethic in the West as follows, indicating the practical goals of literature (his own writing and that of other contemporary authors):

In the American West we are struggling to revise our dominant mythology, and to find a new story to inhabit. Laws control our lives, and they are designed to preserve a model of society based on values learned from mythology. Only after re-imagining our myths can we coherently remodel our laws, and hope to keep our society in a realistic relationship to what is actual. (64)

We've got a chicken-and-egg scenario here. What takes priority, law or story, government or art and imagination? Kittredge, not surprisingly, argues that the imagination forges the cultural values that, in turn, lead to law and public policy. I believe the point of his critique of the dominant mythology of ownership and exploitation in the West, a critique that could surely be applied to any other region of the country, is to exhort himself and his fellow writers to understand the responsibility they bear in evoking their lives, their places, their visions of social reform. Authenticity, in this context, means taking responsibility. A language revolution is one of the keys to achieving a revolution in environmental policy. "If the language among the people changes," Charles Wilkinson writes in *The Eagle Bird,* "the language in the law books will change."

One task is to add new kinds of words to balance out a vocabulary now dominated by board feet and cost-benefit analyses. The other task is to enrich existing words. When we hear a forester comment that timber harvesting will "sustain the productivity of the land," we should ask, "Productivity for voles?" When enough westerners understand that concept, law and policy will fall into line. (15–16)

How shall westerners in general, Americans more generally still, and people throughout the world as well, begin to consider concepts and words such as "productivity" and "value" from the perspective of voles? We can begin to see an answer to this by reading Terry Tempest Williams's "A Man of Questions: A Tribute to Wallace Stegner," published in the 1997 issue of the University of Utah's *Journal of Land, Resources, & Environmental Law;* by examining how David Hoch and Will Carrington Heath begin their 1997 article "Tracking the ADC: Ranchers' Boon, Taxpayers' Burden, Wildlife's Bane" in the journal *Animal Law* by quoting the entirety of Williams's short essay "Redemption"; and by acknowledging Williams's decision to print her cryptic, mythicized narrative "Bloodlines" in the small anthology, *Testimony,* which she and Stephen Trimble distributed to all members of the U.S. House and Senate in 1995. These writings by Williams are, on the whole, oblique and exploratory, full of questions rather than answers, poetry rather than measurements, uncertainty rather than certainty. When Terre Satterfield and I conducted an interview in April of 1998 with the ethnobotanist and nature writer Gary Paul Nabhan, he told us he regards story as "a zone of tension," a form of language that facilitates understanding because it obstructs easy, linear thinking. This interview and eleven others, plus samples of narrative and poetic expressions of environmental values, appeared in the 2004 book *What's Nature Worth?*

Authentic occupancy in the American West requires accepting our geography and our language as zones of tension. More and more western writers, including the various people I've mentioned in this essay, are realizing that it is their responsibility—and by extension the responsibility of critics and teachers—to find ways of getting their language not only to occupy the minds of academics in classrooms and conference hotels, but also to live in law journals and courtrooms and corporate boardrooms—and this is what's happening as we speak.

■ ■ ■ As we speak, one of the major authors of the West continues to lift his voice in an effort to protect wild places and wild species in this region, but he does so from a stance of contingency and uncertainty, from a personal viewpoint that constantly raises questions of belonging and occupancy. Although Rick Bass has now lived in the Yaak Valley in the far northwestern corner of Montana for the past twenty-one of his fifty years, although people are far more likely to refer to him as a "Montana writer" than as a "southern writer," and although his books are not placed in the "Mississippi authors" section at Square Books in Oxford, Mississippi, Bass remains an artist for whom the southern experience and, more specifically, southern landscapes, are deeply generative. His environmental activism became a notable part of his life only after the move to Montana, and yet his southern origins remain unmistakable in his work. Doubts about Bass's "regional affiliation," so to speak, remain evident in the recent scholarly literature, with Michael Kowalewski claiming him as a western author in *Reading the West: New Essays on the Literature of the American West* and Robert H. Brinkmeyer Jr. reclaiming him as a southern author in *Remapping Southern Literature: Contemporary Southern Writers and the West*. Brinkmeyer explains at length how Bass's view of western wilderness is, in a sense, part of the author's continuing process of releasing himself from and reconciling himself to his southern past. Regarding the 1991 volume *Winter,* the critic states: "In a hopeful and unironic dismissal of the past, rare in Southern writing, Bass . . . wholeheartedly embraces the American dream of leaving history behind, of fleeing west into a new world of possibility and potentiality" (81). What interests me, however, is the fact that Bass's westward migration is not merely a flight "into a new world of possibility and potentiality," but rather a process of gaining better, fiercer moral purchase on the interaction between American society and the natural world—by gaining a fresh, firm grip on his own relationship to the physical world, the author aspires to create for himself an authentic, believable voice. By moving geographically to the outer edge of American culture—not only from South to West, but from city to remote mountains—Bass assumes the potent rhetorical role that George P. Landow, in *Elegant Jeremiahs,* attributes to the "sage." As Landow puts it,

the style, tone, and general presentation of the wisdom speaker derive from the fact that his often anonymous voice resides at a societal and cultural center; it purports to be the voice of society speaking its essential beliefs and assumptions. In contrast, the style, tone, and general presentation of the sage derive from the fact that his voice resides at the periphery; it is . . . an eccentric voice, one off center. (23)

In a strange and interesting way, Rick Bass's work combines the familiarity and acceptability of the "wisdom speaker" with the radical aggressiveness of the sage. He writes from the standpoint of a husband and a father and someone who loves his family and his home. But he also writes as someone who loves animals and wild, uncomfortable, and even ugly (to humans) places. One of the central themes of Rick Bass's work, both his fiction and his nonfiction, beginning with the 1985 work *The Deer Pasture* and continuing to the present, is the desire to find, to experience, to appreciate a "wild home." This is, of course, an oxymoron—it's a tension, an incompatibility, one of several that Bass lives with every day. Look through his work, and you'll see again and again, various characters—or the author's various personae—both relishing wild, manic feats of energetic joy and hunkering down in quest of a safe haven to call "home." Where might it be possible to find a "wild home"? How might it be possible? These are what I take to be the questions at the core of this writer's work. They are questions that address the intellectual and physical process by which a nonwesterner strives to attach himself not to a blandly homogeneous western suburb, but to an authentic western landscape—to a place that has not yet been absorbed into mainstream American culture.

When I interviewed Bass in 1993 for the journal *Weber Studies*—an interview reprinted in Alan Weltzien's book *The Literary Art and Activism of Rick Bass*—there was one particular section of that conversation that's always stuck out in my mind because of the weirdness of what Bass said. And because I had to wonder if it were actually true—even possible. We were discussing his writing about the Yaak (remember, he'd lived there only six years or so at the time, and his books about the Yaak, starting with *Winter* in 1991, had been out for no more than two years), and I asked if he was concerned that by publicizing the Yaak he might lure hordes of Winnebagos into his remote, rugged part of the world—or worse yet, that his writing might inspire the hordes to clamor for new roads into the Kootenai region of northwest Montana and southeast British Columbia. So I asked if all of this celebratory writing about the Yaak uses this particular area as a "*kind* of place, not as a homing beacon" (34).

He responded:

Oh goodness, yeah. It's ugly. I mean, it's a homing beacon for me because it's home, but it's ugly, it's not a place people want to go visit. It's got clearcuts and it rains a lot and you can't see anything, there are no vistas. It's an ugly place to visit—it's an okay place to live. It's a perfect place for me to live because it's just what fits my warped mind, the twisted contours of brain—what are those things called?—the loops and coils. . . . Anyways, it fits, it's a good fit for me, but it probably wouldn't be for anyone else in the world. (34)

I've never forgotten his idea that there might be a single, perfect place for a particular individual—the right place for the right mind. I try to imagine, perhaps over-literally, how the clearcuts and rain and the lack of vistas somehow "fit" the "loops and coils" of this one man's brain. It occurs to me that this is a statement from someone trying very hard to justify and explain, for himself as much as for anyone else, why he came to choose, with the whole world a possibility, this particular place to make his home. He's articulating a sort of myth of the perfect home. To me, though, even his brief, derogatory description of the Yaak in the above statement sounds a lot like a description of where he'd just come from, the interlaced pastures and dense woods of Mississippi.

The distinguished German explorer Alexander von Humboldt traversed the globe in the late 1700s and through the first several decades of the nineteenth century, from the Orinoco Basin in South America to the steppes of Siberia, and one of his main goals was to study the "geographical isomorphisms," the extraordinary physical similarities, among certain kinds of places in vastly different parts of the world: for instance, the llanos of South America, the Great Plains of North America, the steppes of Russia, and the grasslands of South Africa. I think it's plausible to argue that, for Rick Bass, the Yaak

Valley of northwest Montana is a wild (and more mountainous) replica of the overly populated and domesticated landscape of Mississippi, and Mississippi represented a less urban, somewhat hillier version of the woods and bayous he grew up with in Houston. Far from being simply a "Montana author," truly wedded to the distinctiveness of the intermountain West, Bass is a southern writer *and* a western writer—someone whose taste for place was formed in Houston, the Texas Hill Country two hundred miles west of Houston, and the mixed pine and hardwood forests of Mississippi and Alabama—who eventually lighted out for a wilder version of his southern home.

To offer a brief recap of Bass's geographical movements, he lived primarily in Houston, Texas, while growing up, with regular November hunting trips to Gillespie County, where he developed much of his affinity for both the natural world and storytelling. In the midseventies, as a high-school senior, Bass visited Logan, Utah, in order to take a scholarship test at Utah State—Logan and Logan Canyon captivated him, and he decided to attend college at Utah State. He graduated with a degree in petroleum geology in 1980 and took a job in Jackson, Mississippi. The job in petroleum prospecting involved a lot of desk work but also some tramping around in the backwoods of east-central Mississippi and northern Alabama. Bass, who had studied nature writing and literary nonfiction with Thomas J. Lyon at Utah State, began writing in a serious way while he was living in the Jackson area in the early 1980s, so he was immersed in the Mississippi landscape as he worked to reimagine himself as an artist. He relates this process in the 1999 Credo book, *Brown Dog of the Yaak*. In the summer of 1987, Bass and his then-girlfriend Elizabeth Hughes, a Mississippian, got in his old truck, together with their two hound dogs, and drove west and north until they found a place that felt right—they stopped just short of the Canadian border. This is all described in the 1991 book, *Winter*. For four years, they lived as caretakers at the Fix Ranch in the Yaak Valley, before buying land in 1991 and building their house on it. More recently, using money brought in by selling his personal papers to the natural history special collection at Texas Tech University (where his papers now join those of Barry Lopez, William Kittredge, David Quammen, Pattiann Rogers, and other major environmental writers), Bass has bought additional land surrounding the lot purchased in 1991, further insolating himself and his family from expected land development in the area.

Bass's early books—*The Deer Pasture, Wild to the Heart, Oil Notes,* and *The Watch* —are mostly about his family's Hill Country hunting lease ("the deer pasture"), Houston, and fictional and actual adventures in Mississippi, Alabama, and North Carolina. Repeatedly, in the nonfiction, we see Bass physically located in one place, while dreaming of another. Often this takes the form of nostalgic self-realization, as if his true self will emerge in how much he misses what he's left behind—people, landscapes, wild experiences. His first book, 1985 *The Deer Pasture,* begins in precisely this vein, as he recounts his move from Logan, Utah, to Jackson, Mississippi, with friends and family placing odds on how long it will take him to quit his job and move back to the mountains. "When I left school for Jackson," he writes,

I was able to stuff everything I owned in the back of my little Rabbit. It was a sad feeling, very frightening, actually, leaving the security of the mountains, traveling downhill like that, out of the crispness of the high country and into the hot torpor of the flatlands, but it was also a good feeling, being able to contain myself and all my possessions in one small orange car that would go forty-two miles on a gallon of gas. I believe I even hummed a little as I drove.

Whistling in the dark.

When I got to Jackson, I was glad I had brought the little cedar tree [from the Texas Hill Country]. It was a pretty one, and until I found a tiny one-room cell of an efficiency apartment to stay in, it so completely filled my hotel room with the sappy, sprightly clean smell of the deer pasture that upon awakening in the morning, for the first few seconds I would forget where I was. Or rather, where I wasn't. (x)

Much of Bass's writing, both the early southern-focused books and the more recent volumes centered in Montana, exhibits the particular form of place-writing that Lawrence Buell has called "the aesthetics of the not-there" (1995, 68). In other words, Bass has an intriguing tendency to describe one place in terms of, or in relation to, another. Buell argues that Thoreau does much the same thing in *Walden,* using elements from exotic European landscapes and other parts of the world to characterize the local features of Concord. In Bass's case, though, I would say the purpose of such landscape juxtapositions, couplings, and transpositions is to evoke a sense of yearning, a restless urge to find his true place in the world and possibly his truest self. So, upon arriving in Mississippi, he savored the smells of his potted Hill Country cedar, which reminded him of Texas. Eventually, he planted his tree "in the center of the City Hall flower garden, right beneath the statue of Andrew Jackson" (xi). As he recounts in the preface to *The Deer Pasture,* he'd spend lunch and coffee breaks in Mississippi visiting the cedar tree—"I . . . close my eyes and take deep, satisfied breaths; it smells so good," he says (xi). Quite a powerful display of the aesthetics—the identity-forming process—of the "not-there."

For me, some of the most memorable early pieces of Bass's writing also exhibit this powerful yearning to be somewhere else. These are the essays called "The Shortest Route to the Mountains" and "On Camp Robbers, Rock Swifts, and Other Things Wild to the Heart," from the 1987 book *Wild to the Heart.*

"The Shortest Route to the Mountains" is about how you can experience mountain wildness without actually getting to true western mountains. In this essay Bass, then still working in Jackson, Mississippi, tells the story of an August escape from the steamy city. Since he doesn't have enough time to go all the way to the mountain West, he heads north to Hot Springs, Arkansas, taking the "shortest route to the mountains." As gradually becomes clear in this collection, though, the author is not seeking just a specific place in the world, a specific geography, but a certain quality of experience that he calls "wild." Synonyms for "wild" would be intensity, passion, richness, energy, freedom, and sensation. The irony of "The Shortest Route to the Mountains" is that Bass begins to experience "wild" things before he's gone far from Jackson and before he's left ordinary, fast-food civilization. The essay opens with a rapturous description of a strawberry milkshake. "The trouble with buying a strawberry milkshake from the Lake Providence, Louisiana, Sonic Drive-In on the left side of Highway 65 going north through the Delta, north to Hot Springs, Arkansas, is that you have got to tag the bottom with your straw and then come up a good inch or so if you want to get anything, the reason being that the Lake Providence Sonic uses real strawberries and lots of them in their shakes" (15). The first three paragraphs rhapsodize about such a milkshake, the joy of this experience accented by the withering heat and humidity of the Mississippi Delta in August. The next several pages of this brief essay offer vivid details of the northward drive, as the narrator stays in his car, sinfully pleased to have the windows rolled up and the air conditioner on. The piece ends with the speaker anticipating his arrival at Hot Springs the following day, but the shortest route to the mountains and what they entail has already been enjoyed through the sensations of the trip itself—the milkshake and the other sensations of the drive. This is sheer Thoreauvian "home-cosmography," relishing the local as if it were the longed-for exotic.

Sometimes, though, it's not enough to stay nearby—the actual, authentic mountains are required. This is the point of "On Camp Robbers, Rock Swifts, and Other Things Wild to the Heart," which recounts the story of Bass's thirty-six-hour, round-trip drive from Jackson, Mississippi, to the Pecos Wilderness Area just west of Las Vegas, New Mexico, in 1981. Unlike "Shortest Route," which focuses on the richness of the drive itself, "On Camp Robbers" elides the drive and opens with the narrator already in the mountains. "I've been waiting a long time for this," he tells us.

Jackson, Mississippi, is the best place for me to make a living, but there's this one small problem. There are no mountains. There aren't even any aspen. . . . That's why I'm here—to drink in the mountains and the aspen for a brief Fourth of July vacation. (38)

One is struck by the calmness, the nonfranticness of the prose, which belies the frenzied journey from Mississippi to New Mexico and back again. Predictably, the New Mexico mountains are placed in relief against the landscape he's just left: "After I woke I shouldered my pack, yawned, consulted my topo map, scarcely believing my luck—just yesterday I was in hot humid flat Mississippi!— and headed up a ridge toward where I hoped the trailhead to Hermit's Peak would be" (40). He continues to write about the mountains, even these mountains he's never seen before, as if he's come home to a long-lost favorite place:

On my way through the aspen I snack on the last of the sausage and biscuits (sweet madeleine!) and suddenly, all is well. Job pressures are gone, as are worries that I might never see aspen or feel the rough wild texture of the mountains on the palms of my hands again. I am back home again, for a couple of days anyway. The sausage and biscuit is always the real beginning of the best part of the trip; I always save one for this purpose. Everything before that last

Grandmother's homemade biscuit is Getting There; everything afterward is There Itself. (40–41)

The Proustian reference—sweet madeleine—reinforces the power of nostalgia for Bass's imagination. What has been lost or left behind, and then regained, at least momentarily, at least by way of a surrogate or a symbol, takes on a richness of meaning not possessed by objects, places, or relationships newly acquired. The Deer Pasture thus assumes a mythic elusiveness for Bass, as a place loved magically for a brief period of time each autumn, in the company of his family, in pursuit of natural experiences (not just through hunting) and the primal bonds of story, and then this place is left behind when the family returns to Houston. The mountain West, first experienced in Logan, Utah, is lost to the author when, giving in to young-adult responsibility, he takes his first job in Mississippi and drives "downhill" to the office in the city in the humid flatlands.

But nostalgia can work in opposite directions. When I refer to ideas such as "geographical isomorphisms" or "the aesthetics of the not-there," I'm not just thinking of how Bass, in his southern writings, looks for traces of mountain wildness in the South or describes certain aspects of the South with language he associates with the non-South or even uses the South as a foil against which to celebrate the yearned-for mountain West. What's also fascinating about Bass's life and work is how he and Elizabeth have chosen to live in a part of the mountain West that resembles certain aspects of their southern experience—clear-cut, rainy, and relatively vista-less—and, further, how Bass's descriptions of the Yaak could, with minor tweaking, sound like descriptions of southern landscapes. One of Bass's most evocative and eloquent essays since the move to Montana in 1987 is the piece he wrote in 1993 for the Nature Conservancy's anthology of writings on favorite, endangered places, *Heart of the Land,* which appeared in 1995; the essay, called "On Willow Creek," waxes nostalgically about the Texas Hill Country and mourns, both explicitly and metonymically, the death of Bass's mother, which occurred shortly before he traveled down to Texas to work on the essay. Three years after he wrote "On Willow Creek," Bass's collection of essays, *The Book of Yaak,* came out. One could make a thorough study of southern-esque descriptions of Montana landscapes in this volume, but when I picked up the essay recently, it took only few minutes to find a passage in it called "The Value of a Place," near the beginning of the book, where the Yaak is celebrated in terms that could just as easily be applied to Mississippi, or Houston, if not to the Hill Country. Bass writes:

> The cycle of dying trees giving birth to living ones—we're all familiar with this, familiar with the necessity of rot, and diversity, in an ecosystem: the way that the richness, or tithing, of rot, and the flexibility, the suppleness, of diversity, guarantees that an ecosystem, or any other kind of system, will have a future. I like to walk—and sometimes crawl—through the jungle up here, examining the world on my hands and knees—watching the pistonlike rise and fall of individual trees—noticing the ways they block light from some places and funnel or focus light into other places—watching the way, when the weaker trees fall, that they sometimes help prop up and brace those around them. Other times the fallen trees crash all the way to the ground to become fern-beds, soil-mulch, lichen pads. It's not a thing we can measure yet, but I like to imagine that each different tree, after it has fallen, gives off a different quality of rot—a diversity even in the manner in which nutrients are released to the soil. The slow rot of a giant larch having a taste to the soil, perhaps, of bread; the faster disintegration of ice-snapped saplings tasting like sugar, or honey. The forest feasting on its own diversity, with grace and mystery lying thick everywhere. (11)

When I read this passage about the Yaak, I find myself thinking of the character Buzbee in the title story of Bass's 1989 collection *The Watch*, a seventy-seven-year-old man who's disappeared into the piney woods and swampy bottomlands of central Mississippi. Although there are few sustained natural descriptions like the one I've given from *The Book of Yaak*, there are many references in the story "The Watch" to fecundity and rot in both the land and the human imagination. I can tell these two texts, one located in the mountains of Montana and the other set in the woods and bayous of Mississippi, come from the same pen. I suppose this is why, whenever I refer to "the Montana writer Rick Bass," I find myself hesitating slightly, knowing that wherever Bass might be living, whatever landscape he's writing about, he's also still "a southern author."

So, one might ask, how does Bass seek to gain moral and political credibility as a defender of wilderness in the mountain West when he continues to write in a "southern voice," from a "southern sensibility," intuitively relying upon the "aesthetics of the not-there"? I began this essay by emphasizing the extraordinary and sometimes comical value placed on long-term occupancy in western states such as Nevada. Implicit in any discussion is the idea that a native or longtime resident possesses more authority, more credibility, than the newcomer regarding any issue of public debate. However, the reality is that most residents of the western mountain states are relative newcomers, straining to be at home, to develop a sense of attachment and caring in places where we might have dwelled, physically, for only a period of months and seldom for more than a decade. For the first decade or so of his life in Montana, Bass's literary representation of the West was particularly notable for its reliance upon the "aesthetics of the not-there," a trope that can be understood as an effort to make the strange familiar, the not-home home. This is, in other words, a technique for bootstrapping oneself into a condition of belonging.

More recently, some surprising new rhetorical shifts have occurred in Bass's work. These shifts have contributed to the author's authentic, pleasing voice and vision and, at the same time, have made his conservation efforts even more credible and convincing than before. Bass's two presentations at the Orion Society's June 1999 millennial extravaganza, Fire & Grit, mark the emergence of a newly detached and philosophical Rick Bass and the return of the charmingly antic storyteller whose comedic sensibility, evident early on in *The Watch,* had become increasingly submerged in activist angst and frustration by the mid-1990s. The essay "The Community of Glaciers" recounts Bass's work on behalf of a small "pro-roadless group" in the Yaak, which resulted in the author's shocking dismissal from the volunteer steering committee of the Yaak Valley Forest Council by a vote of thirty-nine to three. "Wearier, if not smarter," he writes, "I have retreated to the far perimeters of the community, for now. The place where everyone wants me, the place where perhaps even the landscape wants me, and hell, perhaps even the place where, when all is said and done, I myself want to be—though it does not feel that way to me." The essay proceeds to contemplate the processes by which social change and glacial erosion occur, especially the concept of glacial slowness and imperceptibility. "I do not mean to dismiss our little fires, nor our fiery hearts," he concludes: "I mean only to remind us all that our lives, our values, are a constant struggle that will never end, and in which there can never be a clear 'victory,' only daily challenge . . ." (unpublished manuscript). This sounds like the world-weary statement of a wilderness warrior now retired from the battlefield rather than the desperately fierce whoops and pleas of *The Book of Yaak* and *Fiber*. And yet, taken in context, "The Community of Glaciers" can be seen as an effort to retrench and gain perspective, a gathering up of wisdom and resolve for the next phase of the artist-activist's life.

The day before he presented "The Community of Glaciers" at Fire & Grit, Bass read a hilarious, self-mocking essay called "Bear Spray Stories," subtly setting up his audience for the more sober critique of activist hubris. "Every time I get sprayed, I have to laugh. It's like, how dumb can I get? But each time it happens, I tell myself it won't happen again: that there's no way I'll make that mistake twice," he writes (unpublished manuscript). Beneath the guise of a series of slapstick stories, Bass seems to be stating a powerful message: life is funny, painful, uncontrollable, and sometimes all too predictable. Things don't always work out as we want or expect, but it's important to keep striving, loving, and believing.

These two recent essays illustrate a surprising discovery that Bass seems to have made in his quest for an authentic, credible literary voice, a voice that might gain him leverage in the landscape debates of the American West. He has discovered that beyond and beneath a more specific regional authenticity are certain familiar and possibly universal human passions and concerns. "The Community of Glaciers" and "Bear Spray Stories" seem to acknowledge and accept the author's lingering and perhaps insurmountable outsiderness—and in doing so they tap into the sense of unbelonging that many of Bass's readers, particularly his western readers, are likely to feel. Although Bass certainly would not have wished to be voted out of the Yaak Valley Forest Council any more than he would intentionally squirt himself with pepper spray, these experiences of alienation and ineptitude have, in the hands of a brilliant storyteller, become the inadvertent means of achieving a kind of authentic humanity that will inspire future readers and listeners to take up the cry, "Don't hack the Yaak," "Nevada is not a wasteland," and various other slogans and phrases that indicate a growing ethic of responsible occupancy in the American West.

▥   ▥   ▥   As I touched up an earlier draft of this essay in August 2002, a note arrived from Rick Bass, packaged with a form letter from him to members of the Association for the Study of Literature and Environment and a detailed letter from the Yaak Valley Forest Council, urging recipients to write letters to various senators and U.S. Forest Service officials and ask them to speak out on behalf of the Yaak Valley. "Same old story," he writes in his informal cover note. "Our letters against their dollars. Even a short note demanding wilderness designation for Yaak roadless lands would be great." The other materials suggest that Bass and the YVFC have teamed up again, this time providing maps, reports, photographs, and computer-accessible videos and audio feeds to make the "public process" of evaluating wilderness in the Yaak available to students and teachers across the United States, to make the process part of school curricula. The YVFC outsider, it seems, has once again been embraced by his rural community, and the writer and the pro-roadless and pro-sustainable logging group are working to make their place, a remote western valley scarcely known to the outside world a decade ago, familiar to more and more people throughout the country, to give them a little taste of wildness in an increasingly tame America. On another level, participating in this process of activism and public education, side by side with his neighbors, is part of Bass's continuing effort to achieve true occupancy, deep and permanent occupancy, in the place he and Elizabeth chose as their home back in 1987. Bass has now written so many of these help-protect-the-Yaak letters, dozens of them, that they've virtually become a literary genre unto themselves—missives that once may have struck some readers as angry and frantic and postured now come across as measured, calm, and credible.

As I began to touch up this essay, one of my colleagues, a professor with a special interest in Nevada literature, told me she had recently figured out how to go through an elaborate telephone menu system at the state DMV in order to get herself new blue-and-white replica license plates. "It's part of my continuing process of becoming a native Nevadan," said the native Californian. My own western anxiety of unbelonging was piqued, and I felt a desire to become a native, too, well up in me. I called the DMV myself and gathered information about how to use the phone menu and order my own "circa 1982" plates, for a mere one-time fee of twenty-six dollars. Seemed like a cheap enough price for one kind of attachment to place. When I picked up my fifteen-year-old son at school, I told him, "Hey, I figured out how to get blue-and-white license plates for the car. Won't that be cool? The DMV is requiring us to get new plates this year—might as well turn our car into a 'native Nevadan.'"

"Why would you want to do that, Dad?" said Jacinto. "The new plates with the yellow sunset—those are cool. The old plates are ugly, boring. Why do we need special license plates to prove that we belong here?"

The application for replica old-time Nevada license plates sits on my desk, and there it will stay. Later that week I visited the DMV and asked for a set of the new sunset plates. The old car will be driven mostly by Jacinto in a year or two, so it might as well have the plates he wants. He seems content with his own sense of belonging in Reno, in Nevada, and doesn't need blue license plates to authenticate, to legitimize, his residency here. For my part, belonging comes less easily, less surely. I enjoy reading western literature, and especially work by newcomers to the region, because the ambivalence toward place confirms my own sense of tenuousness and transience. The only true antidote I know for the angst of unbelonging is a walk through sage and rabbitbrush, through vanilla-smelling Jeffrey pines, collecting the dust of here and now on my sandal-clad feet. I think I'll take such a walk right now.

7 | Mexico City Declaration (21 January 2000)

A STORY OF NONCONSENSUS

If only the new millennium had somehow dawned on an earth made magically fresh. Instead, we passed that long-awaited midnight on the same planet, tattered with the abuse of the last century. At least in places of privilege the party seems to rage on, with soaring stock markets and swelling trade, but there's a frantic edge to the euphoria. Another decade, another century, another millennium of this? We sense not—we sense that the party is drawing to a close.

The reasons for our foreboding are familiar—perhaps too familiar. The litany of unsolved environmental threats is so well known that we can list them without feeling in our bones their enormity. Soil erodes; aquifers dry; forests fall and burn; species and cultures vanish; incomes diverge, undermining possibilities for human solidarity. Each of these crises has grown more severe in the last decade, and now, looming over them, is the new fact of global warming. No longer mere theory, climatic upheaval already takes a bitter toll—in 1998, the warmest year on record, 300 million of our fellow humans were driven from their homes by flood and fire. Polar ice shrinks, sea levels creep ever higher, even the seasons shift; the world turns ever more unstable, its glorious complexity daily reduced.

The catalog of our perils makes them seem separate, a checklist of crises to be cured with particular doses of expertise. Instead, they are the symptoms of one species demanding too much of the world. They are *signals,* heralding the very real possibility of an environmental collapse so systemic it could undermine the very basis of our civilization.

We do not lack for the tools to address these problems. Engineers offer us alternative technologies from windmills to fuel cells; economists show us how we could bring their costs within the reach of the entire world, developing as well as developed. Our religious thinkers increasingly offer counsel on how we could rally self-restraint and reverence; the World Wide Web lets us spread both alarms and solutions. We even have a few examples of real achievement—international treaties protecting the ozone layer or the breeding grounds of whales, the growing resistance to unrestrained genetic engineering, the falling fertility rates that promise an end to unchecked population growth.

By and large, though, we have not interrupted business as usual—and we will not until we muster the same sense of moral urgency that animated the fight against apartheid or totalitarianism, the battle for civil rights or women's equality. In *our* age this is the mandatory fight, the one that can't be ducked or wished away. It is a fight for an intact planet that can support dignified lives, for all people and for all creation. Survival will require imagination above all else—if the rich world cannot conceive some goal other than endless economic expansion, we will bump from one crisis to the next, ever poorer in spirit and surroundings.

"Globalization" is one of our rallying cries, and yet specialization, entrenchment, and orthodoxy our daily reality. With unprecedented tools of communication at hand, from cell phones to the Internet, we send information more rapidly than ever from one corner of the planet to another. But can any of us be heard beyond our own tribes? Have we ourselves learned to listen to other cultures? We yearn for contact, for new language, for the open-mindedness to think new thoughts.

If we do blunder blithely on, or wait until some catastrophe forces our hand, then we commit a crime against the future. That is no mere figure of speech—those who oversee and justify the continued devastation of the natural world should be no less morally and legally culpable than the sadistic generals of our shabbiest wars. They preempt for generations yet to come the wonders we have known: the great migrations, the deepest woods, the consoling company of our fellow creatures.

And at the same time we commit crimes against the past. As writers and scientists, we are heirs to the achievements of our civilization—its long, halting, bloody trek toward understanding and toward human freedom. But now our carelessness raises the possibility that those struggles will have meant little, that instead, our most important legacy will be clouds of carbon dioxide, ranks of felled trees, catalogs of extinct animals.

Although we represent only a minute fraction of the Earth's human voices, we hope to inspire others to gather and reflect, to offer expressions of vision and commitment. We are, like all modern humans, complicit in the habits and systems that drive this destruction. But we pledge ourselves to resist, creatively and earnestly, the business-as-usual that must soon end.

That resistance will take many forms—research and art, civil disobedience and uncivil speech. And it draws its inspiration from many sources—clouds of monarchs on the wing, small farmers planting another crop, clever alchemists of the new technologies, dying fish of the dying reefs. We proceed with the faith that while it is too late to prevent our troubles, nature nonetheless retains some vigor; if we take a step back, the rest of creation will step forward to bless that space. We proceed with the understanding that we will need to be rude and loud and humble all at once. We proceed with the example of many others who have come before us, and with the confidence that we will be joined by many, many more. The millennial party may be coming to a close, but the hard sweet work of real celebration is only just beginning.

■ ■ ■   But this is only part of the story. Bill McKibben and I drafted this "manifesto" in January 2000 during the International PEN-UNESCO Symposium called "The Earth 2000/La Tierra Año 2000," which was organized by writers Homero and Betty Aridjis and took place at the Museum of Natural History in Mexico City. Actually, when asked by Homero and Betty to prepare a summary statement to be presented at a press conference at the end of the conference, I lent my laptop to Bill overnight, and he returned the following morning with a lyrical first draft of this document, which I then massaged throughout the day, splicing additional perspectives from the week's lectures into the small essay that I've presented above.

The gathering had brought together fourteen writers and a dozen scientists from a variety of disciplines and countries, ranging from Mexico to Sweden, from the United States to South Africa. Bill and I had tried to produce an overarching statement about the "findings" of the meeting that could be released to the public at the beginning of the new millennium, but we found there to be certain ideological rifts and complications that prevented us from speaking in a single, unified voice—in particular, some of the social scientists from developing nations (chiefly, Mexico) felt that social and environmental justice should be foregrounded, while natural scientists and some of the American writers felt that impending ecological disasters trumped (and actually caused) important social problems. It might seem that participants in this conference would have at least been able to come together on a handful of common issues, common concerns about the state of the world. But ultimately our differences in perspective overcame our shared zeal for social justice and environmental protection.

So, what exactly happened during the drafting of this document that blocked its presentation to the media and its appearance in print at the time when it was written? The diverse participants in the Mexico City conference ranged from South African essayist, painter, and antiapartheid dissident Breyten Breytenbach to British cetologist Sidney Holt. Nobel laureate Sherwood Rowland, the American chemist who helped to explain the physical basis for global warming, launched the week's presentations, and prominent Mexican sociologist and former United Nations official Lourdes Arizpe gave a stirring presentation on the implications of poverty and social stratification for environmental protection. The entire week was a smorgasbord of diverse disciplinary and cultural perspectives with a balanced representation of papers from the natural sciences and the humanities, complemented with several lectures on public policy, such as Jerome Delli Priscoli's talk on international water policy.

After an initial draft of the manifesto—this is what the conference organizers called it, what they asked us to write on behalf of the assembled speakers—was shared with the group a few days before the week's end, several scholars immediately agreed to sign on, several luminaries desired to abstain because they felt it inappropriate as public figures to attach themselves to any sort of strident political statement, and a few conference participants vociferously complained about the document, essentially halting the entire process of coming up with a unified statement about the outcomes of this high-profile meeting. The press conference loomed at the end of the week, a statement had been drafted, and the expected signatories to the document were squabbling about the tone and details of the essay. Here's the passage that was especially problematic:

That resistance will take many forms—research and art, civil disobedience and uncivil speech. And it draws its inspiration from many sources—clouds of monarchs on the wing, small farmers planting another crop, clever alchemists of the new technologies, dying fish of the dying reefs.

The public figures among us (government consultants, famous scientists, and so forth) felt uncomfortable attaching themselves to a document that allied itself with "resistance" and seemed to acknowledge and lend credibility to "civil disobedience and uncivil speech." The activists among us insisted on the potential for disobedience and incivility, when necessary. The scientists among us were adamant about the importance of endangered species, from monarch butterflies to organisms of the sea, as celebrated causes, as sources of inspiration to spur conservationist efforts. But the socially conscious scholars refused to place the cause of peasant farmers on par with environmental causes and concerns, refused even to place them in the same manifesto. Shamans of new energy and biological technologies felt their work was a crucial source of vision and inspiration, while ecologists had difficulty stomaching the value of high-tech solutions to global problems that, in many cases, were the product of technology.

At the eleventh hour, just before the scheduled press conference, Bill and I were sent with our laptop to a workroom in another part of the Museum of Natural History while the final lectures of the symposium were being presented in the auditorium. Across the room from where we tinkered with our draft,

Lourdes Arizpe and Homero Aridjis worked on a counterdraft of the manifesto in Spanish and English. Finally, we reentered the lecture hall with our two versions of the manifesto and shared printed copies with our colleagues, hoping to find some common ground and make an announcement to the world. But that was too much to hope for.

When members of the press entered the dark lecture hall (normally a planetarium) and the glaring lights shined on the assembled scholars and writers from throughout the world, we had no unified voice with which to speak, no common message of commitment and resolve, no solutions to the world's grave problems of injustice and degraded habitat. Homero, our leader, addressed the press in his passionate, quavering voice, describing the purpose of the week's conference, applauding the efforts of the participating speakers, and apologizing for our failure to come up with the promised manifesto. I couldn't follow everything he said in Spanish, so it's possible, too, that he slipped in a little bit of the countermanifesto that he and Lourdes had composed.

But the upshot of this experience is that the world's environmental scholars and artists still have a long way to go in achieving effective cooperation, in learning to establish alliances and negotiate functional compromises, with an eye toward long-term goals. As I'll explain in the next chapter, in the context of the relationship between environmental justice ecocriticism and other branches of environmental expression, I believe we must learn to look for *common* ground and take special care not to pick useless fights, to the detriment of all of our interests, all of our causes.

8 | Ecocriticism on and After September 11

On September 11, 2001, I was sitting in my apartment in Houston, Texas, where I'd moved from Reno, Nevada, three weeks earlier to spend the fall semester teaching courses in ecocriticism and contemporary southwestern environmental literature at Rice University. My stay in Houston was part of my usual effort to make environmental literature and ecocriticism available to students who might not ordinarily have an opportunity to encounter these subjects, as they would at a place like the University of Nevada.

I was sitting in my Houston apartment on the morning of September 11, working on an essay about contemporary Oregon nature writer John Daniel that would be included in his book for Milkweed Editions' Credo Series, reflecting on his Wordsworthian "spots of time" echoes in various poems. Talk about spots of time, about memorable moments, distinct from the rest of life. It was around ten o'clock in the morning, and suddenly my wife, Susie, called from Nevada and said, "Turn on the TV—we've been attacked, the U.S. has been attacked." On the television were the astonishing and horrifying images of the World Trade Towers in flames, the repeated images of one airplane and then another smashing into the towers, the fireballs, the falling glass, and, eventually, the collapse of the buildings. It was, I must say, difficult to return to my ecocritical project for the rest of the day. Ecocriticism—environmental writing in general—felt irrelevant at that moment. The world would never be quite the same for any of us who experienced the shock of that day, even if we were not directly impacted by the violence.

I had no classes to teach at Rice on Tuesday, the 11th of September. That was a strange, scary day in the United States, and perhaps elsewhere in the world, too. Nobody really had a clear idea of the extent of the activities of the 11th—the attack. I'm not sure it was clear yet that these events were acts of terrorism. All air traffic was halted for several days in the United States, and perhaps in other countries, too. The two or three days after the initial attack on the 11th were ominously quiet—no planes in the skies above Houston, except for military jets patrolling the air space above the downtown skyscrapers, mainly offices of major oil companies, several miles from my apartment.

But, amid the scary strangeness of the days following September 11, I did continue to meet with my Rice students—we had class the morning of 9/12 and again on 9/14. The business of discussing literature—including environmental literature—continued. In my southwestern literature class, we were talking about Rudolfo Anaya's 1972 novel *Bless Me, Ultima* during the week of the terrorist attacks; this is a book set in rural New Mexico in the 1940s and '50s, telling the story of a young boy growing up and emerging from childhood innocence into an awareness of the traumas and tragedies of life. There is an eerie motif in *Bless Me, Ultima,* whereby the characters attempt to live lives of timeless engagement with the natural patterns of their rural village, the seasonal changes, and local human dramas, but the narrator Antonio's older brothers are called away to fight in World War II and eventually return to the village after several years, changed and hardened, unable to be content with simple village life anymore. One of the messages seems to be that world events can reach even the outposts of rural New Mexico.

I would extrapolate from this and suggest that even nature writers and ecocritics cannot remove themselves from the context—the frightening, unwanted context—of a world of terrorism and social unrest. This is the gist of my assessment of the field since 2001—that the puncturing of pastoral retreat, to use David Gessner's phrase, has affected not only nature writing itself, but the ecocritical response to literature. The vicious frustrations that seem to have led to the events of September 11 and to the ongoing battles of words and bombs in the Middle East and elsewhere in recent years have not evaporated, have not disappeared. It is necessary for all thinking people to worry about, to work through, the issues that led to 9/11 and to other social struggles related and unrelated to 9/11. Ecocritics and environmental writers do not do their work in a historical and political vacuum—in fact, within two weeks or so of the 9/11 attack, a cluster of eloquent responses to 9/11 by distinguished environmental writers was published on the Orion Society's Web site.

The main character of *Bless Me, Ultima* is a young Hispanic boy named Antonio Márez, who begins the narrative at about the age of six (just before starting school) and tells his story up through high school or so. The crux of the narrative is the way in which Antonio, or "Tony," is torn between various opposing forces, his father's family of cowboys and his mother's family of farmers, the childhood innocence of his rural village and the lure of the world beyond the village, and particularly the divergent worldviews represented by the Roman Catholic Church and the pantheistic, animistic beliefs of Native American people. Tony struggles to mesh the various influences on his life, to create a meaningful identity for himself composed of seemingly contradictory ideologies. The novel's narrative style is notable for its gentle, accommodating approach toward so many contrasting perspectives—for its sensitivity and diplomacy. No worldview or set of beliefs is destroyed in order to make room for another. Although in my classes on environmental literature I tend to use Anaya's novel primarily as an example of how indigenous sense of place (including ethnobiological knowledge) is represented in contemporary fiction, it seems to me, in the wake of 9/11, that the novel also has important lessons to offer about how we should feel about conflicting ideologies in the world today. While the United States government immediately responded to the terrorism of 9/11 by vowing to crush and erase the people who hate America and all that it stands for, the message of Anaya's writing is that we must try to be sensitive to divergent and even conflicting worldviews—and we must teach ourselves to be tolerant and not allow rage, fear, and frustration to well up into hatred. Much of what we call "environmental literature" and "ecocriticism" is about cultivating sensitivity toward, appreciation of, "the other." Think, for instance, of the lines on the opening pages of Barbara Kingsolver's post-9/11 essay collection

Small Wonder (2002), where she imagines the parents of an Iranian child who's become lost in the nearby mountains:

I can feel how [the parents'] hearts slowly change as the sediments of this impossible loss precipitate out of ordinary air and turn their insides to stone. And then suddenly moving to the fluttering panic of trapped birds, they become sure there is still some way out of this cage—here my own heart takes up that tremble as I sit imagining the story. (1)

The U.S. administration expressed its pent-up rage and fear by bombing rural Afghanistan "back to the Stone Age," while writers like Kingsolver sought to empathize with people on the other side of the planet, to appreciate the universal human feelings of "the others." One could argue that *Bless Me, Ultima,* like *Small Wonder* and many other examples of environmental literature, is a rather important text for us to be thinking about during these worrisome days.

I have suggested that ecocriticism and environmental literature must exist in a social context, and this means that these activities and ways of thinking and communicating must exist in the context of, with cognizance or awareness of, the events of 9/11 and their aftermath—despite this, writers continue to explore the nuances of their personal experience of the natural world and the broader scientific and social implications of human behavior in relation to nature. And ecocritics have gone on with their work since 9/11, some of them explicitly engaged with issues of social justice, warfare, and globalization (perhaps one of the inspirations for the 9/11 attacks), while others may seem to be doing ecocritical work as if 9/11 were still just an ordinary day on the calendar.

Although my own life was rather startlingly interrupted by the attacks, I have not radically revised my research and teaching to accommodate discussion of 9/11. It has always been my goal to use the insights and eloquence of literature to enhance my own sensitivity and that of my students to important social and environmental concerns. Since 9/11, I have perhaps felt somewhat more urgency to include on my course reading lists works that show an awareness of the fact that Americans are not *alone* on the planet. For instance, I have made a special point of incorporating discussion of Kingsolver's essays from *Small Wonder* and selections from Arundhati Roy's *Power Politics* into my undergraduate humanities courses, hoping to use the writers' insights to provoke my students' appreciation of the tendencies of American culture and the actions of the U.S. government that may be contributing to international tensions. I believe both ecocriticism and environmental writing are, intrinsically, ways of thinking through issues that are important for human society. We need more of both in order to live well and sustainably on the planet. We need this kind of writing and scholarship in order to fathom the implications of social strife that existed before 9/11/2001 and continues to exist today.

It is not my purpose in this essay to offer a survey of ecocriticism since 2001. Others have already offered helpful overviews of that kind: for instance, Kate Rigby's "Ecocriticism" in Julian Wolfreys's *Introducing Criticism at the 21st Century* (2002), Peter Barry's chapter on ecocriticism in *Beginning Theory* (2002), Greg Garrard's *Ecocriticism* (2004), Lawrence Buell's *The Future of Environmental Criticism* (2005), and Ursula Heise's PMLA article, "The Hitchhiker's Guide to Ecocriticism" (2006). But I do believe a kind of "sea change" occurred in ecocriticism, and perhaps in all branches of humanities scholarship, in the wake of the events of 2001. From my vantage point as the editor of ISLE, I noticed that we began to receive more politically aggressive, more urgently expressed scholarly submissions. Perhaps the most explicit of these, an essay that actually articulated a new, succinct definition of ecocriticism, was Camilo Gomides's article "Putting a New Definition of Ecocriticism to the Test: The Case of *The Burning Season,* a Film (Mal)Adaptation" (2006). The new—post-9/11—definition of the discipline he asserts goes like this: "Ecocriticism: The field of enquiry that analyzes and promotes works of art which raise moral questions about human interactions with nature, while also motivating audiences to live within a limit that will be binding over generations" (16). The emphasis here on the explicit raising of "moral questions" and the use of textual analysis to inspire audiences to "live within a limit that will be binding over generations" suggests interesting assumptions about the *power* of scholarship and the appropriate *scope* of academic work (including both research and teaching). I respect the passion of such a definition, while I also feel certain reservations about enforcing such a precise notion of this field. My own approach has always been to cast a wide net, to welcome and support any and all "green readings" of literature and other kinds of texts. But I have noticed the field shift since 9/11 toward a more hard-edged, socially conscious approach.

This way of reading, one might argue, already existed (before 9/11) in what we've now come to call "environmental justice ecocriticism." *The Environmental Justice Reader,* edited by Joni Adamson, Mei Mei Evans, and Rachel Stein, a collection that helped to codify and promote this approach to scholarship, was published in 2002 and was already well underway when 9/11 took place. Nonetheless, in an interesting way, the occurrence of the 9/11 attacks and the almost contemporaneous emergence of environmental justice ecocriticism would prove to be fortuitous for ecocritics suddenly looking to infuse their writing and teaching lives with ideas relevant to the state of the world. To some extent, I would argue, the majority of ecocritics prior to 9/11 were *already* sensitive to and supportive of the ideas foregrounded in environmental justice. T. V. Reed, in his essay "Toward an Environmental Justice Ecocriticism" from *The Environmental Justice Reader,* does an excellent job of identifying and distinguishing several of the major strands of ecocriticism, which he labels "Conservation Ecocriticism," "Ecological Ecocriticism," "Biocentric/Deep Ecological Ecocriticism," "Eco-feminist Ecocriticism," and "Environmental Justice Ecocriticism." I'm actually not sure what kind of ecocriticism I have been practicing throughout my career, as I tend not to identify myself consciously with any of these categories. Perhaps because of my interest in placedness and movement, I've been primarily what Reed would classify as an "ecological ecocritic," although, like most of my colleagues and students, I actually feel I belong in several of these categories, including environmental justice. When the 9/11 attacks occurred in 2001, I happened to be teaching not only Rudolfo Anaya's *Bless Me, Ultima* in my undergraduate class at Rice, but Joni Adamson's *American Indian Literature, Environmental Justice, and Ecocriticism* in my graduate seminar on ecocriticism.

I strongly appreciate the kinds of critical questions Reed links to environmental justice ecocriticism, such as:

How can literature and criticism further efforts of the environmental justice movement to bring attention to ways in which environmental degradation and hazards unequally affect poor people and people of color? How has racism domestically and internationally enabled greater environmental irresponsibility? What are the different traditions in nature writing by the poor, by people of color in the United States and by cultures outside it? (149)

I believe most people who think of themselves as ecocritics and/or environmental writers would also support the lines of investigation suggested by these important questions, even if we don't all make these questions the central issues of our own research, teaching, or storytelling. For this reason, though, I found myself both inspired and dismayed by Reed's powerful essay when I read it in 2002, disappointed chiefly by the apparent hierarchy of socially conscious ecocriticisms, with the new environmental justice emphasis clearly being promoted as more important and morally acceptable than the others. Immediately after pronouncing the central questions of environmental justice ecocriticism, Reed vilifies—I don't think this is too strong a word—Scott Russell Sanders, whose essay "Speaking a Word for Nature" appears in the discipline's foundational anthology, *The Ecocriticism Reader* (1996). Reed points to the "pre-sumptuousness of the title [which] is matched by the content of the essay, which in essence condemns virtually all of contemporary American literature as un- if not antinatural." He proceeds then to celebrate the ecological and socially conscious dimensions of Don DeLillo's novel *White Noise,* which is criticized mildly in Sanders's essay. But in castigating Sanders for a full page, Reed ignores the eloquent insights of the article, first published for the mainstream readers of the *Michigan Quarterly Review* in 1987, which concludes:

The gospel of ecology has become an *intellectual* commonplace. But it is not yet an *emotional* one. For most of us, most of the time, nature appears framed in a window or a video screen or inside the borders of a photograph. We do not feel the organic web passing through our guts, as it truly does. While our theories of nature have become wiser, our experience of nature has become shallower. . . . Thus, any writer who sees the world in ecological perspective faces a hard problem: how, despite the perfection of our technological boxes, to make us feel the ache and tug of that organic web passing through us, how to *situate* the lives of characters—and therefore of readers—in nature. (*Ecocriticism Reader* 194)

To my mind, Sanders's statement sums up some of the essential goals of environmental literature, from before 9/11 and after, from all social strata, from within the United States and abroad. I ardently support the mission of the environmental justice movement, both within literary studies and beyond. And yet I do not support the *factionalizing* of social and environmental consciousness. Rather than simply taking the Sanders essay a step further or highlighting and correcting certain aspects of Sanders's work that tend to be more explicitly stated through other modes of analysis, Reed tosses out the baby with the bathwater. This is, I must say, the grave failure, too, of Dana Phillips's 2003 volume of witty slander, *The Truth of Ecology: Nature, Culture, and Literature in America,* and Michael P. Cohen's 2004 rant, "Blues in the Green: Ecocriticism under Critique," the latter of which was, strangely enough, published in the journal *Environmental History* rather than in a literary journal, where the author could have approached his colleagues diplomatically and urged them to consider new directions. Rants, whining, and self-promoting manifestoes aside (is that what I've been doing myself in the preceding paragraphs?), there has been a striking new emphasis on political urgency and international relations in post-9/11 ecocriticism and environmental writing. One of the impressive examples of this focus is *Caribbean Literature and the Environment: Between Nature and Culture,* coedited by Elizabeth M. DeLoughrey, Renée K. Gosson, and George B. Handley and published in 2005, a project that operates within the frameworks of social justice and postcolonial critique without blaming or denouncing scholars working in other branches of literary scholarship. In articulating the aims of their collection, the editors state simply:

Although North American ecocritics often describe an idealized natural landscape that is devoid of human history and labor, the colonization and forced relocation of Caribbean subjects preclude that luxury and beg the question as to what might be considered a natural landscape. Against the popular grain of U.S. ecocritical studies, we argue that addressing the historical and racial violence of the Caribbean is integral to understanding literary representations of its geography. As Wilson Harris reminds us, this is "a landscape saturated by traumas of conquest." (2)

Enough said. This is the sort of scholarly approach that will lure converts to an important mode of reading rather than splintering the community of ecocritics.

■ ■ ■   I know of no ecocriticism and little environmental literature—aside from David Gessner's "The Punctured Pastoral" and Susan Hanson's "Homeland Security: Safe at Home in the World"—that has explicitly explored the implications of 9/11, but it's possible that scholars and nature writers in the United States or elsewhere will increasingly come to terms with that event and the broader phenomenon of globalization in future work. Gessner's piece tells the story of his own 9/11 experience, beginning with the story of his hike in the Colorado Rockies the day of the attack and exploring his efforts to return to normalcy back home on Cape Cod in the following months. His entire life, as a nature writer in rural, coastal Massachusetts, had been one of pastoral "retreat" in a "place apart" from the pressures and concerns of urban America. He recalls, "Perhaps, after the horror of the deed, that was the immediate message we took away from September 11. *Welcome to the world.* There is no place apart" (172). After 9/11, the nature writer wonders:

was heading for the hills, even the metaphorical hills, a cowardly retreat in the face of this new world? How could I spend another year observing and writing about ospreys or snails? I suspected very few nature writers were working in Israel, for instance. What use was it now to write of titmice or the migratory pattern of the semipalmated plover? Wasn't this a time to think only of war and politics? (173)

So Gessner's immediate response to the crisis, like that of many writers and scholars, was to feel that his vocation—observing, contemplating, and describing nature—was irrelevant and even somehow irresponsible. Like Anaya with his subtle message in *Bless Me, Ultima* that retreat from the throes of the world is impossible, he now understood that "there is no world apart." As time passed, however, Gessner came to realize that distance and detachment were crucial to achieving a deeper understanding of the meaning of 9/11. In "The Punctured Pastoral" he explains how his post-9/11 wanderings in nature reinforced his sense of humility, the vulnerability of life, and the need sometimes to feel modestly empowered by doing small, constructive things. "It's hard to respond to crisis with creativity," he writes, "but I found I was a little better at it when walking out by the bluff. One of the things living by the bluff had taught me was that 'I don't know' is often the best answer, at least initially, to the questions the world poses. I needed to rebuild on the foundation of this uncertainty" (175). Not only does nature provide innumerable mysteries (forcing the honest human observer into an inevitable stance of uncertainty), but it also makes life and death—mortal frailty—plain at every turn. Gessner writes: "In this lack of a safe place, we joined not just the citizens of the rest of the world, but the other species that populate this planet. Vulnerability is a reality of life on earth, a fact we have tried so desperately to bury under layers of control" (176). This realization reminds him of the strange unity between his own sense of frailty and the migrating monarch butterflies he had observed in Colorado, "engaged in their great and preposterous enterprise" (177). News from the Massachusetts Audubon Society's Wellfleet Bay Wildlife Sanctuary that a hypothermic loggerhead turtle (a "threatened" species) he and his wife had recently rescued on the beach near their home would likely survive provides a glimmer of hope, a slight sense of the power to have a positive effect on the world. "In a time when the daily environmental news was overwhelming," states Gessner, "it was heartening for me to take things down to an individual level: one person saving one turtle, feeling for a moment that my actions could have some influence" (179). Reading Gessner's thoughtful essay, which approaches the implications of 9/11 so explicitly and gracefully, propels me back to my daily fare of eco-criticism and environmental writing, where I find that similar themes—so useful in times like ours—abound in this work. Writing about nature—and the *study* of this literature—intrinsically prepares us to weather the challenges and complications of the world.

Susan Hanson's approach in "Homeland Security: Safe at Home in the World" is more oblique than Gessner's, but the title and the content clearly evoke the global context of the changes brought about by 9/11. In this essay the narrator "walk[s] along the bare caliche road, as [her] sandals crunch across the gravel, drowning out the mid-September songs of birds." One senses, because of the reference to the month, that the speaker is fully conscious of the ominous meaning of the phrase "mid-September" for American readers following 2001. What ensues is Hanson's delicate marveling at the fact of her own life in a dangerous and lovable world. She writes:

It is morning when suddenly it occurs to me that, for reasons unexplained, I am not being struck by lightning. I am not falling into a crevice and disappearing into the earth. I am not bursting into flames or whirling into space. My body is intact.

It is a morning in mid-September when I wonder why it is that I so seldom marvel at the fact that I'm alive. Why does it seem so ordinary to be occupying time and space?

I hold out my hand and see the veins, see the knuckles, tendons rippling underneath the skin. I see the tiny scar there on my middle finger where I accidentally burned it as a child, the callous [*sic*]where I gripped the pruning shears too long. (136)

The humble, richly accessible narrative voice here, typical of the many lyrical stories in her 2004 collection *Icons of Loss and Grace,* achieves two important things, I think—two things essential to any of us trying to write about nature in the post-9/11 world. First, the story of this simple walk down the rural road in central Texas does not *ignore* the fact that we live in a world of danger, unpredictability, terror, and suffering. Though the focus here is on the dangers of nature, the topic of terrorism does come up briefly:

Should we be concerned about possible terrorist threats? Only the very naïve would say the danger's not real. There are malevolent forces at work to destroy the things we hold dear. There is evil in the world. There are cruelty and anger and misuse of power. There are arrogance, intolerance, and greed. (141)

Nonetheless, the narrator is determined not to "live a life fed by fear" (141). Perhaps the ultimate tragedy of 9/11 is that American culture and much of the world were inculcated with a sense of fear following the attacks. True, we have always experienced fear, and some have even argued that fear and insecurity are underlying motivations for much of what passes for civilization—see, for instance, Michael Moore's discussion of fear and American culture in the documentary film *Bowling for Columbine.*

But, though conscious of fear and danger, Hanson does not allow such a preoccupation to usurp her fundamental love of life. She makes a curious literary gesture in the final brief paragraphs of her essay, switching from first to third person, making the narrator an anonymous "everywoman" or "every-man." In the willful loving of herself and the world—a celebratory perspective that acknowledges darkness—Hanson accomplishes what I consider to be the second major achievement of this essay. Here's what she writes:

Walking along a rough caliche road in mid-September, a woman is jolted by the mental image of herself alone on a gravel bar, staring in amazement at her empty hands. This is your life, the stones in the river tell her. Pick it up and hold it tightly; turn it over and over; let it go. Let it gently fall into the flow of the river. Let it be carried away like sand. Let it disappear from sight, becoming a part of the current as it goes. Let it not matter any longer that you have lost it. Let the losing of it set you free.

Walking with the wind against her back, with the sun on the side of her face and the sound of crunching gravel underneath her feet, the woman is grounded in this time and in this place. She knows that the world is dangerous, that life is dangerous, but she also loves the way her body feels as it travels across the earth. Holding both hope and fear in her heart, she is, she knows, safe at home. (144)

The final lines of this essay do a wonderful job of describing the state of mind many of us try to achieve as we toil in the field of ecocriticism and environmental writing in the world today, trying to hold "both hope and fear" in our hearts. We could not live, we could not work as well, without either the hope or the fear. In a peculiar way, the explicit locus of fear—the fact that we live in a world where events like the 9/11 attacks could occur—offers motivation to care more, to try harder, to engage more fully with the world's injustices. But without loving the feel of our bodies passing across the earth, what would be the point?

Hope in the dark. Life's flavors and its risks. Human imagination, tipping toward life or tipping toward death. Saving, savoring. This is the state of ecocriticism in the wake of 9/11.

9 | Gated Mountains

In July 2002, having spent the better part of a Saturday in the office catching up on paperwork, I decided to treat myself to a taste of Nevada wilderness. I'm not talking about an impromptu jaunt to one of the state's remote mountain ranges. I'm talking about proximate wilderness, about the possibility of a hike through sage, bitterbrush, mountain mahogany, Jeffrey pines, and multicolored rock, serenaded by the sound of mountain water, just fifteen minutes from downtown Reno.

Tired of my sunless office, eager for the bracing smell of the mountains, I raced home to pick up my wife and our dogs. Susie had been thinking about a walk somewhere in the direction of Mount Rose—perhaps the Thomas Creek area. But I had in mind another familiar hiking area, a place where I've often walked with my graduate students from the University of Nevada's Literature and Environment Program. I pictured the striking ochre and gray cliffs of Hunter Creek Canyon, the many shades of green tracing the route of the creek from the Mount Rose Wilderness Area down to the Truckee River.

I arrived in Reno in 1995 to teach in UNR's English Department. One of the primary attractions of the move was the opportunity to live near mountains, to live *in* the mountains. I had been working for several years in the Texas Hill Country, just southwest of Austin, and was starved for genuine alpine climate and vistas. It didn't take long to discover the popular Steamboat Ditch Trail and the Hunter Creek Trail, both of which were accessed via an informal parking lot in the new Juniper Ridge housing development, just south of the Truckee River, two or three miles west of Virginia Street in downtown Reno. Both of these trails had obviously been used by Reno hikers and runners for many years. The Steamboat Ditch Trail was a favorite location for mountain bikers as well.

But almost immediately it was clear that trail access would be a serious issue in Juniper Ridge, as McMansion after McMansion cropped up on the west-facing ridge. This is nothing new in Reno. All over the city, access to spectacular wild places is threatened by metastasizing urban sprawl. There's Hidden Valley State Park on the eastern side of the city, Peavine Mountain to the north (just a few minutes from the UNR campus), Galena Park and Thomas Creek and Whites Creek to the south, and Steamboat Ditch/Hunter Creek to the west. Wise urban planning would preserve public access to these beautiful areas, much as Boulder, Colorado, has created Chautauqua Park in the nearby Rocky Mountain foothills. The public parks remain open; but, increasingly, Reno's traditional places of outdoor recreation, including the Hunter Creek and Hunter Lake Trails, are on the verge of inaccessibility. They are becoming private viewsheds for wealthy new arrivals.[1]

So the Saturday afternoon hike on Hunter Creek Trail in July 2002 would be a kind of experiment. Susie and I, and my son Jacinto, had recently returned from spending a sabbatical semester in Brisbane, Australia. In addition to our research and lecturing activities in Australia, we'd traveled much of the eastern and central regions of that vast country, hiking both rugged and highly engineered trails, dodging lightning on Mount Kosciuszko in the Snowy Mountains of New South Wales and shivering in the foggy highlands of Tasmania's Cradle Mountain.

We'd been impressed by the enlightened efforts of Australia's state and national governments to create parks and promote public access to wild places and, at the same time, to set aside many pristine wild areas as trail-less habitat for the country's extraordinarily diverse plants and animals. In some ways, our outdoor experiences in Australia reminded Susie of her native Colorado, including the maintenance of lovely trails in the Front Range near Denver and the Flatirons in Boulder. Even in Brisbane, a city of more than a million people, it was possible to leave behind the city noises and vistas while on Mount

Coot-tha or in the more distant parts of the Brisbane Forest Park or on nearby North Stradbroke Island and Moreton Island. Wandering around Australia, I often found myself thinking of my hometown of Eugene, Oregon, and the many trails for hiking, running, and biking in the Cascades, just to the east. Like many people, I tend to hold up my own favorite childhood places as a kind of fixed standard of beauty and joy, thinking, "This is what the world should be like."

I chose Hunter Creek Trail as an experiment in "urban wilderness trail access," knowing as soon as we began the short drive from our house to the trailhead that the experiment would be completed even before we stepped out of the car to begin walking and knowing, too, that the results would not be pleasant.

We drove west along the south side of the Truckee River and after a few minutes turned left past the faux gate at the entrance to Juniper Ridge. Up the hill a minute further, and then a right turn onto a street named "Mountaingate." I'd never noticed this name before, but it seemed ominously appropriate. For several years I've been tracking the progress of the extraordinarily ugly and pretentious mansions of the nouveau riche up this ridgeline, facing the Steamboat Ditch to the west and Hunter Creek Canyon and Mount Rose Wilderness Area to the south. Rocky lots, scattered with cheatgrass and sagebrush, were being replaced, one by one, by bloated stucco castles and greener grass than could be found in nature.

Sure enough, when we arrived at the lot that had served as the public parking area for the past seven years (and probably longer), there was no empty lot. During the past six months, yet another castle had been erected, a monument to the privatization of wilderness access in the American West. The gating of Mount Rose Wilderness Area, at least from this popular access point, was now almost complete. We drove down the block and found a surreptitious route between two mansions, then slipped through with the dogs and made our way to the Hunter Creek Trail. But it felt as if we were doing something illegal, trespassing in order to get to public land. At the same time, our simple walk felt like an act of necessary defiance. It was a warm July afternoon, and I felt my blood boiling as we hiked. I thought of the man I had seen standing on his greener-than-green "mountaingate" lawn when we drove by, his arms proudly crossed, watching his dog take a shit. His stance seemed to say, "I own this place, this grass, this dog, this shit, this entire valley. I own the Hunter Creek view. No riffraff allowed." I wanted to say to him, "Up yours!" And I wanted to say the same thing to the civic leaders who had allowed Reno, and still allow Reno, to be sold out to distant developers (often located in California and the Midwest, according to scuttlebutt) who have no concern for the beauty and livability of this place, only for the money that can be extracted from it.

■ ■ ■ As a scholar of environmental literature, I know the many historical and philosophical views of wilderness that have percolated in both public and academic circles during recent years and for many decades, even centuries. My bookshelves at home and at the university are loaded down with such statements.

Every morning when I look at distant Mount Rose from my bedroom window and when I kick up the dust on any mountain trail in Reno or elsewhere, I think of Wallace Stegner's elegant proposal, from his so-called "Wilderness Letter" of the early 1960s, that wilderness is the "geography of hope."

I think, too, of Edward Abbey's provocative claim, from *Desert Solitaire,* that we need wilderness even if we never go there (or never can go there), for its mere existence, or the thought of it, gives us a form of refuge from our right-angled, human-made environments. I remember supporting this claim years ago, as a graduate student in New England, when the memory of wild places in the West helped to sustain me as I wrote my dissertation in stuffy offices on the Brown campus. Western wilderness, the idea of it, filled my dreams and inspired my pen.

And then I moved to Nevada in 1995, just as William Cronon was publishing "The Trouble with Wilderness" in venues suitable for academics (*Uncommon Ground: Toward Reinventing Nature*) and for the general public (*The New York Times*). Cronon's work problematized the concept of wilderness, revealed its social constructedness and artificiality, and made it easier for developers and road builders and loggers and miners to buy (or rent at bargain-basement prices) and despoil land that has not for a long time been what "romantic idealists" call "wilderness." While Cronon's ideas may have intellectual merit, they are also a practical fiasco. Sometimes it's simply best for academics to stay in their offices and chatter to each other.

As I walked the Hunter Creek Trail on that July day in 2002, blood boiling, I found myself remembering Robert Michael Pyle's phrase "the extinction of experience" from his book *The Thunder Tree*, published in 1993. Remembering the High Line Canal from the Aurora, Colorado, of his childhood, Pyle eloquently argues that we are increasingly removed from the more-than-human world in our daily experience of urban America. He argues that many routes to self-understanding and ecological awareness are traveled not by abstract thinking, but by ordinary, daily experience, by using our senses to see, smell, hear, and touch the world. We need urban wildlands, says Pyle, in order to have access to the experience of the world and in order to appreciate who we are and what's important in our lives. The "extinction" of wild experience, even the moderate forms of wild experience that one can have in a city park or a nearby mountain trail, is one of the significant crises of our time.

As a scholar and a teacher, I, like many people in my city, spend much of my time indoors. Even though I often talk about nature with students and colleagues, we tend to conduct our discussions in built environments, referring abstractly to the world beyond our making. But I also love being outside, and I seek access to the world wherever I can find it. I am not content merely to look at the world from a glorious distance. Although I occasionally find time to wander over to the Ruby Mountains or to the more remote reaches of the Sierra Nevada range, I have always felt that access to the Reno area's small wildernesses is one of the special blessings of living in this place. As this access frays and vanishes due to the greed of corporate developers and the shortsightedness of city planners and officials (and perhaps even the local electorate), I find myself brooding over our collective "extinction of experience."

Here in Nevada we have another "gated mountain" to make our blood boil and to threaten us with "extinction of experience" in an even more literal sense. If people throughout the United States know nothing else about Nevada, most have now heard of Yucca Mountain, a place that, according to the Bush Jr. administration, will solve the nation's energy worries by storing seventy-seven thousand tons of high-level radioactive waste and enabling nuclear power plants to continue operating and producing more waste ad infinitum. If Yucca Mountain were located in just about any other American state, it would be recognized as a beautiful place, even a sacred place. Because it's located in a state with more than three hundred mountain ranges, and because it's located on the Nevada Test Site (part of the federal land that constitutes more than 80 percent of Nevada), it's relatively easy for a White House with its hands in the pockets of the nuclear industry to run a farce of a review process, launch a national publicity campaign loaded with logical and scientific and ethical fallacies, and ram approval of the nuclear-waste repository through Congress. Who will ever know the difference? How many people will ever see firsthand the beauty of this mesalike topography? How many people know about the twenty species of reptiles that live there?

Yucca Mountain is a secret place. It's located one hundred miles north of Las Vegas on gated, Test Site land. Just as wilderness areas in the Reno area are increasingly becoming inaccessible to recreational visitors, Yucca Mountain and other military locales in the state are places where the federal government does things it doesn't want scrutinized by the public. For the current federal administration, Yucca Mountain signifies a safe, politically expedient solution to the nuclear-waste conundrum. To citizens of Nevada, Yucca Mountain signifies the culmination of a greedy, shortsighted, and scientifically unin-formed (or incomplete) energy industry, working in cahoots with a corrupt, self-serving administration. Increasingly, if the predicted waste-transportation accidents occur, citizens throughout the nation will come to share the critical perspectives of Nevadans—and they'll remember that it was the Bush-Cheney government that stamped its approval on this repository site. Rebecca Solnit wrote in an August 2002 editorial for the *San Francisco Chronicle* that "the bumpers of the trucks that will carry tens of thousands of loads of nuclear waste to Yucca Mountain should read, 'We're gambling with the inheritance of our children and grandchildren and countless generations after them.'" Yucca Mountain is a "gated" Nevada mountain that gives new meaning to our reputation as a gambling state.

I watch a covey of California quail, a few grownups and a brood of nervous chicks, gather seeds from my backyard. We can wait for nature to come to us, and we can view the world from behind glass. Or we can organize ourselves, as individuals and as communities, to speak out for access, for the opportunity to experience our place in the world. And for a responsive, responsible government that does not perceive wilderness, particularly desert, as "a good place to throw used razor blades," in the words of an Atomic Energy Commission official quoted in Terry Tempest Williams's *Refuge* (242).

■ ■ ■ Should we be content with mountaingate mansions gating access to proximate wilderness in Reno, in Nevada, in the American West? Are we powerless to act for preservation of trail access in our part of the world? Should we allow Nevada's wild mountains to become synonymous with "nuclear waste"? We should ask ourselves these questions. And we should let our elected officials, and our mountaingate neighbors, know that the public needs and demands access to nearby wild places, to the world's beauty. And that we'd prefer not to have our mountains hollowed out and filled with radioactive garbage.

NOTES

1. The department of Regional Parks and Open Space for Washoe County has planned construction in 2008 of the Michael D. Thompson trailhead for the Hunter Creek Trail. Land dedicated by the owner will provide trail access, parking, and restroom facilities at the end of Woodchuck, off Plateau Road.

10

Animals and Humans

IN APPRECIATION OF RANDY MALAMUD'S
POETIC ANIMALS AND ANIMAL SOULS

The human experience of the world is permeated through
and through, on every possible level, by animality—by our
relationships with other animal beings on the planet and by
our own animal ways of feeling and sensing. Randy Malamud, in his eloquent
2003 study, *Poetic Animals and Animal Souls,* throws down a challenge to Western
civilization, and particularly to American readers, to acknowledge the ethical
and psychological flaws inherent in our attitudes toward and interactions with
nonhuman animals. Although this is a work of literary criticism, it begins with
a powerfully aggressive moral assertion, noting that "from the beginning God
authorizes an ecologically perverse hubris" (3). The task of his project is to make
readers more conscious of this unconscionable arrogance—this hubris—in their
own lives and to reveal the dire implications of our arrogance toward animals
and, by implication, toward the rest of nature and toward people different
from ourselves. It may not be popular in some circles to say this, but the harsh
critique Malamud directs toward our views of animals mirrors (or echoes) the
criticisms that one also hears from ecofeminist scholars and environmental
justice scholars—at its most fundamental and universal level, it is an attack on
all cultural structures built upon premises of priority and exclusivity. Malamud's
opening lines make this concern piercingly plain: "The relationship between
human and nonhuman animals is codified in social culture as hierarchical and
fundamentally impermeable: we are in here, they are out there" (1).

Malamud's book is divided into two parts: part 1, An Ecocritical Ethics of Reading; and part 2, Poetic Animals. By beginning with an extended, multipart essay on the ethical aspects of our reading of literature, Malamud adheres to some of the central concerns of the new field of ecological literary criticism, which many scholars have recently argued is essentially a scholarly movement devoted to advancing particular ethical concerns about the state of the world and the state of society. Much of the opening part of the book explores how humans fall short of truly "knowing" other animals, despite our fervent efforts. Zoos, for instance, seem to indicate human devotion to the preservation and understanding of other species. However, for Malamud, zoos merely salve society's guilt "toward environmental pillaging . . . that supports our consumptive appetites, . . . justifying the small-scale extrication from the plundered biota a few, token exotic animals" (5). Like so many human actions, the "saving" of endangered animals from their natural habitats and their placement in cages and artificial landscapes for our own viewing convenience is easy on our collective conscience but does little to correct the destructive force our kind exerts in the world.

So what could be better than zoos? Although he acknowledges the inevitable limitations of human imagination in understanding realms of experience beyond our own, Malamud claims ultimately to be a believer in the "powers of our intellectual aspirations" (7) and argues that "The empathizing imagination can be enlisted to enhance the awareness of sentient, cognitive, ethical, and emotional *affinities between people and animals*" (9). This is where literature begins to factor in—despite the tendencies of writers and others to commit what philosopher Thomas Nagel sees as "anthropomorphic fallacies" (7), the artistic imagination also provides crucial gestures of affinity beyond the oppressive attitudes of a particular culture. Malamud relies upon formulations of Gilles Deleuze and Félix Guattari in suggesting that the "empathetic imagination" operating in certain examples of literary and visual art "connects us with other species in a meaningful way." Early in his study, the critic points out several poetic examples to illustrate the dynamic and even transgressive tendencies of the best animal poetry, such as Mexican writer José Emilio Pacheco's "empowered, exuberant, hyper-animated" lyric titled "Investigation on the

Subject of the Bat" (8), Gary Snyder's propulsion of the human reader toward the experience of being a bird in "Straight Creek—Great Burn," and Pattiann Rogers's appreciation of the specific and multifarious significances of animals in her work "Abundance and Satisfaction." Throughout his ethical, theoretical, and analytical discussions, Malamud maintains a passionate wittiness, such as his pronouncement in the context of Rogers's poem: "As Hereclitus might have said, one can never look at the same blackbird twice" (16).

Part 1 of Malamud's book is ultimately not only a pronouncement on behalf of the mysterious and authentic autonomy of animals, but a defense of *literature,* and especially poetry. He writes: "I will propose a defense of literary value, and not just on cerebral or intellectual merits, but as a springboard for ethical replenishment: a platform for real-world improvements of our modes of engaging with nature" (19). The basic argument suggests that without an ethical evolution, we're bound to continue our current destructive societal tendencies—and without good literature that acknowledges and celebrates animals with "authenticity, complexity, and nobility" (27), we'll be gravely challenged in our capacity to assume a healthy ethical stance toward other beings. Of course, animal literature is nothing new, but writers have seldom done full justice to our brethren on this planet, according to Malamud. He argues, in surveying the history of American writing about animals, that authors ranging from Theodore Roosevelt to Mary Oliver have generally accepted the idea of "human power over animals" and have operated from the perspective, at least implicitly, that "The animal subject exists for our pleasure and at our pleasure" (28). Leavening his unashamed—and well deserved—critique of Western civilization and specific writers, Malamud's first-person plural pronoun implicates himself in the flaws he observes, and his intermittent confessions, along with the wit of his prose, reveal him as an evolving animal advocate, not as a supersensitized champion of all species apart from our own. He writes, for instance, "I read books, try not to do too much harm to the ecosystem, and hope to change, for at least a few people, some cultural attitudes that seem to me demonstrably undesirable" (35). What more could a literary critic hope to accomplish?

The final section of part 1, "An Ecocritical Aesthetic Ethic," lays out Malamud's notion of an "advocacy methodology," built upon the central premises of Marxist and feminist criticism and assuming three things: (1) the oppression of the subject ("the proletariat, women . . . here, animals"); (2) that exploitation must be understood in a historical context; and (3) that this understanding must lead to an evolution of consciousness and, in turn, to better treatment of those who have been oppressed (43). It would be easy for readers to assume that Malamud is, paradoxically, seeking both to bash his fellow humans and, at the same time, to stand apart from the rest of us in serving as champion of the planet's voiceless species. But he takes pains to claim that his is not a holier-than-thou project, nor does he mean his criticisms of particular authors and particular poems as restricted, personal attacks. Rather, he seeks to spur his readers to become aware of—and then work to transcend—the unspoken "cultural conspiracy" in our treatment of animals and animal habitats (48).

The second major part of his book probes in detail the specific "poetic animals" offered by such twentieth-century and contemporary writers as José Emilio Pacheco, Marianne Moore, Stevie Smith, Philip Larkin, Gary Snyder, Seamus Heaney, and Pattiann Rogers. He begins this half of the book, though, with a provocative chapter on "Meso-American Spirituality and Animal Co-essences," foregrounding the traditional Central American concept of "'animal souls'—the idea that a person's soul is implicitly connected with an external animal counterpart, or co-essence" (51). The purpose of offering this concept is to provide a possible alternative to the limited, reifying view of animals that typically operates in Western societies, although the critic also feels it necessary to apologize to readers for the possible perception that he is being culturally imperialistic even in investigating ideas of animals in Central and North America in pursuit of admirable alternatives to his own culture's limited perspectives, hoping that the realization of his goals—an "enlightened coexistence" between humans and other animals (63)—will "justify this intercultural exercise" (53). Malamud's methodology, he explains at one point, is to try reading selected examples of poetically imagined animals through the "lens" of the concept of animal souls (63). He is appropriately tentative about this projection of different cultures onto each other, but he is also disarming in the spiritual and ethical ambitiousness of his project—this is not the business of literary analysis being performed merely for career advancement.

The entire book builds toward the critic's climactic discussion of Pattiann Rogers's four-page poem "Animals and People: 'The Human Heart in Conflict with Itself,'" which is reprinted in full from Rogers's 1997 work *Eating Bread and Honey* as Malamud's final pronouncement. Having already completed most of this manuscript, Malamud discovered Pattiann Rogers's work and felt, humbly, that she had said in her poetry precisely what he was trying to articulate in his scholarly prose, except that she had said it "more concisely and immensely more effectively" than he (182). What particularly moves Malamud about Rogers's "Animals and People" is her prescient juxtaposition of ideal human treatment of and attitudes toward animals and the ways we actually act and think, working toward her ultimate revelation that "Their blood is our blood, and their fate is our fate. . . . In our compulsions concerning animals, and in our ambivalent adoration of animals, Rogers finds our very life force, our connection to life, our inspiration to live" (183). This realization of our deepest life urge in the being of animals is what Malamud means when he adopts the concept of "animal souls" from traditional Meso-American cultures.

Despite the fact that Malamud humbly yields the podium to Pattiann Rogers at the end of the book, his own scholarly voice is passionate and imaginative enough to do the poet proud. At a time when literary criticism in general—like ecocriticism more specifically—is trying to find its proper place in a world of rampant social and ecological trauma and brazen, callous plays of global power brokers, *Poetic Animals and Animal Souls* breathes new life into the practice of humanities scholarship, taking exciting and productive risks, going well beyond business as usual.

11

Chimeric Opinions

XENOTRANSPLANTATION AND THE

CONCEPT OF "MIXING"

People come from far and wide to take risks in Reno. Our economy here has long been dependent on visitors who perceive this as a place where they can get away with things that are beyond the pale elsewhere—first it was prizefighting, then getting divorced. Although it's illegal in Reno and Las Vegas, you can still pay for sex elsewhere in Nevada. And, as the billboards advertise on all the highways heading toward the state, there are plenty of opportunities to try "loose slots" or make a killing at the casino gaming tables. More recently, Reno—and especially the University of Nevada—has achieved notoriety for the research in genetic engineering that now takes place in the College of Agriculture, Biotechnology, and Natural Resources. All of these activities, from betting on boxing to experimenting with recombinant DNA, involve going out on financial or biological limbs, sometimes both at once.

I've taught environmental literature at the University of Nevada, Reno, for a decade now, and it's never been a secret that my colleagues and students in the "College of Ag" were "doing research with animals." Barney Nelson, my first graduate assistant at the Center for Environmental Arts and Humanities, lived in a cottage on the grounds of the university's agricultural research facility, six miles east of campus, near the sage-covered slopes of Hidden Valley State Park. I remember driving past grazing cattle and sheep on my way out to meet with Barney—they looked like regular cattle and sheep to me. Until the biotech studies hit the national news in 2004, I had always assumed that "agricultural research" focused on better ways of raising healthy livestock. Now it's come to light that scientists are implanting human stem cells in their research animals as a way of growing organs that could eventually be transplanted to the human donors from which the cells originally came. This mixing of human and animal bodies has created organisms that journalists are calling "chimeras," bringing to mind mythological monsters, freaks of nature. Lead researcher Dr. Esmail Zanjani insists, "They're still sheep. But they have significant amounts of human cells in their different organs."

Despite the clamor in the national media, the UNR campus has been surprisingly silent about this ethically touchy line of research. Local concerns have focused in recent months on an ag professor's claims about improper disposal of dead animals and mistreatment of research animals (not due to the actual research processes, but because of insufficient access to drinking water)—these claims have recently been supported by findings of the U.S. Department of Agriculture.

More interesting, perhaps, is what the stem-cell research teaches us about our own thinking. It occurs to me that beyond the medical implications of stem-cell work, this line of investigation is an elaborate inquiry into the phenomenon of *mixing*. In cultural circles, this idea has long been associated with miscegenation—with intermarriage or "mixed blood." In my various courses, I routinely teach Leslie Marmon Silko's celebrated novel *Ceremony* (1977), which encourages readers to appreciate the value of change and convergence. Tayo, the book's hero, is a man of mixed Anglo/Laguna Pueblo blood. Tayo's climactic revelation occurs when he realizes that the world has "no boundaries, only transitions." However, despite our cultural metaphors of melting pots and salad bowls, our myths of diversity and cooperation, Americans—like people elsewhere—still adhere viscerally to a belief in segregated sameness.

I think, too, of *Animal Heart* (2004), Brenda Peterson's recent novel about *xenotransplantation*, in which one of her characters (a mixed-blood Scottish-Hāwaiian undersea photographer) suffers a heart attack while diving and, in an emergency transplantation procedure, receives the heart of a baboon. "I do know what science is capable of doing—and how little we think about the consequences," says another character (92). And Marshall McGreggor, the "animal heart" recipient, tells his sister, "Here I am, a miracle of science, a freak of nature" (98). Despite the initial shock and abhorrence Peterson's characters express upon learning of this trans-species mixing, the story unfolds in a way that complicates and deepens the emotional and ethical issues. Patience and uncertainty win out over knee-jerk revulsion.

Still, as I write these notes, I find myself watching a pair of robins outside the window. The brown-breasted female perches on her nest, warming a trio of blue eggs, as the male (who looks much like his mate) dashes back and forth from the lawn to the nest, placing insects into the female's mouth. This is how nature seems to work. "Birds of a feather flock together," as Aristotle famously put it.

And yet, cultures appear to work better—especially in a globalized, post-colonial era—when diverse people can get along together. Harmony and hybridity are good things, aren't they? I recall Gloria Anzaldúa's mestizo paean *Borderlands/La Frontera* (1987), eloquently articulating the virtues of "mestizaje," of cultural and linguistic and, yes, biological mixing.

Like many people, I feel ambivalence, a mix of resistance and support, toward bioengineering of all kinds, due to uncertainties about the health effects of GM foods, the corporate patenting of seeds, the demonstrated value of engineered crops as an alternative to massive use of pesticides in order to feed the world's hungry people, and the hopeful medical possibilities of current stem-cell work. I feel compelled to learn more about the scientific implications and the ethical concerns associated with this work rather than leaping toward reflexive opinions.

I'm also fascinated by what the stem-cell work might teach us about the psychology of mixing. Could it be that the creation of human-sheep chimeras has simply ramped up the stakes that have always been at risk when "others" have come together? In their powerful study *New World New Mind: Moving Toward Conscious Evolution* (1989), Robert Ornstein and Paul Ehrlich argue that human survival in a changing world requires new ways of thinking, new ways of overcoming some of our genetically programmed responses to the world. "Birds of a feather flock together" may be an appropriate way for robins to behave, but imagine the grave social implications of such a marital policy in a multicultural community. Likewise, given today's technical possibilities in recombinant DNA and stem-cell research, perhaps it makes sense for us to strive for a "new mind" to match this "new world" of technological mixing.

But I don't really know for sure. When I read news accounts of the UNR stem-cell research, and when I scan the university Web site to get a sense of what biotech graduate students are working on, I'm struck by the casual enthusiasm these researchers express about the ethically and biologically risky work they're engaged in. In our culture, we tend to be blithely absolute in our support for or criticism of complex, uncertain phenomena. In her oft-cited book *The Argument Culture: Stopping America's War of Words* (1998), linguist Deborah Tannen explains how ancient and pervasive our "adversarial approach to knowledge" is. She urges readers to progress "from debate to dialogue."

These days, as I drive past BT sheep at home on the Nevada range, I feel neither horror nor joy. I wonder what they mean. I wonder what to think. My opinions about these animals, about this entire line of research, are as chimeric as the cells beneath the wool. Perhaps we should all try to learn more, perhaps we should engage in open-minded dialogue, before rushing to argue.

12

The Story of Climate Change

SCIENCE, NARRATIVE, AND SOCIAL ACTION

I really appreciate the invitation to come and speak here this morning, and I especially appreciate the effort that Kirsten and Kayla have put into organizing today's service.[1] I've often felt I was "preaching to the choir," but I've never had a chance to preach to an actual choir—so this is a treat for me. I should say it's especially meaningful for me to address a religious gathering in light of the recent criticisms that have been directed toward the American religious community, particularly toward the apocalyptic sects that seem to have had such an influence in the November 2004 elections. Some of you may have seen printed versions of journalist Bill Moyers's December 1 speech when he received the Harvard Medical School's Global Environmental Citizen Award, in which he expressed the frightening realization that "the delusional is no longer marginal," that really kooky ideas have "come in from the fringe" and "now sit in the seat of power in the oval office and in Congress." Moyers describes an article by the journalist Glenn Scherer that explains how many of our fellow citizens feel about the world these days:

Why care about the earth when the droughts, floods, famine and pestilence brought about by ecological collapse are signs of the apocalypse foretold in the Bible? Why care about global climate change when you and yours will be rescued in the rapture? And why care about converting from oil to solar when the same God who performed the miracle of the loaves and fishes can whip up a few billion barrels of light crude with a Word?

So this is the perspective on the world that increasing numbers of people in our society share—I have to say, at the risk of seeming ungenerous, that I find it to be wacky, ignorant, lazy, and scary. And it is in this context that I do my own work as a literary scholar devoted to exploring how the refined use of language—through literature (like the beautiful poetry Kayla and Kirsten have read this morning) and also journalism and science writing and political discourse and the common language we use every day—might enable us to understand better our relationship to the rest of the planet, our physical and psychological needs, and what we might do in order to correct some of the injustices and imbalances that are occurring throughout the world as a result of human actions.

I really have only a few minutes to speak here today, so let me get right to the point. Your congregation has decided that it would be a good thing for the next two years to think about the issue of global warming and social action. What can we do at this point in history in order to live meaningful lives and help to correct vast and complicated problems such as global warming?

You might wonder, in particular, why someone like me would bother emphasizing the role of language—and specifically literature—in this kind of context. Well, to me, language is crucially important in exploring and even *shaping* our sense of personal values and in communicating these values. Language is also essential to the communication of the evolving scientific ideas that are so deeply necessary to our understanding of such phenomena as global warming. Without paying close attention to language, we can't be entirely aware of how our own ways of thinking are being shaped—some might say "controlled"— by certain terminologies. Also, when the *scientific* community concentrates primarily on communicating its discoveries and theories to the public in purely statistical (or quantitative) ways and through inaccessible technical jargon, it becomes all too easy for government officials and the general public simply to blow off these ideas—and what we're left with is the "road to environmental apocalypse."

"GLOBAL WARMING" OR "CLIMATE CHANGE"? ISSUES OF SCIENTIFIC
ACCURACY AND RHETORICAL POTENCY

Let's talk first about the phrase "global warming." This phrase itself, embedded as it is in our popular vocabulary, doesn't quite describe the complexity of the actual phenomenon of global *climate change*. According to the science, what's happening in the world is not simply a process of warming temperatures throughout the planet. Yes, temperatures are rising on the whole—but other weather patterns have also been noticed. Both warming and cooling are occurring, and sometimes from year to year an alternation of the two, with an overall trend toward warming. What scientists actually seem to be observing and predicating are very slow and subtle warming trends and also increased volatility of weather patterns in general—tremendous storms and devastating droughts. If you read works like Arthur Upgren and Jurgen Stock's *Weather: How It Works and Why It Matters,* published in 2000, you begin to realize that climate is as variable as it is visible. We can walk out the door each day and see what the weather is, but it's much harder for us, without careful attention, to notice subtle climatic changes over time—and changes in the chemical composition of the planet's *atmosphere* can be discerned only through special scientific measurements. When members of the public walk around with a phrase like "global warming" in their heads while it's snowing several feet in a day here in Reno—or in Washington, DC—and then freezing fog settles in for a week, people start to think, "Those crazy scientists! Global warming is just a hoax, another example of the failed predictions of ecological nerds." It seems to me that our tendency to latch onto certain popular phrases, phrases that can be controverted by powerful personal experiences (like shoveling snow in Reno two weeks ago), makes it that much easier for people to downplay science and drive their gas-guzzling cars with clear consciences. For *rhetorical* reasons, I think it makes sense for us to talk about the worrisome implications of "climate change" rather than "global warming"—but, that said, I should admit that much of the scientific and popular literature still uses the term "global warming."

However, some of you may have read Michael Crichton's new novel, *State of Fear* (2004), in which he caricatures environmentalists as fear mongers who will go to almost any lengths in order to frighten the public and secure funding to support their activist agendas. Crichton's activists use paramilitary tactics in their attempts to fracture the continental ice in Antarctica, seed vicious storms in the American Southwest, and instigate tsunami-causing undersea rockslides in Southeast Asia—all in the name of public relations and in defiance of scientific findings that discount the theory of global warming. One of the central characters in the novel, Nicholas Drake, the villainous leader of NERF (the National Environmental Resource Fund), declares out of frustration,

"I *hate* global warming. . . . It's a goddamn disaster. . . . [I]t *doesn't work*. . . . That's my point. You can't raise a dime with it, especially in winter. Every time it snows people forget all about global warming. Or else they decide some warming might be a good thing after all. They're trudging through the snow, *hoping* for a little global warming." (295)

To which Drake's PR advisor, John Henley, responds,

"So what you need . . . is to structure the information so that whatever kind of weather occurs, it always confirms your message. That's the virtue of shifting the focus to abrupt climate change. It enables you to use everything that happens. There will always be floods, and freezing storms, and cyclones, and hurricanes. These events will always get headlines and airtime. And in every instance, you can claim it is an example of abrupt climate change caused by global warming. So the message gets reinforced. The urgency is increased." (314)

The environmentalists in *State of Fear* come across as self-interested, ignorant, arrogant, and deceitful, as perpetrators of a vast pseudoscientific hoax. In his concluding "Author's Message," Crichton states: "I conclude that most environmental 'principles' (such as sustainable development or the precautionary principle) have the effect of preserving the economic advantages of the West and thus constitute modern imperialism toward the developing world. It is a nice way of saying, 'We got ours and we don't want you to get yours, because you'll cause too much pollution'" (571). The MIT professor John Kenner, who leads Crichton's band of lawyers and philanthropists in a fight to thwart environmental extremism, calmly cites scientific articles and guns down ELF (Environmental Liberation Front) terrorists, working on behalf of a clandestine U.S. government agency to preserve the American way of life. Throughout the novel, Crichton provides footnotes citing articles from such periodicals as the *Journal of Glaciology* and the *Bulletin of the American Meteorological Society,* suggesting that when his characters—usually Kenner—contradict the theories of global warming and climate change, this information is derived from actual science. Unable to rebut the professor's scientific claims, several of the moderate environmentalists in the novel actually convert to Kenner's side and help him to stop the ELF extremists. And even some of the author's comments in his "Author's Message" seem so neutral and, in a way, *liberal* as to lure progressive readers to appreciate his narrative debunking of global warming. This is, in many ways, a rhetorically impressive work.

The actual model for Crichton's John Kenner character seems to be, in part, MIT professor Richard Lindzen, whose work is cited several times (more than any other individual author) in the novel's extensive bibliography. I recall Ross Gelbspan's rather detailed portrayal of Lindzen in the 1997 treatment of climate issues, *The Heat Is On,* in which he recounts visiting the professor at his home in 1995: "Both he and his wife are exceedingly gracious and hospitable people. In contrast to his often tortured scientific pronouncements, I found his social and political expressions to be lucid, succinct, and unambiguous. Indeed, I found him to be one of the most ideologically extreme individuals I have ever interviewed" (52). Just as journalist Gelbspan sees through Richard Lindzen's gracious hospitality and ascertains the role of his ideological extremism in his contributions to national climate policy, I believe it's important for readers of Crichton's novel—and, indeed, any other fictional or nonfictional writings about climate issues—to realize that an engaging and lucid story does not represent the final word on this complex, elusive, and still-unfolding phenomenon. Still, in the context of our discussion of the *rhetoric* of climate change, it is important to remember Crichton's forceful critique of the rubric of "climate change" as an alternative to "global warming." The novelist has clearly anticipated this rhetorical gesture.

The year before Crichton's *State of Fear* was published, British essayist Mark Lynas produced a similarly forceful statement, *High Tide: The Truth about Our Climate Crisis,* from the opposite perspective, emphasizing the *urgency* of the current situation and the need to reduce carbon emissions in order to mitigate humans' damaging impact on climate. Although much of Lynas's study (like

Crichton's novel) is richly documented with scientific citations and experiential information, he is not above resorting to mockery (as he does in the preface), just as Crichton's work uses caricature as a rhetorical tool. Lynas asserts:

> The only remaining question is whether enough of us will realise our peril before it becomes too late to act.
>
> Some may never be able to face up to it. The current political leadership in America is a clear example, demonstrating a collective myopia which is as illogical as it is selfish. A confusion of politics and corporate self-interest—Exxon, Enron and Halliburton come to mind—surrounds the Bush White House and its policy decisions from Dick Cheney's "Energy Task Force" to the President's repudiation of Kyoto. Like the townspeople of Pompeii who laughed and turned their backs on the threatening volcano, President Bush and his Administration have met the global warming challenge with responses ranging from obfuscation to pretence to outright denial. Their worldview is founded on various assumptions such as "economic growth is essential," "we need more cars," "we must drill all our oil," all of which conflict utterly with the new paradigm that climate change represents. "I don't believe it," runs their argument. "And therefore it can't be true." (xviii–xix)

Lynas's work is not a novel, but it does offer a strong narrative thread, as he travels through Asia and the South Pacific to the Peruvian Andes and coastal Alaska, offering evidence of climate change and its implications in the form of travelogue, backed up by data. All of this is presented up front to readers in the form of a challenge: "If you can see all this and still remain unmoved, then you have lost some essential part of your humanity, and history will judge you for your lack of compassion. If you want to remain in ignorance then that is your choice too—but do not claim to be a leader" (xix). Between the extreme examples of *State of Fear* and *High Tide,* the rhetorical and ideological lines are clearly drawn.

Apart from Crichton's persuasive nay-saying and Lynas's insistent yea-saying, there is a significant tradition of environmental journalism, history, literature, and popular-science writing that describes the process of climate change, the uncertain ecological impact of this phenomenon (including the possible impact on human comfort and survival), and the political complications of developing policies in a country like ours, that does so much to contribute to the emission of so-called "greenhouse gases" and yet refuses to sign the Kyoto

Protocol, which would help us to reduce our damaging behavior. I use a lot of this material in a class I occasionally teach at UNR called "The Literature of Population," in which we study how various authors approach such topics as human overpopulation, extinction and biodiversity, and climate change—major contemporary environmental topics that seem implicitly to require abstract, quantitative scientific discourse. What we investigate in that class is the possibility of addressing such topics in ways that will be intellectually and emotionally meaningful to general readers. How, one might ask, is it possible to use *narrative* language for this purpose, to tell the *story* of something as abstract and complicated as climate change?

Let me run through a few quick examples in my limited time. First, I highly recommend historian Gale Christianson's 1999 work called *Greenhouse: The 200-Year Story of Global Warming*. I should say that the reason Christianson uses the term "global warming" is that the long-term planetary trend *is* toward warming temperatures, but the history he presents, going back to the dawn of industrialization in Europe, shows that this large-scale warming trend actually consists of occasional cooling occurrences (even mini-Ice Ages). What I find particularly useful about the book *Greenhouse* is how the author shows the extended history of climate change, making it clear that this is not simply a recent faddish concept among today's scientists and alarmist environmental ideologues. Along with Christianson's book, which takes a broad historical view of global climate change, I would recommend journalist Bill McKibben's 1989 work, *The End of Nature*. In addition to offering a well-informed, yet engagingly presented, overview of atmospheric chemistry, McKibben excels at offering a moving philosophical context for this phenomenon. Instead of making a sky-is-falling-and-we're-all-going-to-die sort of argument (of the sort we see in Hollywood's recent *The Day After Tomorrow*), he writes eloquently in the final lines of the introduction to the tenth anniversary edition of the book that

the sadness that drove me to write this book in the first place has not really lifted. This home of ours, the blessed hunk of rock and sky and biology that we were born onto, becomes each day a less complex and more violent place; its rhythms of season and storm shifted and shattered.

We didn't create this world, but we are busy decreating it. Still the sun rises; still the moon waxes and wanes; but they look down on a planet that means something different than it used to. Something less than it used to. This buzzing, blooming, mysterious, cruel, lovely globe of mountain, sea, city, forest; of fish and wolf and bug and man; of carbon and hydrogen and nitrogen—it has become unbalanced in our short moment on it. It's mostly us now. (xxv)

McKibben adopts a more philosophical approach to global warming and the greenhouse effect than we can find in most other journalistic and "infotainment" approaches, such as *State of Fear* and *The Day After Tomorrow*. Because he back-pedals from narrow, argumentative assertions, he invites readers to contemplate implications of different future paths for civilization and for the planet. Unlike some of the more defiant and breathlessly frantic commentators on global warming, McKibben limits his moral pronouncements to the sphere of his own behavior. He writes:

I have no great desire to limit my way of life. If I thought we could put off the decision, foist it on our grandchildren, I'd be willing. As it is, I have no plans to live in a cave, or even an unheated cabin. If it took ten thousand years to get where we are, it will take a few generations to climb back down. But this could be the epoch when people decide at least to go no further down the path we've been taking—when we make not only the necessary technological adjustments to preserve the world from overheating but also the necessary mental adjustments to ensure that we'll never again put our good ahead of everything else's. This is the path I choose, for it offers at least a shred of hope for a living, eternal, meaningful world. (213–14)

While McKibben skirts overarching, accusatory styles of argumentation, opting—which he does elsewhere, too, as in his 1998 book, *Maybe One,* about the issue of reproductive responsibility—for stories of personal choice and humility, other climate commentators have also, in the interest of scholarly detachment, shied away from direct assertions of cultural responsibility.[2]

A particularly distinguished effort to put the climate debates into perspective is Andrew Ross's 1991 study *Strange Weather: Culture, Science and Technology in the Age of Limits,* in which he points out the curious timing of the popularization of global-warming theory in the late twentieth century, just in time to serve "as an added ingredient for the rich stew of popular millenarianism" (199). He explains the cultural paradigm shift that brought climate issues to the forefront of environmental debates in the 1980s as the result of social changes and challenges rather than the coming to light of new scientific information:

It is perhaps no coincidence that this new threat is often described in terms usually reserved for the liberal market economy, and that human intervention is demonized in the same manner as "state intervention" in that economy. As one climatologist put it, "we still have to learn to live according to our climatic income." Nor is it a surprise to find the moralizing burden for this interference shifted on to humanity as a whole, further Christianized by the language of retribution and penitence. As another commentator put it, global warming must be seen as "the wages of industrialization." Certain elements of the new world-view that is being constructed to accommodate the global warming theory resemble pre-enlightenment conceptions of Nature as a providential interpreter of human affairs, repaying the whole of humanity for its sins with the visiting of meteorological scourges. (198)

In a section of his study titled "Science as Culture," Ross offers a telling analysis of two weather-related novels, Zora Neale Hurston's *Their Eyes Were Watching God* and Saul Bellow's *Henderson the Rain King*, showing how each reveals the "knowledge/power relationship" between native understanding of nature and white science (216). From Ross's perspective, the rise of global climate theory represents a power play on the part of Western science, further marginalizing other ways of understanding nature. He explains that these novels

about the relations between cultural power and climatic prediction do not *seem* to be part of the same interpretive system as, say, the eminently scientific theory of global warming, and yet it could be argued that the only difference is that they appeal to differently organized systems of rationality. Global warming theory claims universal scientific truth for itself, against which climatic interpretations like those of the Seminoles [in *Their Eyes*] or the Wariri [in *Henderson*] are seen as local belief-systems, or, at best, *ethnometeorology*. (217)

Although this approach to telling "the story of climate change" may seem to obscure the basic questions about whether human actions are affecting the global climate and, if so, what the implications of these effects may be, this kind of analysis helps readers to step back and understand the historical and ideological contexts in which knowledge, even natural science, is developed. Especially in the case of a phenomenon such as climate change, so vexed with claims and counterclaims, citations and countercitations, it seems important for people throughout the world to grope for a kind of skeptical open-mindedness, not settling for once-and-for-all beliefs, but rather assembling and reassembling information in pursuit of reliable, practical understanding.

The year 2004, when *State of Fear* appeared, also saw the publication of the book *Red Sky at Morning: America and the Crisis of the Global Environment*, by James Gustave Speth, dean of the Yale School of Forestry and Environmental Studies. The new wrinkle in the climate story provided by Speth's work was its central focus on environmental issues—not just climate—from a *global* perspective. Although he draws on considerable information from scientific sources, Speth focuses primarily on issues of public policy, asserting:

I hope this short book will be a wake-up call to those of us, including many in the environmental community, who may believe that all the international negotiations, treaties, and other agreements of the past two decades have prepared us to deal with global environmental threats. They haven't. The current system of international efforts to help the environment simply isn't working. The design makes sure it won't work, and the statistics keep getting worse. We need a new design. (xi–xii)

Despite publications to the contrary (like those cited copiously in *State of Fear*), Speth unequivocally adheres to the validity of climate change. He opens his section on "Global Climate Disruption and Energy Policy," stating, "For the past quarter-century, the international scientific community and others have been sounding ever-louder warnings that earth's climate, the climate that has sustained natural and human communities throughout history, is now seriously threatened by atmospheric pollution" (55). Urging a multifaceted remediation strategy that includes reducing carbon emissions (by improving efficient use of energy and shifting away from carbon-intensive fuels) and adopting high-tech chemical processes for carbon sequestration (keeping carbon dioxide from being released into the earth's atmosphere), Speth focuses the core of his discussion on the importance of improving what he calls "global environmental governance," meaning the cooperation of governments and for-profit and not-for-profit organizations throughout industrialized and developing societies.

Far from adopting the haughty, first-world attitude toward the concerns of developing nations criticized in Crichton's "Author's Message," Speth acknowledges that one of the reasons for past failures in global governance has been the reluctance of the "wealthy North" to deal fairly with "the South . . . in a way that recognizes their aspirations and special challenges" (108). Among the many competing claims to "truth" in the literature of climate change, Speth's work—despite the somewhat theatrical title—comes across as serious, sober, uninflammatory, and realistic, calling for global cooperation more forcefully and precisely than most other writing on this issue. He also acknowledges the importance of finding the right language for the slippery and contentious environmental concerns we now face around the planet: "A new vocabulary or way of discussing the issue can help this along. No group could be better suited to undertake such a redefinition and new articulation than the young people I see on campuses across the country. I hope that they can lead in making the grand challenges of today have the same immediacy as the local environmental threats of the 1970s" (200).

One of the major themes in the literature of global climate change is the question of whom we, as readers, should trust. Do we simply assume that the people wearing literal or figurative lab coats deserve our passive trust? Should we believe the technocrats? Or should we say, as many people do, that since those scientists can't agree about the precise processes or implications of climate change, we don't have to do anything about it ourselves? (This seems to be the attitude of the Bush administration, inspired in no small part by a devotion to growing the economy and supporting the oil industry.) There is ample writing about the technical phenomenon of climate change by scientists such as Stanford's Stephen Schneider, author of the 1996 work, *Laboratory Earth: The Planetary Gamble We Can't Afford to Lose.*[3] In the public eye, however, Schneider's sometimes bland and sometimes inflammatory descriptions of climate change and its implications have been effectively blunted and countered by works such as Gregg Easterbrook's voluminous and apparently authoritative work from around the same era (the mid-1990s), *A Moment on the Earth: The Coming Age of Environmental Optimism.* Easterbrook has chapters on global cooling and global warming and concludes, conveniently, that nature does as it pleases and humans cannot predict or control its behavior—so why panic? Paul and Anne Ehrlich, in the 1996 book *Betrayal of Science and Reason,* point out that Easterbrook's work "contains so many serious errors that it has spawned a virtual cottage industry among scientists trying to correct them" (40)—they refer to the work of Easterbrook and other nay-saying writers as "brownlashing." And the Ehrlichs, in their own chapter devoted to "Fables about the Atmosphere and Climate," lend their voices to rebutting Easterbrook as well. Ross Gelbspan, in a fascinating chapter called "The Battle for the Control of Reality" from his book *The Heat Is On: The Climate Crisis, the Cover-up, the Prescription* (also published in 1997), points out that the preponderance of scientific evidence shows that climate change is a real phenomenon and one that warrants serious attention from government, industry, and the public, but, as he puts it,

the tiny group of dissenting scientists have been given prominent public visibility and congressional influence out of all proportion to their standing in the scientific community. . . . By keeping the discussion focused on whether there really is a problem, these dozen or so dissidents—contradicting the consensus view held by 2,500 of the world's top scientists—have until now prevented discussion about how to address the problem. (40)

Obviously, science doesn't advance merely through a democratic process, with the majority necessarily outweighing the dissenting voices. And obviously, dissent and discussion are important in any academic and social arena. But Gelbspan expresses concern that the small group of scientists, many of whom are doing industry-funded research and seem to be "ideologically extreme individuals" (52), are able to deflect the vast amount of data collected by other members of the scientific community and the arguments mounted by environmentally attuned politicians.

A somewhat different approach to the issue of trustworthiness in telling the story of climate change is offered in Susan Gaines's 2001 novel, *Carbon Dreams*. This book tells the story of a young, female Latin American scientist whose research in the field of paleoclimatology (the study of ancient climates through the gathering of core samples from the ocean floor) leads her unintentionally into the public controversy regarding global warming and climate change. The novel is not simply an indirect way of espousing the politically controversial idea of global warming. It also explores the predicament of a scientist who merely wishes to understand the planet's natural history and tries to avoid extrapolating from her findings in statements about today's environmental issues. But *other* scientists get wind of her findings and, she believes, misinterpret the data in support of their own political goals, so she is forced to become involved in the public discussion despite her wishes. Gaines's novel explores the role of science in contemporary society and, in a sense, tells the story of climate change by showing how none of us, scientists and nonscientists alike, can simply sit back passively and ignore the political implications of our actions or inaction. Fictional paleoclimatologist Dr. Cristina Teresa Arenas is all the more credible for her *reluctance* to join the fray of scientists scrambling for power, publicity, and money ("funding") by insisting upon the relevance of arcane research to headline topics of the day. Arenas, to her credit, claims:

The science doesn't take sides. The science just is whatever it is, and if I'm going to communicate with the press then that is what I have to communicate. I can't say I know, when I don't. I can't make knowledge absolute, when it isn't. It doesn't matter what I might imagine or dream or even feel is true. I can only repeat what the data says, what the science is. (334–35)

Gaines's character, despite her reluctance, gradually comes to realize that the public and the press hunger to understand what's going on with the earth's atmosphere, and her research on ancient core samples from the ocean floor might hold certain subtle clues to the relationship between carbon dioxide and climate. But her authority and persuasiveness are earned through faithful empiricism and cautious conclusions, not through rhetorical games or flamboyant leaps of logic.

Those interested in reading fiction relevant to climate change, such as *Carbon Dreams* and *State of Fear,* might also want to go back and reread John Steinbeck's 1939 *The Grapes of Wrath* with the climate change issue in mind—it puts an entirely new spin on that novel about the 1930s Dust Bowl when you think of it as a book about how people struggle to survive in a landscape radically altered by drought (to give the novel additional context, you can read it together with environmental historian Donald Worster's fine book, *Dust Bowl: The Southern Plains in the 1930s*).

Both of these books, Steinbeck's and Worster's, are discussed in the recent article, "After Tomorrow: The Peril of Ignoring Global Warming," by Columbia University earth scientist Peter DeMenocal. A particularly important passage in DeMenocal's article is his discussion of how other cultures have been affected by previous "megadroughts." In particular, he refers to the Mayan culture of Central America, writing: "The Maya had thrived for nearly two thousand years and their cultural achievements were comparable in many ways to those of any modern G-8 nation." Nonetheless, he continues, "this thriving civilization collapsed at the peak of its cultural and scientific development, between 750 and 950 A.D., and the decline coincided precisely with a 150-year drought that gripped the region" (20). Much of the scientific and political discussion about climate change in recent decades has focused on the question of whether or not human activity has caused changes in the earth's atmosphere, resulting in climatic shifts. DeMenocal points out, echoing Speth, that most scientists now adhere to the notion that humans have produced much of the warming that's occurred in the past century and that it's unlikely we, as a species, can do much at this point to reverse the warming process. But this does not lead him to advocate continued denial, continued avoidance of this issue among policy makers and the public. Instead, like many of his scientific colleagues, he urges his readers to call for "serious discussion on immediate implementation of political solutions to reduce emissions and increase adaptive capacity" (23). What's at issue here is not simply short-term economic prosperity in industrialized nations, but the long-term survival of our species on a planet that may, through drought or freezing, become devastatingly inhospitable.

ASKING "WHY" QUESTIONS, PAYING ATTENTION, AND MAKING A DIFFERENCE

I'd like to conclude with a last word about why people in the humanities do what we do—how this kind of work, in the context of an issue like climate change—is a form of intellectual activism. And also a practical word about what we might do in our community with regard to this issue. I often find myself thinking about Donald Worster's comment from his 1993 book, *The Wealth of Nature: Environmental History and the Ecological Imagination,* where he said:

Why are we in a state of crisis with the global environment? Scientists of many disciplines have described that crisis with impressive precision. . . . They can pinpoint with amazing detail the sources of that carbon in the tailpipes and smokestacks of the industrialized, automobilized societies. But having done all that, the scientists still cannot tell us *why* we have those societies, or where they come from, or what the moral forces are that made them. They cannot explain why cattle ranchers are cutting down and burning the Brazilian rain forest, or why the Brazilian government has been ineffective in stopping them. They cannot explain why we humans will push tens of millions of species toward extinction over the next twenty years, or why that prospect of ecological holocaust still seems irrelevant to most of the world's leaders. . . . All those "why" questions are rooted in culture, which is to say, in ethical beliefs. . . .

We are facing a global crisis today, not because of how ecosystems function but rather because of how our ethical systems function. Getting through the crisis requires understanding our impact on nature as precisely as possible, but even more, it requires understanding those ethical systems and using that understanding to reform them. Historians, along with literary scholars, anthropologists, and philosophers, cannot do the reforming, of course, but they can help with the understanding. (26–27)

It seems to me that a better understanding of how our personal and cultural beliefs—our values—are formed will enable us to do a better job of considering why we live as we do and the ways in which our lifestyles match or contradict our deepest values. Obviously, in the context of climate change, our dependency upon fossil fuel for transportation and other energy needs seems to require further examination. Why is it that most of us use our cars so much? What can we do to advocate for more governmental and corporate investment in research in the field of alternative energy? And what other lifestyle and infrastructural changes can we recommend if we're concerned about the issue of climate change . . . and the larger, related issue of the survival of our species on this planet? Upgren and Stock, the authors of the book called *Weather,* which I mentioned earlier, suggest that "Heat is the main energy consumer in [American] domestic life" (189). In cities like Reno—and throughout the arid West—it seems strange that we don't insist upon the adoption of passive solar architectural principles (and when possible the use of geothermal heating as well) in all new housing developments, the use of which could radically reduce the amount of energy needed for domestic purposes in our communities. The authors of *Weather* quote the Ehrlichs' statement that while on the one hand, we applaud the grassroots efforts on behalf of environmental protection (such as curbside recycling, ecotourism, and enthusiasm for things "organic"), we can't help but fear that *these useful but utterly insufficient steps may also help to distract attention from the much more basic issues.* Society needs to recognize that to be sustainable, the economy must operate in harmony with rules set by Earth's ecosystems—and needs to act accordingly. (188)

The same people who are willing to recycle their cans, bottles, and newspapers will not give up their snowmobiles and SUVs, or their oil- or coal-heated homes.

I feel as if I've barely scratched the surface of this huge topic, but I hope my comments here have made it clear there's a lot of interesting literary and journalistic material to read in the area of climate change—work that will provide important background information about the greenhouse concept and the implications of our society's inaction on this issue, will make connections between vast environmental topics and our lives as individuals, and will point out significant ways for us to alter our daily behavior in order to lessen our impacts on the Earth's atmosphere. Allow me to close by saying how impressed I am to know that congregations like yours are committing themselves to think about and act on issues like climate change—you're providing a positive model for other communities in this country and throughout the world.

NOTES

1. This sermon was presented to the Unitarian Universalist Fellowship of Northern Nevada in Reno on 30 January 2005.

2. Bill McKibben's more recent writing about climate change is available in his powerful essay "Year One of the Next Earth," collected in the 2006 volume *In Katrina's Wake: Portraits of Loss from an Unnatural Disaster.* An elegant journalistic treatment of climate change that brings the science of *The End of Nature* fully up to date is Elizabeth Kolbert's *Field Notes from a Catastrophe: Man, Nature, and Climate Change,* also published in 2006.

Perhaps the single most effective effort to convince the general public of the urgency of global warming/climate change is Davis Guggenheim's 2006 documentary, *An Inconvenient Truth,* featuring former vice president Al Gore, which received an Academy Award in February 2007. The compelling Powerpoint presentation and narrative digressions in the documentary are extended by numerous additional images and informative explanations in Gore's 2006 book, *An Inconvenient Truth: The Planetary Emergency of Global Warming and What We Can Do About It.* For his tireless work to communicate the significance of global warming (not only in the film and book versions of *An Inconvenient Truth,* but in hundreds of lectures, articles, and interviews delivered on this subject), Gore shared the 2007 Nobel Peace Prize with the Intergovernmental Panel on Climate Change. I believe that the essential rhetorical strategy in *An Inconvenient Truth* resembles the telescoping strategy that McKibben used so effectively in *The End of Nature* and *Maybe One* and various other publications: the movement back and forth between intimate personal stories and broad, impersonal information. For me, one of the best examples of this occurs in the apparent digression (in the film and the book) that Gore titles "My Sister" in the book. The book's previous section concludes with a quotation attributed to Mark Twain: "Denial ain't just a river in Egypt." The following story about Gore's sister Nancy develops her personality in a warm and vivid portrait and also discusses the smoking habit she started at the age of thirteen (despite the fact that scientific warnings about the harmfulness of cigarette smoking began to appear in the early 1960s) and her eventual death by lung cancer. Most of the portrait of "My Sister" seems irrelevant to the global warming focus of the book (just as the corresponding clip in the film seems to digress from the global-warming Powerpoint lecture). But the final paragraph of this chapter shifts dramatically back to global warming: "just as the scientists of 1964 clearly told us that smoking kills people by causing lung cancer and other diseases, the best scientists of the 21st century are telling us ever more urgently that the global warming pollution we're pumping into Earth's atmosphere is harming the planet's climate and putting the future of human civilization at grave risk. And once again, we are taking our time—too much time—in connecting the dots" (259). Al Gore's powerful use of story to convey ideas about the apparently abstract and highly technical phenomenon of global warming corresponds to what I discuss in chapter 14, "Seeking a Discourse of Environmental Sensitivity in a World of Data."

3. See Joan Hamilton's cover story "Danger Ahead" from the September/October 2005 issue of *Stanford Magazine* about the work of Schneider and his Stanford University colleagues on climate change, including some such as Hoover Institute economist Thomas Gale Moore, who says, "I don't argue that we're having global warming, but I find the effects are going to be small" (53). In the current era of confusion and controversy, it seems that almost any perspective can be uttered with blithe impunity—economists can quarrel with climate scientists, ministers with geologists. And the public is left to scratch its collective chin . . . while driving the family SUV down to fill up the gas tank again.

13 | There's Something About Your Voice I Cannot Hear

ENVIRONMENTAL LITERATURE, PUBLIC POLICY, AND ECOCRITICISM

"I'm sorry, Ms. Williams, there's something about your voice I cannot hear." There's something about your voice I cannot hear. This was Utah congressman Jim Hanson speaking to nature writer Terry Tempest Williams after she had presented her essay "Bloodlines" as testimony during a public hearing in southern Utah regarding wilderness preservation in that part of the state in the mid-1990s. The idea that there are certain kinds of voices—certain modes of discourse—that are unheard, and perhaps unhearable, in public discussions of environmental values and policy is what inspired me to join up with Canadian anthropologist Terre Satterfield to work on the book that became *What's Nature Worth? Narrative Expressions of Environmental Values,* which was published in 2004. The images and stories embedded in "nature writing," "environmental literature," or what is sometimes called "the literature of place" are now widely recognized as some of the most potent literary creations in recent years and throughout history. But what does such achievement mean if we are doomed to lose the places and species that have inspired such eloquence? What do any artistic and scholarly achievements mean if we are fated in the coming decades to see our own species contort itself to pass through what American environmental journalist Bill McKibben has called "the ecological bottleneck"?

We must find a way, I believe, to help those toiling in the realms of politics, economics, law, and public policy move beyond the constraining discourse of those fields and appreciate the values-rich language of story and image. As Charles Wilkinson argues in *The Eagle Bird,* it is crucial to "change the language of the law in order to change the terms of debate" regarding species, habitat, and natural resources in the American West. He laments that "legal language . . . is bloodless. It seems that attorneys are imbued with an absolute compulsion to wring every last drop of emotion, passion, love, and grief out of every single sentence" (10). Somehow, this professor of law maintains, we must find a way to deepen and enrich the language used by the public—and by public officials—when talking and writing about our relation to the natural world. He states:

If the language among the people changes, the language in the law books will change. One task is to add new kinds of words to balance out a vocabulary now dominated by board feet and cost-benefit analyses. The other task is to enrich existing words. When we hear a forester comment that timber harvesting will "sustain the productivity of the land," we should ask, "Productivity for voles?" When enough westerners understand that concept, law and policy will fall into line. (15–16)

The process of transforming our official legal, economic, and governmental language from that of bloodless contractual arrangements to empathetic stories that might enable us to imagine the issue of forest productivity from the perspective of a vole (a small, mouselike mammal) will require monumental ambition and verbal acrobatics. This is, and has perhaps always been, the ultimate ambition of writers and critics exploring nature and culture, at least in the United States. Barry Lopez famously remarked in *Antaeus,* "I suppose this is a conceit, but I believe this area of writing will not only one day produce a major and lasting body of American literature, but that it might also provide a foundation for the reorganization of American political thought" (Contribution 297). Environmentally oriented literary scholars have been tracking this trans-formative process in such works as Daniel G. Payne's *Voices in the Wilderness: American Nature Writing and Environmental Politics* (1996) and Daniel J. Philippon's *Conserving Words: How American Nature Writers Shaped the Environmental Movement* (2004). *What's Nature Worth* seeks to contribute in a different way, spurring the process of merging literary images and stories with the discourse of public policy by presenting interviews with twelve leading environmental writers about the connection between story and environmental values, providing brief samples of their work that illustrate this connection, and contextualizing each example in a framework that should be accessible to economists, lawyers, and policy specialists. Although many environmental writers and ecocritics prefer to work for social reform through the gradual, subtle media of traditional literary and scholarly publication, classroom instruction, and occasional public talks, others are opting for more direct approaches—writing to public officials, joining the boards of activist organizations, and preaching to audiences other than the choir.

■ ■ ■ Allow me to backtrack a bit and discuss two central facets of environmental literature: how this writing guides us to pay deeper attention to our physical senses and enables us to appreciate our own embeddedness in the world, and also how this writing enables us to develop and clarify and articulate our feelings about the world's meaning, its value.

As I mentioned in chapter 8, Scott Russell Sanders's 1987 essay "Speaking a Word for Nature" (collected several years later in his book *Secrets of the Universe*) is a key articulation of what literature needs to do if it's to get us to acknowledge the ecological implications of our presence on the planet. In this essay, he laments the tendency in popular contemporary American writing, especially fiction, to ignore nonhuman nature. He calls such writing "pathological" for its avoidance of reality, its neglect of questions and issues crucial to the current and longtime survival of our species. Sanders writes:

However accurately it reflects the surface of our times, [literature] that never looks beyond the human realm is profoundly false, and therefore pathological. No matter how urban our experience, no matter how oblivious we may be toward nature, we are nonetheless animals, two-legged sacks of meat and blood and bone dependent on the whole living planet for our survival. Our outbreathings still flow through the pores of trees, our food still grows in dirt, our bodies decay. Of course, of course: we all nod our heads in agreement. The gospel of ecology has become an *intellectual* commonplace. But it is not yet an *emotional* one. (226)

As Sanders suggests, the great difficulty encountered by writers who tend to be attuned to their personal experience of the world and the implications of that experience is how to communicate their ideas to a readership that, first, may be more interested in watching television or film than in reading, and, second, has little direct experience of the nonhuman world. I live in a fairly typical suburban neighborhood in the United States, where large houses cover entire lots and the most prominent features of many homes are the multiple garages for cars (sometimes as many as four or five garages per house). I seldom see my neighbors—they drive home from work, electronically open their garages, and then close the garage doors by remote control after they drive in. This is a metaphor for how they live their entire lives, more or less, enclosed within human constructions. Encouraging such people to think of the ecological implications of their lives is an uphill challenge. But it's a challenge that many contemporary writers and artists nonetheless feel compelled to take on.

I believe we need literature—or art more generally—to help us use our senses more fully and intensely. We need to overcome the abstractness of our ecological awareness and learn to *live* through such awareness, to *feel* our presence in the world. Writers in general—and I find this particularly true of so-called environmental writers—serve as extensions of our own nerve endings. They feel for us, they exhort us to feel more intensely, more fully, and they demonstrate the processes of sensation in a way that we can then enact more consciously. Lamenting the interiority and human-centeredness of many sophisticated, academic readers of literature, Lawrence Buell asks in *The Environmental Imagination,* "Must literature always lead us away from the physical world, never back to it?" (11). Close attention to environmental literature and art draws us inevitably into the realm of sensory ecology—an appreciation of our own presence in the physical world and our connections with other beings.

"How sense-luscious the world is," writes essayist and poet Diane Ackerman in the preface to *A Natural History of the Senses* (xv). How many of us actually go through our lives thinking this, aware of how our senses are connecting us moment by moment to the rest of the world? It's the purpose of most if not all of the people we call environmental writers to do just that—to help us overcome the idea of ecological connectedness as an arid abstraction and to feel it as a vivid, visceral reality. Read Australian essayist Eric Rolls's *A Celebration of the Senses* (1998), for instance, or Japanese-American farmer and nature writer

David Mas Masumoto's 2003 book of nonfiction, *Four Seasons in Five Senses: Things Worth Savoring*. Read novelist James Dickey's 1970 classic, *Deliverance*, for an allegory of sensory awareness, showing how several characters overcome the ennui and alienation of their suburban lives by experiencing the vivid beauty—and the pain—of a direct encounter with wild nature.

Fiction is often a particularly good genre in which to present narratives that are readily perceived not only as specific stories but as allegories that mirror readers' experiences. There are many fine examples of environmental fiction that function allegorically to demonstrate how engagement with the world through our senses might somehow revitalize us and enable us to live more conscious, meaningful lives. One fine example is David James Duncan's 1983 novel, *The River Why*, in which the narrator is a fishing prodigy who comes to learn that it is important for him not only to know *how* to catch fish, but to appreciate *why* he finds it useful and meaningful to have such interactions with fish, with nature. Another is Tim Winton's 2001 novel *Dirt Music*, in which the character Luther Fox "goes bush" and finds himself profoundly enmeshed in the reality of nature, realizing, "The world is holy? Maybe so. But it has teeth too. How often [have I] felt that bite in a slamming gust of wind" (361).

The idea that we can begin with personal sensory experience and then quickly build upon such experience in order to develop a better understanding of large-scale ecological processes is well explained in environmental education scholar Mitchell Thomashow's recent book *Bringing the Biosphere Home: Learning to Perceive Global Environmental Change* (2002). Thomashow suggests that we can use our senses to explore connections between our own specific places in the world and the rest of the planet. He argues that it's crucial, if we're to know what's happening in the world during this time of significant changes, for us to think in terms of relationship—particularly, the relationship between our place and other places, our moment in history and other times, past and future. Several of Thomashow's points specifically tie in with the role of literature in helping people to "bring the biosphere home," to understand the big picture of the "biosphere" (the planet and its atmosphere) by way of close attention to "home" (where we are at any given moment). Here is his explanation of the methods of his own practice of "biospheric perception":

First, I emphasize the importance of routine experience. In the course of your daily affairs and adventures, you have all the material you need for interpreting global environmental change. Biospheric perception is a practice you can engage in wherever you may be. In the time and space between your busy tasks, you can take a few moments to reconsider where you are, have a look around, and notice the sky, the landscape, and other life forms. In just a few moments you can travel a considerable conceptual distance through the biosphere. Second, I accentuate the narrative experience. I probe the stories that emerge from childhood memories, travels, and conversations, in conjunction with imaginative forays. To perceive the biosphere requires comparing times and places, different views you've had of the same spot through many years, understanding how your perceptions change by presence or absence. Imagination and memory often work together to conjure impressions that you may not attain in any other way. Third, I encourage you to carefully observe what you observe—knowing your proclivities and interests, assessing your insights, figuring out your perceptual and ecological strengths and weaknesses, the things that you see as well as the gaps, and using good teachers to help you in this. Fourth, biospheric perception is a community practice, something you engage in with other people. It takes lots of folks pointing things out to each other to reap the deepest insights. Fifth, I emphasize the importance of global change science as a means to provide balance and ballast for your observations. The biosphere is not necessarily what you project it to be. It involves processes and patterns that are empirically derived.

Finally, I wind through a shifting phenomenological and existential passage. By phenomenology I refer to the great insights that can be derived from one's direct sensory impressions. To practice biospheric perception you must aspire to probe the full potential of your sensory awareness. By existential I convey the impression that we are investigating ideas and concepts that we can never fully understand. (16–17)

All of these cognitive processes—attention to routine experience, articulation via story and image, exploration of memory and imagination, precisely focused sensory attention, engagement with other people, absorption of formal scientific theories and information, and the asking of deeper phenomenological and existential questions—characterize the standard elements, both subtle and overt, of so-called environmental writing, environmental literature.

▪ ▪ ▪   So far I've been discussing how environmental writers guide readers to pay attention to the world. One of the crucial questions about literary accounts of such sensory experiences of nature is how they will affect readers and, further, how such writing might eventually have an impact on environmental laws and policies and on the daily behavior, even the conscious and unconscious worldviews, of other members of society.

Remember the passage with which I began this essay, the oft-quoted statement by Congressman Jim Hanson—it may someday be printed on his tombstone—"I'm sorry, Ms. Williams, but there is something about your voice I cannot hear." Comfortable with and accustomed to the discourse of law and economics, but less so with the language of story, at least in a public-policy context, Hanson could not pick up the usable, values-related aspects of Williams's narrative—they somehow eluded his hearing, his comprehension. Here are the opening brief paragraphs of Williams's two-page statement:

> There is a woman who is a tailor. She lives in Green River, Utah, and makes her livelihood performing alterations, taking in a few inches here, letting out a few inches there, basting in hems, then finishing them with a feather stitch.
>
> While hiking alone in the San Rafael Swell, this woman was raped, thrown down face-first on the sand. She never saw the face of her assailant. What she knew was this: in that act of violence she lost her voice. She was unable to cry for help. He left her violated and raw. (Qtd. in Satterfield and Slovic, 80–81)

The woman responds to her experience by returning to the site of her attack and leaving symbolic "fetishes" here and there in the desert: "The woman cut pieces of thread and placed them delicately on the desert. Six inches. Three inches. Twelve inches. They appeared as a loose stitched seam upon the land." Eventually she approaches a particularly magical place that has been named "the birthing rock" by Native people. Here,

> The woman picks up an obsidian chip that has been worked by ancient hands; the flaked edge is razor sharp. She holds it between her fingers like a pencil, opens her left hand and traces her own lifeline from beginning to end. The crescent moon below her thumb turns red. She places her palm on the boulder and screams. (81)

This story has no simple, explicit message about environmental policy or wilderness preservation, but in its richly emotive and imaginative language it suggests that human life is deeply associated with specific places on the planet. The woman character, when attacked in a beloved landscape, must restore her attachment to that landscape by using thread and scissors—the tools of her craft—to stitch herself back into place. She has lost her voice, her sense of empowerment, in the initial attack, but when she guides the sharpened, pencil-like stone across her hand and imprints her blood upon the land, her voice, her scream, her sense of power and pain return.

For the *What's Nature Worth?* project, Terre Satterfield and I conducted in-depth interviews with a dozen distinguished U.S. environmental writers, ranging from Native American authors such as Simon Ortiz and Ofelia Zepeda to former rancher William Kittredge and celebrated ethnobiologist Gary Paul Nabhan. It was our goal specifically to use these writers as "lay ethicists," as people who devote their lives to using language as a way of understanding the value of nature. We view such writers not as academic specialists in the field called "environmental ethics," but as storytellers who work every day to understand the value—the meaning, the importance—of their experiences in the world. We asked them questions about their approaches to writing stories, essays, and poems. We asked them to reflect on how information might be packaged within the medium of story. We asked them whether they wrote to convey their values to audiences or to explore, for themselves, the value of particular experiences or phenomena. We asked them to speculate about the broader social impact of narrative discourse that conveys a sense of environmental values.

In the lengthy introduction and the contextualizing essays at the beginning of each chapter, Terre Satterfield and I explain the current state of environmental-values research in the United States and Canada and discuss how environmental law and policy tend to rely almost exclusively on economic processes for determining the value of natural phenomena (thinking of nature, for the most part, as a set of "resources" rather than as a realm of phenomena that may have value, or meaning, beyond human economic purposes). The primary method for determining the value of resources, particularly when certain kinds of degradation have occurred and compensation must be provided, is an economic tool known as "CV" (or contingent valuation), which involves the positing of a hypothetical market for whatever is being assessed—if you were going to purchase the Great Barrier Reef, for instance, how much would you pay for it? Put together a cluster of such evaluations, basically pulled from thin air, and, voilà, there you have it: the value of the Great Barrier Reef. Our project emerges from a fundamental distrust of merely economic means of determining environmental values, our feeling—shared by many people in the arts and humanities and in the general public—that certain important facets of human values are getting left out of the economic processes, the economic equations. These aspects of our values systems cannot easily be reduced to numbers—to dollar amounts or ratings. Often the only way we can initially communicate such meanings, such values, is by telling stories that express our intuitive appreciation for certain places or phenomena.

In our interview with Terry Tempest Williams, the author suggested that the tension between the language of story and the language of law, economics, and policy is not necessarily a bad thing. She argued against neatly merging the various modes of expression. "I don't think you can manufacture or manipulate this connection," she said. "Stories arise out of the moment and that's where the power lies. You can't know what story is appropriate for any given moment. I mean the stories are born out of an organic necessity, out of the heat, and that is the source of their potency" (67–68). According to Williams, formal ideologies and mindless, inherited language start to break down when narrative language is introduced into policy discussions. Williams hopes, through her work, to help our culture "fall in love again with language and stillness and slowness," believing that this will enable us to make better, more sustainable decisions about how to live on the planet (69).

"I'm sorry, Ms. Williams, there's something about your voice I cannot hear." Despite the inability of one impatient politician to "hear" the message of a nature writer's story, this kind of language—narrative discourse, steeped in values born of specific landscapes, specific homes—plays a vital role in the lives of everyday people around the world. Laypeople, artists, and government officials, when asked what's really important to them, often turn to tales of experience and hope. One of the crucial roles of ecocritical scholarship is to help make such tales audible in the halls of power.

14

Seeking a Discourse of Environmental Sensitivity in a World of Data

THE DIVIDE BETWEEN LITERATURE AND SCIENCE

In American culture, we live today in a condition of inundation. We are up to our necks in fragments of information, in facts and figures and the prognostications of experts—we are drowning in data, and we don't know what to do. I'm speaking in particular about my own country, the United States, and about such countries as Germany and Japan that I know especially well; but I suspect my comments will be relevant to the experience of people living in most industrialized, technology-oriented societies. Scott Russell Sanders vividly describes the current situation in "Telling the Holy":

For all of my conviction, the watchdog of reason inside me still raises its hackles whenever I talk about stories, and when I talk about the sacred it bares its fangs and barks. Where are the hard data? it snarls—for this is a talking watchdog, straight out of fairy tale—where's the proof? Where are the equations? the formulas? Where, oh where, are the *numbers?*

Anyone who tries to live by stories—by hearing, by reading, and especially by making them—is likely to be nagged by the yapping of doubt. Hasn't science made myth obsolete? Even someone as firm in her vocation as Flannery O'Connor admitted feeling "a certain embarrassment about being a storyteller in these times when stories are considered not quite as satisfying as statements and statements not quite as satisfying as statistics."

I very much doubt that we can live by statements, and I am certain we cannot live by statistics. Not even scientists can bear a steady diet of numbers. After Ruth [Sanders's wife] comes home from the lab, we often talk over the day's experiments as we are fixing dinner, and she will often say, when the results have been confusing, that she and her colleagues haven't yet figured out a plausible story for the data. The data themselves only make sense, only add up to knowledge, when they are embodied in narrative. (156–57)

I want to begin by asking several basic questions. First, what is the relationship between information and meaning? To phrase this another way, what is the relationship between the meaning or import of scattered pieces of information and what we might call "an integrated worldview"? To push this a little bit further, it seems significant to ponder the relationship between such a worldview and daily behavior. I wonder, too, what so-called experts can tell us about the world that will impress us and offer acceptable guidance and perhaps enable or inspire us to change our lives and work toward keeping the planet inhabitable for our species. Perhaps most importantly, I find myself asking the following question: *how* should we be *communicating* with each in order to express our thoughts and feelings about the world—what would a "discourse of environmental sensitivity" look like? These are the kinds of questions I find myself asking these days—they are the questions of a literary scholar who feels himself to be living in a threatened world.

I suspect that all of us come from various cultures that appear to believe in numbers, that trust quantitative information as a relatively firm version of "the truth," while anything nonquantifiable tends to come under suspicion. In the United States, people want to know "the bottom line." What does it all add up to, what does it cost? We're ready to pull out our wallets and pay for whatever we want at a given moment, and yet we're likely to fight to avoid changing our lives if that's what's called for to achieve our purposes. We have difficulty realizing that changing our lives may *be* the cost of certain things we profess to want.

We believe in numbers in my culture, but we do not really understand numbers any better than people elsewhere in the world. Perhaps it's the very alienness of numerical information that seems authoritative and impressive—trustworthy. We've tended to put our lives and the well-being of the planet in the hands of people who can speak a quantitative language: the food distributors who make sure the shelves in our supermarkets are well stocked; the engineers who design our automobiles and the roads we drive on; the physicians who deliver our babies and care for us when we're not feeling well; the technicians who hook up our telephone and cable TV service. Sometimes we notice things aren't going quite right: smog hangs in the valley where we live and even brisk winter winds can't clear the air; a power outage at the office knocks us off e-mail for a weekend and underscores our excessive attachment to this technology; a glance out the window at home shows the steady creep of urban development up the side of a nearby mountain, making population growth a visible phenomenon. Vaguely troubled by these experiences, we try to ponder their implications, what sort of corrections might be needed, and then, overwhelmed, we suspend our worries and rationalize that "the experts have everything under control." We reimmerse ourselves in the daily activities that we can manage.

"Truth" inheres in numbers, and people who speak (and write) the language of numbers *appear* to know what's going on in the world. In the past decade or so, American writers have offered several powerful investigations of this numerical fetish of ours. One of the particularly potent meditations on the phenomenon of quantification is Annie Dillard's 1999 book, *For the Time Being*. In the past year, I've found myself thinking a lot about a brief passage from that book. "There are 1,198,500,000 people alive now in China," writes Dillard. "To get a feel for what this means, simply take yourself—in all your singularity, importance, complexity, and love—and multiply by 1,198,500,000. See? Nothing to it" (47). Who can perform such a simple act of multiplication? "Nothing to it," jokes Dillard. Simply do the math. It would be difficult to state more graphically that we struggle to understand big numbers, whether these numbers describe quantities of *things* or the kinds of vast processes—either sudden cataclysms or slow, barely perceptible systemic changes—that we're told are occurring in the natural world.

I shift my attention from Annie Dillard's teasing, philosophical treatment of the meaning of numbers to examples of our efforts to process the latest environmental news. A good illustration of what happens when we try to respond to quantitative information about the environment comes in Terry Tempest Williams's statement in the "Getting It Right" symposium in the pages of the January/February 2000 issue of *Sierra* magazine. I'm singling out a passage that emphasizes what I take to be a common response to information presented in an abstract or numerical form. "When I hear all of the statistics," writes Williams,

the losses we are incurring, the truth and weight of issues like genetically manipulated foods, a population of 6 billion and rising, the loss of diversity of species and land, the control wielded by global corporations, I become mute, my spirit crushed by information that becomes abstracted into despair. My human frame cannot accommodate it all. I become listless, apathetic, impotent, and turn inward, turn to pleasure, to distraction, to anything that will move me away from what I perceive to be the true state of the world. (Pope 45)

Although Williams suggests focusing on her own local experience, on the good, constructive work that her neighbors in small-town southern Utah are doing, or that people in other specific communities are doing, to restore and protect their immediate environments, I'm afraid that this sense of solace is like whistling in the dark. It can make us feel better for the moment, but it seems simply to avoid the bigger issues, to defer or deflect them.

In an essay called "The Blood Root of Art," published in his 1996 volume *The Book of Yaak,* Montana author Rick Bass gets right to the heart of this discussion, stating: "The numbers are important, and yet they are not everything. For whatever reasons, images often strike us more powerfully, more deeply than numbers. We seem unable to hold the emotions aroused by numbers for nearly as long as those of images. We quickly grow numb to the facts and the math" (87). This perception, intuited by the Montana nature writer, is precisely what contemporary social scientists, chiefly psychologists and economists, are corroborating in their research on framing and processing information for making decisions and determining attitudes and values. "Still," Bass continues, "the numbers are always out there" (87), and he proceeds to offer a page of statistics about forests, roads, and logging in the Pacific Northwest. Two pages later, though, he switches tactics and writes, "I meant to use numbers throughout this essay—I had a bunch of them lined up, all of them perverse and horrible—but I got tired of them right away" (90). The writer then frets about the possible inadequacy of art, of language, for the communication of solid information that might have the power to sway government and corporate officials away from the excessive harvesting of natural resources, the destruction of wild places and nearby communities. "I had, once again," he states, "meant for this whole essay to be numbers, a landslide of numbers, like brittle talus. But I cannot tolerate them, at present. There is a space in me, this short winter day, that cries out for words" (93). In truth, I believe there is a space in all people, even in the scientists and economists whose daily currency is the system of measurement, the worldview we call "quantification," that "cries out for words"—and for images and stories, for the discourse of emotion. One of the central concerns of this essay is to explore the function of language—and, chiefly, "literary language"—in helping us, scientists and laypeople alike, to appreciate the *meaning* of our environmental quandaries.

Many people in contemporary, industrialized societies accept without question the special form of veracity that seems to attach itself to numbers, but this is the result of cultural determination, not some rarefied, absolute insight. In his fascinating book, *The Measure of Reality: Quantification and Western Society, 1250–1600,* historian Alfred W. Crosby documents the emergence of quantitative measurement as a forceful—perhaps the predominant—gauge of truth in thirteenth-century Europe. "What shall we call this devotion to breaking down things and energies and practices and perceptions into uniform parts and counting them?" asks Crosby:

Reductionism? Yes, but that is a baggy category; it does not help us to place in relation to other developments Niccolo Tartaglia's answer in the 1530s to the question of how much a cannon should be tilted upward to fire a ball the farthest. He fired from a culverin two balls of equal weight with equal charges of powder, one at 30 and the other at 45 degrees of elevation. The first went 11,232 Veronese feet, the second 11,832. This is quantification. This is how we reach out for physical reality, push aside its darling curls, and take it by the nape of the neck. (11–12)

Despite the compelling power of quantification, despite our sense of the usefulness of numbers, there persists an underlying skepticism toward numbers as a medium of communication and a gauge of reality. W. H. Auden once stated, with a tinge of bitterness, that we live in societies "to which the study of that which can be weighed and measured is a consuming love" (qtd. in Crosby 12). Rick Bass and Terry Tempest Williams express their own frustration at the limitations and impenetrabilities of numerical discourse in the context of contemporary American environmental discussions.

Yet another eloquent statement of this notion comes in the foreword to *The Nature of Economies,* the extraordinary 2000 book by Toronto social theorist Jane Jacobs. Jacobs presents her thoughts about the intersections between industry, politics, economics, and the sciences of biology, evolutionary theory, ecology, geology, and meteorology in the form of eight fictional dialogues. But first she explains her project as follows: ·

Theories and other abstractions are powerful tools only in the limited sense that the Greek mythological giant Antaeus was powerful. When Antaeus was not in intimate contact with earth, his strength rapidly ebbed. The aim of the talkative characters in this book is to bring rarefied economic abstractions into contact with earthy realities, meaning universal natural processes of development, growth, and stability that govern economic life. (ix)

One of the premises of the particular branch of environmental writing that I'm exploring here is that numbers themselves, far from being the concrete core of reality, are a form of "abstraction." They remove "feeling" from experience and leave us with "data." Some people would argue that the removal of emotion from any body of information enhances the possibility of rational thinking and improved decision making. Still others would argue that without emotion, we as a species are incapable of thinking effectively about the implications of information we're given—we can't sort out our values and attitudes and determine what's important, how to behave . . . how to vote, what kind of car to drive, or whether to drive at all, whether we should have children or take special steps to avoid having children, what to eat, what to wear. While Jane Jacobs's book aims, through the relatively narrative medium of dialogue, to associate economic theories with biophysical theories, much of the important contemporary environmental writing takes the Antaeus paradigm even further, rooting all theories and numbers in the realm of recognizable human experience by telling stories of the authors' (or characters') lives in the world.

What's at stake here? Why does this matter so much? Perhaps the best way to appreciate the virtue of merging "data" with emotive discourse is to consider the implications of *not* doing so. I'm reminded of Robert Jay Lifton's notion of "psychic numbing," an idea elaborated in his distinguished 1967 book *Death in Life: Survivors of Hiroshima* and in many essays since then. In a 1995 article called

"The Age of Numbing," Lifton and coauthor Greg Mitchell define "psychic numbing" as "a diminished capacity or inclination to feel." They explain that

Hiroshima survivors remember witnessing at the time of the bomb terrible scenes of suffering—nothing less than a sea of death around them—but found very quickly that they simply ceased to feel. They spoke of "a paralysis of the mind," of becoming "insensitive to human death," of being "temporarily without feeling." This useful defense mechanism prevents the mind from being overwhelmed and perhaps destroyed by the dreadful and unmanageable images confronting it. (58)

Apathetic responses to the daunting unprocessability of environmental statistics are, I believe, comparable to the self-protective numbness that human beings come to feel when faced with an extraordinary physical crisis, such as the experience of a nuclear explosion. "Psychic numbing," as originally articulated in *Death in Life,* is a survival mechanism, a way of dealing with trauma. But, as Lifton and Mitchell speculate,

Over time, the boundaries of numbing can blur. By closing ourselves off from the human costs of our devastating weapon, we are more able to do the same when confronted with other instances of collective suffering—the 1994 genocides in Bosnia and Rwanda, for example. We can become increasingly insensitive to the physical violence around us, as well as to the institutionalized violence of poverty and homelessness. The tendency toward numbing can even extend to everyday forms of human interaction. (59)

Although Lifton and Mitchell argue it is our habit of ignoring the phenomenon of the atomic bomb that spurs the "tendency toward numbing," I would suggest, too, that we are inundated with information about devastating losses, from earthquake victims in Turkey to the extinction of species in North America, and numbing seems to be the automatic and widespread psychological response. Faced with the ubiquity of suffering, presented to us by way of nerveless numerical discourse and the glaring graphicness of contemporary journalistic photography, what hope do we have of surmounting the deadening effects of numbness and our corresponding failure to act in positive, constructive ways?

Sven Birkerts's 1999 essay "American Nostalgias" builds implicitly upon Bill McKibben's 1992 book *The Age of Missing Information* and observes some of the fundamental shifts of consciousness that occurred during the twentieth century and continue to intensify. "We have . . . shifted from a simple, direct, unmediated sense of reality," Birkerts writes,

to one that is complexly mediated, saturated with information and with the possibility of information. We once knew the world with our senses, or at one remove, and now we know it increasingly as a field of data. . . . The original world was determined in many essential ways by the brute realities of nature—by weather, by terrain, by the time required for various processes, and the intervals of long-distance communication. The new reality is significantly cut off from nature, largely unaffected by weather, global in reference, and premised on instantaneous communication. For the real we are substituting the virtual. (27–28)

What does it take to impress human beings with a sense of vivid reality, to bring us beyond where we've been, to new worldviews and new sensitivities? We are a plodding, intransigent species, truth be told. As Henry David Thoreau once put it, "We need to be provoked,—goaded like oxen, as we are, into a trot" (*Walden* 108).

Neurologist Robert Ornstein and population biologist Paul Ehrlich use more academic phrasing in their 1989 book *New World New Mind,* explaining:

We don't perceive the world as it is, because our nervous system evolved to select only a small extract of reality and to ignore the rest. We never experience *exactly* the same situation twice, so it would be uneconomical to take in every occurrence. Instead of conveying everything about the world, our nervous system is "impressed" only by *dramatic changes.* This internal spotlight makes us sensitive to the beginnings and endings of almost every event more than the changes, whether gigantic or tiny, in the middle. (3)

The irony of the human tendency to generalize, to make caricatures of experience, is that we yearn for specificity and uniqueness. Our nostalgia for physicality within the contemporary sea of abstract information, to use Sven Berkerts's notion, belies the even deeper biological tendency to ignore the specific and look for a broader pattern. Broad patterns of experience can be most efficiently described with numbers. This concept is readily understood by social and physical scientists and almost universally deplored by all others. Yet even for scientists, human as they are, it is difficult to overcome the impressiveness of the representative case. As Ornstein and Ehrlich state, "One or two dramatic events can have a striking influence; statistics can be easily ignored. It is the phenomenon that psychologists Daniel Kahneman and Amos Tversky call representativeness" (113). This psychological tendency seems to result from our ancestors' need to respond to immediate, nearby threats, to live in the here-and-now or perish.

Ornstein and Ehrlich proceed to offer a pragmatic explanation of how the human brain evolved, and a chilling pronouncement about the consequences of our failure to evolve beyond this level of adaptation. True, in the distant past the individual who reacted powerfully to sudden danger was more likely to survive than someone who "pondered the evidence more calmly" (113). If the threat—perhaps the potential danger of a large predator—proved to be false, the consequences of responding would still be minor compared with those of not responding. The world today is presenting to us a host of worries that, in many instances, fail to trigger any alarms at all:

Threats in our world have changed, but not our responses to them. Individuals and society as a whole are especially susceptible to anyone who can exploit the parochial focus of the old mind. In the modern world that focus leads to the vulnerability to terrorism, to brutality spreading as a result of watching violence in movies and on television, and to the election of incompetent politicians who look good and sound good and thus make us feel good. But its focus also leads to the slighting of the hazards of acid rain, CO_2 buildup, desertification, and other unprecedented perils approaching too gradually to trigger our "fight-or-flight" responses. (114)

The consequences of this evolutionary tendency are not minor. Journalist Edith Efron would disparage such a claim as apocalypticism as a hyperbolically dire warning. But if the warning proves to be false, what are the potential consequences of our heeding it? And if it proves to be accurate, more or less, what would be the implications of *not* heeding it?

Ornstein and Ehrlich, like many scholars and artists, prefer the option of sensitivity. They seek, in their writing, to reach toward a new level of sensitivity beyond the immediate, hands-on version of our biological ancestors. "The probability of global disaster goes up each year," they warn,

but our consciousness of it does not. We seem to need shocks and tragedies to goad us into action. The old mind quickly tires of being cautioned, especially about dangers that cannot be averted by immediate, *personal* action.

But if blindness to threatening gradual change continues, eventually a weather report might sound like this: "Clear skies on Thursday, followed by scattered nuclear explosions in the Northwest—with possible unseasonable freezes for a few months." (118)

This passage, though published only two decades ago, obviously emerges from the fears of the cold war. Today's political reality may be different from the context that inspired *New World New Mind,* and yet many of the concerns that preoccupied Ornstein and Ehrlich persist. Some have now intensified.

Given that we are a species inclined to care about individual cases and to be daunted by (or disinterested in) vast processes and numerical descriptions, how might we ever learn to think in a way that will enable us to adapt to the dangers of the modern (and future) planet? Ornstein and Ehrlich point to such problems as acid rain, CO_2 buildup, and desertification. Add loss of biodiversity, vast increase of human population and resource consumption, gradual (but ultimately dramatic) shifts in temperature, and various other almost imperceptibly vast changes in the human and environmental realms, and we're facing potential systemic transformation that will likely change the Earth into a different planet than the one we currently live on. And yet it would be difficult to convince most people in the United States that there's anything going on that might require them to alter today's habits, their use of resources and production of waste. What kind of language might break through this apparent insensitivity and trigger new alertness to the potential hazards our civilization faces?

■ ■ ■ Since the 1960s, there has been an extraordinary surge of important North American writing about the relationship between human beings and the natural world. But contemporary environmental writers in the United States and Canada are not an isolated group, nor is their influence limited to the American literary community. I can think of many international examples, from the work of Homero Aridjis in Mexico to the writings of Michiko Ishimure in Japan, Judith Wright in Australia, Kole Ade-Odutola in Nigeria, Oliver Friggieri in Malta, and many other writers throughout the world (a few years ago I read an M.A. thesis by Nadia Su in Taiwan, mostly a study of Annie Dillard with a concluding chapter about the contemporary Taiwanese writer Liao Hung-chi, who worked for years as a fisherman before quitting to establish the Black Current Society for the Preservation of the Ocean Environment and to write)—and all of this environmental literature and the ecocritical response to this literature have ramifications that go far beyond the realm of aesthetics. I would argue that this body of literature, known variously as "nature writing" or "environmental writing," has the potential to help readers reimagine their relationship with the planet and overcome crippling fears and feelings of alienation—and through a kind of ripple effect this literature will reach beyond the people who actually read it. This is what Terry Tempest Williams was getting at when she concluded her comments in the January/February 2000 issue of *Sierra* magazine by urging her readers not only "to become biologically literate," but "to make the abstract real, to be unafraid to speak of what we love in the language of story, to remember we are engaged in bloodwork, one day at a time" (qtd. in Pope 45). .

One of the reasons environmental literature has become and continues to emerge as such a powerful force in contemporary literary expression is that writers such as Sanders—as well as Dillard, Williams, Bass, McKibben, Aridjis, Robert Michael Pyle, Wendell Berry, Gary Snyder, Robert Hass, Rudolfo Anaya, Barry Lopez, William Kittredge, Linda Hogan, Peter Matthiessen, and dozens of other environmental writers—understand their work as the effort to achieve not only beautiful, lyrical language, but an understanding of human society's relationship to the actualities of the planet.

Ecologist Garrett Hardin once expressed suspicion about literary language as a means of articulating environmental ideas. In his 1985 volume *Filters Against Folly: How to Survive Despite Economists, Ecologists, and the Merely Eloquent,* he stated:

Poetry is least dangerous when the typographical arrangement of words reveals the author's poetic intent. It is most dangerous when the argument is cast in the form of prose, in sentences heavily infected with unacknowledged poetic claims of non-negotiability. In our time the claims of recognized poets are no longer a serious threat to rational thought. The gravest threats to rationality now come from those who employ the rhetorical weapons of poetry from behind an ambush of prose. Popularizers of ecology and advocates of the environment are not the least of the offenders. (33)

I would argue, though, that this is an unnecessary fear. Hardin seems to worry that contemporary nature writers, working in the subtle guise of poetic prose, will undermine rational thinking about the environment. However, much of what we think and feel about our relationship to nature *should* not, and perhaps *cannot,* be expressed in wholly rational terms. Of course, it's important for any environmental writing to be rooted in the most current and most accurate scientific information; it's crucial, for writers and scientists to be talking with each other, and that's what I take to be the fundamental purpose of gatherings I see happening all over the world now. The best way to develop combinations of affectively meaningful discourse and empirically based ideas is to foster ongoing, cross-disciplinary communication so that economists, ecologists, and artists can work together to avoid the oversimplifications and extremes toward which our disciplines, in isolation from each other, might be inclined.

Writers seeking to achieve an understanding of the actual condition of the planet and projections for the future must have a sturdy appreciation for, and a firm grasp on, the scientific world. The lessons of modern environmental science—including the work of ecologists, environmental historians, and environmental anthropologists—are often extremely abstract and difficult for the public to believe, difficult even to decipher. What is an ecosystem and why is it so delicate? How do we know that hundreds and hundreds of animal and plant species are disappearing each year, becoming extinct? Why does this matter, especially if extinction itself is a natural process? There are now many eloquent works of environmental literature that explore these and other, related topics in a way that is designed to compel the general public to think independently about the state of the world, to provoke concern and wonder and a desire to learn more. I'm thinking of two particular examples: Nebraska biologist John Janovy Jr.'s 1997 work, *10 Minute Ecologist: 20 Answered Questions for Busy People Facing Environmental Issues,* and Bill McKibben's *Maybe One: A Personal and Environmental Argument for Single-Child Families,* which came out in 1998. These two books are examples of writing that takes numerical information and presents it by way of images and stories, that attempts to explain the context in which the information was derived. Works like these, together with more metaphorical and indirect writings such as the poetry of A. R. Ammons and the stories of Ursula K. Le Guin, have the potential to help readers gain a new sensitivity to their place in the world—a sensitivity that goes beyond the mere accumulation of inert information.

Janovy and McKibben are two of the authors I have featured in my University of Nevada course "The Literature of Population." The goal of the course is to examine selected samples of the body of recent American literature that exists at the borders of environmental science, environmental journalism, and environmental literature, focusing not only on the topic of human population (or *over*population), but on global climate change (the so-called greenhouse effect) and biodiversity/extinction. We make a special effort to discern the literary and rhetorical dimensions of everything we read, although at times it's difficult not to get sidetracked into discussions—even debates—about the issues and arguments raised by our authors. We read David Quammen's *The Song of the Dodo* to see how he uses extended metaphors, historical and contemporary narratives, biographical profiles of scientists, and humor to convey the urgent intricacies of "island biogeography." We read Paul and Anne Ehrlich on population and on the implications of distortive, complacent, antienvironmental "brownlash" literature. We study the efforts of Donella and Dennis Meadows and Jorgen Randers, in *Beyond the Limits,* to convey the feedback loops and overshoot theories of global systems by way of computer modeling and charts and graphs, in contrast to the more narrative and conversational approaches of recent authors such as Alan AtKisson, who wrote *Believing Cassandra: An Optimist Looks at a Pessimist's World.* Our discussions of population literature per se focus on various works by the Ehrlichs, on Gregg Easterbrook's "eco-realist" dismissal of environmental doomsayers like the Ehrlichs, on the work of Janovy and McKibben, the Meadows, and AtKisson.

▨   ▨   ▨   Now let me move toward a conclusion by focusing on a few specific authors and texts. John Janovy holds an endowed chair in the biology department at the University of Nebraska, where his teaching and scientific research focus on the field of parasitology. He is the author of many scientific papers and maintains funding for a research lab at the university. In the mid-1970s, shortly after attaining tenure in the biology department, Janovy became frustrated with the politics of academia and began to divert some of his attention and energy to literary expression and projects that would explain scientific ideas to general readers. In 1978 he published *Keith County Journal,* a collection of personal essays on subjects related to his field research. Two years later the novel *Yellowlegs: A Migration of the Mind* appeared, telling the story of an individual migrating bird. Since then, Janovy has published such books as *Back in Keith County* (1981), *On Becoming a Biologist* (1985), *Fields of Friendly Strife* (1987), *Vermilion Sea: A Naturalist's Journey in Baja California* (1992), and *Dunwoody Pond: Reflections on the High Plains and the Cultivation of Naturalists* (1994). But the particular book that interests me in the context of this discussion of alternative modes of environmental discourse, and especially those approaches that seek to express complicated scientific phenomena in nonquantitative language, is *10 Minute Ecologist,* which appeared in 1997.

Janovy explains the genesis of this book in his preface:

I was sitting in a meeting one day listening to one of the world's most distinguished scientists talk about biodiversity. His audience was made up mainly of business executives and attorneys who, because of various factors such as government regulation or marketplace events, suddenly found themselves dealing with environmental issues. As I looked around the room, I could see the audience paying close attention to the speaker. But afterward someone said to me: "I loved that speech but I still don't know what biodiversity really means or why it's so important." At that point I decided all these businessmen needed help. But they didn't have the time to go back to college and major in biology. That's when I decided to write this book. (xi)

Keeping this audience in mind, the biologist has attempted to present a series of complex ecological topics in a manner that should be accessible to an educated but nonscientific group of readers. In the United States, children often play a game called "Twenty Questions," where several players are invited to ask twenty questions in order to figure out what another person has in mind (a person, place, or object). Janovy offers his readers twenty questions pertaining to "ecology" and twenty brief responses, mini-essays that he thinks readers should be able to get through in about ten minutes each—this idea of brevity is important, as many people who need to know things about the environment simply don't have much time in their daily lives to read long, complex articles on these subjects. Despite the difficulty of responding to such questions as "What is biodiversity?" and "What is an ecosystem?" and "Why study islands?" in five or six pages for each topic, Janovy throws himself into the project and attempts to find an accessible and scientifically legitimate mode of communication. "I've tried very hard to make reasonably complex ideas accessible to the same audience that reads paperbacks and watches television," he states (xii).

Because one of my other important textual examples in this essay is Bill McKibben's *Maybe One,* a project that attempts to make population and human reproduction meaningful to a general audience on both intellectual and emotional levels, I'd like to comment on John Janovy's population chapter from *10 Minute Ecologist* as well. The first thing one notices about this chapter is the indirect title: "How many is too many?" The avoidance of politically and emotionally charged terms such as "population" and "reproduction" is quite important—the author does not want to scare away readers at the outset. But he does quickly get to the issue of overpopulation in the first sentence. Janovy opens his five-page essay by offering a brief, simplified history lesson, showing readers that the concept of "too many" dates back at least a few centuries (in other words, this is not merely a modern social and environmental problem). "In most people's minds," begins Janovy, "the name 'Malthus' connects with the concept of overpopulation, and the adjective 'Malthusian' refers to the dire consequences of reproducing to the point that we run out of resources, as predicted by the British economist Thomas Malthus in 1798." Janovy continues,

In his *Essay on the Principle of Population,* Malthus noted that populations tended to grow exponentially, so that the population increase, as measured in numbers of individuals, was greater with every new generation, whereas food supplies increased by only a constant amount over time. Eventually, Malthus reasoned, populations would outgrow their food supply, and would then become limited by disease, famine, and war. (76)

Notice how this opening paragraph delicately avoids emphasizing *human* populations and instead speaks about "populations" and "individuals" without denoting species. The next several paragraphs explicitly avoid focusing on the issue of human overpopulation, instead discussing the population biology of plants and animals and observing that most studies in this field indicate "some needed resource is usually shown to be a limiting factor on the population" (76–77). This is very clear and species-neutral language—not exciting perhaps, but not treading on the delicate moral and religious questions of human reproduction . . . yet.

On the third page of the essay, Janovy gestures toward the human relevance of the topic, but in a relatively safe and nonargumentative way, stating, "'Too many' is clearly a human idea, and it refers to the numbers that can be supported by a particular set of resources. Nature really doesn't care whether organisms live or die; only humans care. But we can explain 'too many' in a rather neutral and practical way by considering what ecologists call carrying capacity" (78). This emphasis on apparent neutrality and practicality is one of the keys to Janovy's discourse of accessible ecological information. He is trying not to be boring or offensive to his readers, so he attempts to make his prose clear and to find cleverly oblique ways of approaching sensitive issues. The term "carrying capacity" has everything to do with human population, but Janovy initiates his "neutral and practical" discussion by talking about plant seeds in boreal forests, and then he moves into a two-paragraph story, a kind of parable, about talking bacteria in a test tube. The bacteria reproduce themselves actively, and by the end of the day, "the bacteria," writes Janovy, "have flourished, multiplied, and diversified into a large community that includes bacterial politicians, businessmen, ecologists, and of course college students" (79). The bacteria then begin to debate what to do about resources and population. "Remember, it's only a story," Janovy reminds his readers, suggesting that there's no need for humans to take umbrage at the debate. He writes:

And what do these talking bacteria say at 11:58 p.m.? The ecologist, of course, says what ecologists have been saying for quite a while—namely, that *we're about to run out of resources*. The politician, likewise, says what politicians have been saying for quite a while, namely that *the ecologists are idiots; we have three times as many resources as we've used throughout all our history, so don't worry (and vote for me because I'm so smart)*. In a similar manner, the bacterial businessman says what businessmen have been saying forever and forever, namely that *our political leaders are right; we have three times as many resources as we've used throughout all recorded history, so we should sell some to another test tube (and gimme a tax break to create the new jobs produced by these sales)*. And the bacterial college student is asking what young people ask all the time, namely: *Whom should I believe?* I think we should listen to the ecologist, but I'm biased. (79)

Even while expressing his own personal perspective on this debate, Janovy tries to avoid stigmatizing himself as a liberal, environmentalist intellectual. Rather than belaboring his endorsement of the ecologist's perspective, he jokes about his "bias." Still, he concludes this section of his essay by offering a fundamental, apparently incontrovertible principle. "The point of the story is fairly obvious," he writes: "No matter what you want to believe about the natural world, we are still very much a part of that world, and there are certain fundamental ecological principles that operate on all organisms no matter what they believe. One of these principles is that environments possess carrying capacities and will not support populations larger than those capacities, no matter what politicians and businessmen claim" (80).

The rhythm of the entire essay stresses the idea of things building up to an inevitable conclusion by way of a subtle and gradual approach. It's obvious from the outset that Janovy will eventually be talking about human reproduction and overpopulation, but he takes his time getting there. It's obvious in the parable about the bacteria in the test tube that the creatures will eventually have to figure out how to manage their own numbers and their increasingly limited resources. At last, in the eleventh of the essay's twelve paragraphs, Janovy turns to the inevitable crux of the matter:

To what extent does this principle apply to humans? That is a good question with many answers. Mathematicians, as well as many college students, can easily calculate the year at which the mass of humanity comes to exceed the mass of Earth, assuming that human reproductive rates remain what they are today. It doesn't take a rocket scientist, or even a ten-minute ecologist, to figure out that some time prior to that date, humanity will begin to live a rather Malthusian existence, in which our resources become increasingly scarce. On the other hand, something may happen to stop human population growth well before it reaches the Earth's carrying capacity. (80)

And the author then offers a few suggestions about what we might do to avert the Malthusian outcome of unchecked human population growth. Although certain kinds of readers, especially religious fundamentalists, are unlikely to soften their views on contraception and reproductive responsibility as a result of Janovy's delicate rhetorical dance, it seems unlikely that such readers would even open a book like *10 Minute Ecologist* in the first place. However, many people in the United States, including businessmen and lawyers and politicians (people with substantial social influence), want to know more about the relation between human activity and the environment—they realize they don't know it all and feel some urgency for the improvement of their ecological knowledge. By not attacking these kinds of readers and flouting their religious and political beliefs, by adopting at least the guise of authorial neutrality and by moving very gradually toward the vexed human relevance of population biology, Janovy manages impressively to open up new perspectives on population issues to an important audience. The other nineteen essays in 10 Minute Ecologist likewise explore appropriate modes of discourse in which to make complex and sensitive ecological topics understandable and interesting to nonscientists.

Like Janovy, Bill McKibben has made a name for himself by addressing challenging scientific topics and controversial political issues in clear, engaging language. He would most likely describe himself as a journalist, not as a literary artist. But I believe there's an exceptional level of craft and sophistication in his writing. McKibben earned his BA in government from Harvard in 1982 and after graduation went to work as a staff writer for the New Yorker, one of the most widely read American magazines. He wrote hundreds of columns and feature articles for the New Yorker before becoming a freelance writer in 1987 and moving to a house in the rural Adirondack Mountains of upstate New York. In 1989 he published his first book, The End of Nature, a study of ozone depletion and environmental disturbance that has become pervasive as a result of human activity. In 1992 The Age of Missing Information appeared, examining the complicity of television in the contemporary environmental crisis and the implications of television for the ineffective communication of environmental information. His 1995 book, Hope, Human and Wild, describes examples from Brazil, India, and the United States of environmental situations that offer some hope for environmental recovery. In 2000, he published Long Distance: A Year of Living Strenuously—a study of cross-country skiing and the human body. The book of McKibben's I'd like to comment on in a bit more depth is his 1998 meditation on population and reproduction, Maybe One: A Personal and Environmental Argument for Single-Child Families.

If the key to John Janovy's treatment of population is indirectness and gradualness, McKibben's approach seems to be a process of telescoping, of moving inward toward intimate, personal aspects of human reproduction and then moving out to the broader, more abstract aspects. This movement back and forth from the intimate to the global is an attempt to make the topic accessible and meaningful by way of narrative prose without compromising the scientific information that the author feels his readers need to have in mind in order to make informed decisions about reproduction in their own lives. From the very beginning of the book he acknowledges the sensitivity of the subject matter and apologizes for intruding on his readers' private lives:

> Population is a subject I've been trying to avoid for years, and not just because I know it will cause turmoil and angry controversy. It scared me more because it forced me and my wife to confront head-on the issue of how many children we were going to have, a decision which probably affects each of our lives more than any we will ever make. It's as intimate a topic as there is, one of the last subjects we avoid in this taboo-free society. At some level, it's not any of my business how many kids anyone else has.
>
> And yet my work on environmental issues kept bringing questions of population front and center. (9)

McKibben goes on in his introduction to explain why he finds it necessary to confront the issue of population in the book. *Maybe One* differs from more conventional examples of population literature not only because of the author's use of personal narratives of reproductive decision making, but because of his interest in the emotional and developmental experience of growing up as a single child. As he explains, "I did it because of Sophie, my four-year-old daughter. I wanted to make sure that growing up without brothers and sisters would not damage her spirit or her mind." Likewise, the book's final chapter examines what it means to be parents raising "much smaller families than tradition dictates, or to raise no families at all." By focusing on children and parents, and not just on their material existence but on their "souls" (their emotional well-being), McKibben hopes "to make what has usually been an abstract question very personal and immediate" (11).

The opening chapter of *Maybe One* begins with a paragraph about the author's fears that his approach to parenting will "screw up" his daughter Sophie, and the final chapter concludes with a description of a delightful (and implicitly *routine*) afternoon and evening with his daughter as they play and learn together. In between these "bookends," these frames, McKibben offers clusters of chapters devoted to Family, Species, Nation, and Self, presenting research on topics ranging from child psychology to population biology, resource economics, pollution, and contraception, mixed with personal stories and narratives of his research practices, including stories of working in the basement of the library at the State University of New York in Albany and meeting scholars such as psychologist Toni Falbo for an interview in Washington, DC.

Perhaps the best way, in brief, to explain the ecological discourse of *Maybe One* is to refer to the opening of chapter eight, which begins the section of the book devoted to "Self." The chapter starts with a narrative of McKibben's own experience having a vasectomy performed at the Ottawa Vasectomy Clinic. We learn about the doctor: "Then Dr. McGuire came in, wearing khakis, old Nikes, an earring, a plaid shirt. So far that day, he said, he'd done nine vasectomies, pruned the branches of nine family trees. He was calm, gentle—sweet." And then comes the procedure: "So I sat on the table, and pulled my pants down around my ankles, and he swabbed my scrotum with iodine . . . , and then he injected a slug of anesthetic into each side of my testicles" (182). The whole story takes only three pages, but it makes the entire subject of vasectomies profoundly personal and accessible. This is clearly an author who has lived the subject he is discussing. After telling the story of the medical procedure, McKibben backtracks and explores the emotional, philosophical, and even religious dimensions of reproduction, asking why it is that humans seem biologically programmed to reproduce ourselves and how we might come to act in a way that goes against this programming. The discussion is reasonable and respectful, even sympathetic. McKibben seems to appreciate both the dogmatic and personal reasons for having children, pointing out that in his own "circle of friends and acquaintances, the single most common route to maturity has been through raising children, often lots of children." But he then walks the reader through his own decision-making process, his choice not to have additional children, as a result of exploring the fact that "now we live in an era . . . when parenting a bunch of kids clashes with the good of the planet" (196).

One could argue that there will be a limited audience for any work of literature, and perhaps an even narrower audience for literature (or literary journalism) that explicitly addresses issues of ideology, politics, and biology. However, the process of dispersing ecologically enlightened ideas to the general public requires the development of new modes of discourse—new ways of describing experience, new strategies for translating statistics into stories. Writers such as Janovy and McKibben may be writing, to some extent, for the "choir" of already converted readers, but their words are giving these readers more refined ways of thinking about such complex topics as population and reproduction, and these readers in turn are learning new ways of expressing their own thoughts and experiences to friends and colleagues and sometimes to their own readers. Sometimes, as in the case of McKibben, the essays that eventually appear in books are first broadcast to general audiences in the pages of mass-market magazines such as *The New Yorker* or *The Atlantic*. Without sacrificing their sense of humor or their compassion for human beings (as individuals and as a species), Janovy, McKibben, and other environmental writers are inventing a discourse of ecological sensitivity that is helping to communicate important scientific and ethical information to an ever-increasing readership.

Glen Love claimed in 1991 that "the most important function of literature today is to redirect human consciousness to a full consideration of its place in a threatened natural world" (213). He did not limit his statement to *American* literature, but implied that writers in every country—as well as artists working in other media—must assume responsibility for guiding their audiences to a deeper, more sustainable relationship with nonhuman nature. It is easy for people in many parts of the world simply to live from day to day, satisfying their immediate needs and trusting that there will always be a tomorrow for our species. The challenging task for environmental writers, and for the scholars and teachers who use their work to bridge the divide between literature and science, is both to create an interest in nature among their readers and to impress these readers with the value of living with a long-term vision of our relationship to the rest of the planet.

15

Oh, Lovely Slab

ROBINSON JEFFERS, STONE WORK,
AND THE LOCUS OF THE REAL

One of the deepest urges in American environmental literature—and perhaps in all environmental writing and even
in literature and art more generally—is the urge to achieve
contact with "the real," with that which is authentic and true. "I . . . / Felt its
intense reality with love and wonder . . . ," says Robinson Jeffers in the 1937
poem, "Oh, Lovely Rock" (*Wild God* 163). Most of us would rather be sobered
and moved by an experience we take to be part and parcel of this phenomenon
we call "reality" than dazed and deluded by a transient fantasy—at least this
seems to be an essential dimension of what we refer to as "environmental
writing" (both original literature and the critical commentary about that literature). When we say "environment," we seem to mean what's "out there,"
what's hard and fast and externally verifiable, not merely what individual
humans or groups of humans *imagine* into being.

This quest for contact with external reality (and suspicion of that which
seems not to be ultimate reality) emerges in the earliest moments of Euro-
American literature. One of the great examples of this quest, and the uneasiness
with illusory haze, is surely Jonathan Edwards's eighteenth-century *Images or
Shadows of Divine Things* (unpublished until Perry Miller's edition in 1948), which
considers the physical reality of nature to be mere "images or shadows" of truer
things, "divine things"—this was the approach to reality known as "typology"
(physical things existing as "types" or emblems of deeper reality). But the locus

classicus of the quest for reality in American environmental writing, at least in the modern sense of the tenaciously empirical ascertaining of truth, could well be Henry David Thoreau's *Walden* (1854), especially the passage in chapter two, "Where I Lived, and What I Lived For," where he writes:

I went to the woods because I wished to live deliberately, to front only the essential facts of life, and see if I could not learn what it had to teach, and not, when I came to die, to discover that I had not lived. . . . I wanted to live deep and suck out all the marrow of life, to live so sturdily and Spartan-like as to put to rout all that was not life, to cut a broad swath and shave close, to drive life into a corner, and reduce it to its lowest terms, and, if it proved to be mean, why then to get the whole and genuine meanness of it, and publish its meanness to the world; or if it were sublime, to know it by experience, and to be able to give a true account of it in my next excursion. (90–91)

To live deliberately seems to mean living with self-awareness and self-consciousness, with an acute appreciation of one's most essential needs and passions. When writers in the era of modern environmentalism express the importance of knowing and living "within limits," they seem to be echoing Thoreau's notion of "deliberateness." For Thoreau, though, the reasons for such careful, mindful living were mainly spiritual and psychological (to overcome the "quiet desperation" evident among so many people at the dawn of the era of industrialization) rather than ecological, means of averting ecosystemic collapse. There is also, in the famous passage by Thoreau, well known to both scholars and members of the public who happen to spend the afternoon walking around Walden Pond and find themselves reading these lines carved and painted on a wooden sign at the site of his house on the eastern shore of the pond, the notion that somehow it must be possible for the human mind to apprehend reality by close observation of the physical world: "to front only the essential facts of life." This seems to articulate the fundamental goals of modern biological science, of ecology, founded on a faith in empirical observation.

Leap forward to the late twentieth century, and we encounter in Edward Abbey's *Desert Solitaire* (1968) some of the most memorable statements of the same urge to know reality, to grasp something more substantial than flights of imagination or brain-fabricated belief. He famously articulated this effort as the struggle to negotiate the relationship between "bedrock" (verifiable truth, as firm as geology—however firm that might be) and "paradox" (the fickle, shifting realm of ideas and ideologies). As he put it in the first chapter of his book (one of the cornerstones of modern American nature writing):

I am here not only to evade for a while the clamor and filth and confusion of the cultural apparatus but also to confront, immediately and directly if it's possible, the bare bones of existence, the elemental and fundamental, the bedrock which sustains us. I want to be able to look at and into a juniper tree, a piece of quartz, a vulture, a spider, and see it as it is in itself, devoid of all humanly ascribed qualities, anti-Kantian, even the categories of scientific description. To meet God or Medusa face to face, even if it means risking everything human in myself. I dream of a hard and brutal mysticism in which the naked self merges with a non-human world and yet somehow survives still intact, individual, separate. Paradox and bedrock. (7)

Of course, anyone who reads some modern geology quickly learns that even rock (within an appropriate time frame) is fluid and impermanent—that its apparent firmness is permanent only to temporary beings such as ourselves. So even Abbey's geological metaphor for ultimate truth, "bedrock," is simply a metaphor, a kind of truth we might begin to fathom, but not exactly the ultimate explanation of why and how that the human mind might *dream* of discerning. In the canyonlands of southern Utah, where the red (fleshlike) rock stands fully exposed to the observing eye, not clothed in soil and vegetation as is commonly the case in Thoreau's Massachusetts, Abbey struggled to appreciate the meaning of his own existence in relation to this durable (and apparently permanent) evidence of something real and essential, something more lasting at least than his own living, aging, and (all too soon) dying self. The process of considering the human subject *in relation* to something demonstrably *other* than the self is at the very heart of the task of environmental literature.

The quest to know a kind of truth and to articulate this truth—and this quest—through meditations on geology finds its prosaic apotheosis, in American environmental writing, in such works as John McPhee's *Annals of the Former World* (1999) and Wallace Stegner's *Angle of Repose* (1971). But perhaps the most *succinct* and *profound* statement of and about the human fascination with the reality of rock may be Robinson Jeffers's 1937 poem "Oh, Lovely Rock," inspired by an August 1936 backpacking trip into the Ventana Creek gorge several miles east of California's Big Sur coast and about twenty miles south of Jeffers's home in the town of Carmel. Ironically, this meditation on stone quickly becomes, for the poet, a meditation on *change*, on *mutability*. It's impossible, it seems, for humans to look at any part of nature, particularly stone, without becoming intensely aware of the fact that we are simply passing through. But what's the value of knowing this, of being *reminded* of our mortality through the observation of nature and through writing literature on this issue and reading such literature? And how does the literary treatment of mutability somehow enhance our appreciation of life and our ability to achieve ethical responsibility during our relatively short lives? I would like to consider these questions, and also, by telling the story of a recent expedition to find Jeffers's "lovely rock," to consider why literary critics love the idea of finding "the precise place" where literary inspiration occurred and became manifest in language.

When readers think of natural elements in Robinson Jeffers's work, they are likely to dwell on such motifs as the sea, hawks, and stone—apparent metaphors (especially the first and last of these) of durability and emotionless stoicism. All three are potentially images of fierce indifference to human life, what scholars have come to call "inhumanism." Readers might think, initially, of the poet's profound emphasis on *stone* as the *antithesis* of change—as a stable and sturdy phenomenon in direct contrast to the transience of the human mind, the temporariness of the entire human species. Robert Brophy has written that "Rock [in Jeffers's work] is a consistently divine image, a mysterious, chthonic presence and stoic endurance," while "Mountains and headland are a measure of the heavens and reminder of human life's precariousness" (10). There is something ironically calming about such reminders of our fragility, as in the beautiful passages in Jeffers's poetry and prose where he articulates the unexpected solace that comes from acknowledging human mutability. Think, for instance, of the conclusion of the 1927 poem "Credo":

> The water is the water, the cliff is the rock, come shocks and flashes
> of reality. The mind
> Passes, the eye closes, the spirit is a passage;
> The beauty of things was born before eyes and sufficient to itself; the
> heart-breaking beauty
> Will remain when there is no heart to break for it. (*Wild God* 48)

The frail human mind "passes," and even the human *spirit* is merely a "passage," in contrast with the solidity of the "cliff"—which "is the rock." Even water is somehow more substantial and permanent than that which is human, for "the water is the water"—no matter what its temporary incarnation may be, water is always, on the most fundamental level, the same chemical phenomenon. And the sea, despite its restless movement, is inevitably an emblem of fixity and permanence—its vastness and power, like the firmness of rock, reach the human mind as "shocks and flashes of reality."

And then there's the wonderful conclusion of "Credo," with its paradoxical claim that "heart-breaking beauty / Will remain when there is no heart to break for it." If asked whether a tree falling in the forest would make a sound even with no person there to hear it, Jeffers would surely have replied affirmatively—the human presence in the world, it seems, as far as Jeffers was concerned, has little to do with creating or perceiving beauty. Instead, if we're to acknowledge the logic of this inhumanist credo, our purpose on this planet is simply to experience and contemplate our emotive selves, our breaking hearts—there is no alternative to such pain. And indeed, the pain that comes from contemplating human mutability—and the mutability of all living things—is perhaps the ultimate source of beauty, at least as humans know it. Think of the famous lines from Wallace Stevens's "Sunday Morning" (1915), where he considers the tedium of a heavenly realm in which the fruit hang in permanent ripeness from the trees—"Is there no change of death in paradise?" asks Stevens. "Does ripe fruit never fall? Or do the boughs / Hang always heavy in that perfect sky . . ." (283). Recall, as well, the fundamental aesthetic principle of haiku poetry—the Japanese concept of "aware"—which denotes the sweet sadness of fleeting things, such as falling leaves in autumn, delicate cherry blossoms in spring, and even the brief sound of a frog jumping into an old pond (the frog and its sound being transient, in contrast to the pond itself). Without transience, without *change,* the concept of *aware* suggests, there can be no beauty, no yearning for attachment.

The final selection included in Albert Gelpi's recent collection of Jeffers's poetry and prose, *The Wild God of the World,* is the poet's statement "To the American Humanist Association," dated March 25, 1951, which contains the following blunt assertion of human ephemerality: "Man is a part of nature, but a nearly infinitesimal part; the human race will cease after a while and leave no trace, but the great splendors of nature will go on" (201). I love the confident suggestion here that humanity will ultimately "leave no trace," despite all that we do to torment each other and diminish the planet's ecosystems—viewed from the detached perspective of evolutionary time, it may not matter whether or not individual backpackers leave their traces on the trail, because in the long run the wild will take back the trail, will take back everything. What's really at issue is the kind of trail—the kind of planet—we get to experience as long as our kind remains.

The next few lines in the 1951 statement (written two years following the publication of Aldo Leopold's landmark articulation of "The Land Ethic" in *A Sand County Almanac*) could serve as manifesto for the entire genre of environmental literature. Jeffers says that despite our puniness and inevitable extinction,

most of our time and energy are necessarily spent on human affairs; that can't be prevented, though I think it should be minimized; but for philosophy, which is an endless search of truth, and for contemplation, which can be a sort of worship, I would suggest that the immense beauty of the earth and the outer universe, the divine "nature of things," is a more rewarding object. Certainly it is more ennobling. It is a source of strength; the other a distraction. (201)

It seems to me that this statement about the goal of philosophy goes to the heart of Jeffers's so-called inhumanism and also reveals some of the basic motivations of the larger genre of writing about humans within the context of the more-than-human world. Why might it be a good idea for humans to contemplate the "immense beauty of the earth and the outer universe"? Who cares if such contemplation might be "ennobling" for the people who engage in it, as writers or readers? The phrase "source of strength" explains what I take to be one of the central issues in contemporary environmental literature, at least in North America. Something about the act of observing—and writing about—phenomena that are more durable than ourselves places us in relation to those phenomena, connects us to them, makes us part of them and them part of us. So much of Jeffers's work, especially when he refers to natural phenomena such as rocks and hawks and the sea, seems sneeringly scornful of human beings—"I'd sooner, except the penalties, kill a man than a hawk" (*Wild God* 49). But, on a deeper emotional level, what's going on is the poet's effort to identify with phenomena that seem more lasting, noble, and real than himself and his fellow humans. This is what one finds when inspecting more recent American writing about nature as well—as we see when examining the work of Scott Russell Sanders and John Calderazzo, looking at their geological nature writing and considering how these contemporary writers have taken on a somewhat different view of geological mutability.

■ ■ ■ Essential to the idea of *reality* in environmental literature is the concept of the *local*—the nearby, the here and now. In many ways, the idea of the local has become one of the favorite ideas of contemporary environmentalism, an idea that scholars routinely trace back to Henry David Thoreau. "I have travelled a good deal in Concord" (4), Thoreau states cryptically in the opening pages of *Walden*—and eventually he concludes his famous tome by quoting William Habbington's paradoxical seventeenth-century admonition not to travel far and wide, but to look inward and "be / Expert in *home*-cosmography" (320, my italics). Environmentalists are famous for sporting bumper stickers declaring "Think Globally, Act Locally." And related to this slogan, in the 1980s, "bioregionalism" became a political movement that spearheaded a new enthusiasm for local social and environmental activism in response to the feeling that big government, like big corporations, was ineffectual and more interested in self-perpetuation than in achieving healthy relations between communities and the places where they exist; Jim Dodge, in his 1990 manifesto titled "Living by Life: Some Bioregional Theory and Practice," defined bioregionalism as "government by life" and declared that "If you can't imagine that government by life would be at least 40 billion times better than government by the Reagan administration, or Mobil Oil, or any other distant powerful monolith, then your heart is probably no bigger than a prune pit" (231). Around the same time, Kentucky author Wendell Berry made a statement that explained the core logic of bioregionalism: "Love is never abstract," he wrote in his 1989 essay "Word and Flesh." "It does not adhere to the universe or the planet or the nation or the institution or the profession, but to the singular sparrows of the street, the lilies of the field" (200).

Dodge and Berry emphasize the *politics* of localism in their statements, arguing that good government must function through an awareness of what's going on in specific places on the planet. Others, such as cultural critic Lucy Lippard, in her 1997 book *The Lure of the Local: Senses of Place in a Multicentered Society,* adopt a more detached and ironic view of the concept of the local in contemporary American society. Lippard writes:

> The lure of the local is the pull of place that operates on each of us, exposing our politics and our spiritual legacies. It is the geographical component of the psychological need to belong somewhere, one antidote to a prevailing alienation. . . . These days the notion of the local is attractive to many who have never really experienced it, who may or may not be willing to take the responsibility and study the local knowledge that distinguishes every place from every other place. (7)

In a strange way, as Lippard suggests in the very title of her work, *The Lure of the Local,* our multicentered, placeless culture (think of travel writer Pico Iyer's recent book *The Global Soul* [2000]) has actually fostered an intensified enthusiasm for, a *need* for, local knowledge and a sense of local experience. One might argue that this sort of experience is almost unattainable for those who dwell in cyberspace and in the generic urban wilderness of strip malls and highways.

It seems to me that, at this time in history when there is such a hunger for the local, for contact with something "real" and lasting, there could well be a resurgence of interest in the work of a poet like Robinson Jeffers. Obviously, the pull toward something more meaningful and durable, less transitory and mobile, than the human is nothing new—we see this impulse in Thoreau's journal, in Jeffers's work, and certainly in Edward Abbey's effort to navigate between "bedrock and paradox" (between hard stone and the mirages of the mind) in *Desert Solitaire* and his many other works. But Robinson Jeffers remains the quintessential voice of the meaning of stone in American environmental literature, perhaps in American literature altogether. In his introduction to *Stones of the Sur,* Jeffers scholar James Karman writes:

Jeffers' feeling of kinship with the granite on Carmel Point served as the basis for his love of the coast.

The ocean's ceaseless rhythm, the cries of the gulls and other shorebirds, the scent of seaweed and wildflowers, the fog-bound chill night air, the moon rising over the mountains — all this became infinitely precious to him, far more important in its permanence and majesty than the cramped, agitated, and transient world of human affairs. Indeed, a key aspect of the awakening that occurred while he was building Tor House was the realization that, within the context of geological time, human life is ephemeral. (14–15)

Much of Jeffers's "stone work" (my phrase), both his building of his Carmel home (Tor House) from local California granite and his literary reflections on the meaning of stone, emphasizes the immediacy and vividness of this natural phenomenon — its heaviness, its physical and intellectual weight. And yet even Jeffers, as Karman suggests in his description of Tor House in *Robinson Jeffers: Poet of California,* experienced a push-pull tension between the local and the global that seems akin to the current impulse in American culture. According to Karman, the house was built between 1920 and 1925 from "local granite boulders" (48), but using a design from a Tudor barn in Surrey, England, and with far-flung artifacts (stones, carvings, tiles, fossils, and even an arrowhead) from as far away as Mount Vesuvius, Angkor Wat, the Great Wall of China, and the American Midwest embedded in the walls of the tower (49–51).

The tensions between permanence and transience, local and global, become particularly poignant when we consider Jeffers's famous poem "Oh, Lovely Rock" in the context of the present-day American adoration of stone. Until recently, it had never occurred to me that there is, at the beginning of the twenty-first century, an enormous global trade in stone, much of it making its way from the far corners of the earth to the United States — and I'm not talking about pebbles, but rather huge blocks of granite and marble and slate weighing several tons each, quarried in Colombia and Indonesia and Zimbabwe, all of it traveling first to Italy to be cut into eight-hundred-pound slices an inch or less in thickness (called "slabs") and then most of it crossing the ocean again en route to North America, where it will become floors and walls and kitchen counters. The ironies of this contemporary stonework, this commercial explosion, are multiple. First, the geographical mobility of contemporary Americans has caused in us a spiritual malaise, a sense of dislocatedness—so we yearn for something cold and hard to stand on, to prepare our food on, to give us the sense of placedness, and we situate this emblem of longevity in our homes in order to appreciate the short-lived *feeling* of solid ground until we pick up and move to another home in an average of 6.6 years (using information from www.census.gov suggesting that the average American will live to an age of 77.6 and will move 11 to 12 times in a lifetime). Second, the financial sleight of hand known as "home equity," which in the 1990s became a common way for home owners to "refinance" their homes and pay off credit-card debt or cover the daunting costs of home improvements, now serves as a means of creating money for the purpose of purchasing stone—something solid and heavy and (in some ultimate sense) *real*. Third, even when people live in stony parts of North America—remember, I come from Reno, Nevada, on the eastern slope of the Sierra Nevada range, John Muir's famous "range of light," where there is abundant white, pink, and golden granite—even in places like Reno, it is cheaper for homeowners to purchase granite and other building materials that have been mined in the Third World, shipped to Italy for initial cutting, and then shipped to the United States for warehousing, sale to consumers, and "fabrication" (refinement for home use). And fourth, the notion that *stone,* the ultimate locus of the local (the physical material we pull from the ground when we work in our yards or till our farmlands), has increasingly become, for many Americans, a *symbol* of fixity and local reality that we procure from *distant* reaches of the globe.

So, in case this hadn't occurred to you, I am writing from personal experience—as someone concurrently going through a home-remodeling process and reading Robinson Jeffers's work. When I was working on the initial draft of a project on the Yucca Mountain proposed nuclear-waste repository in southern Nevada, it occurred to my wife, Susie, and me that we should embark on the long-anticipated retrofitting of our Reno home for the dual purposes of increasing energy efficiency and aesthetic enhancement. Since we live in a city where home values have essentially doubled in the past four years, we were able to refinance our home (which we bought in 2001) in 2005 for twice the amount of our previous mortgage. The architects completed the plans for our kitchen before finishing plans for the improvement of our passive solar walls and the roof, where photovoltaic panels will eventually be placed, so we ended up working on the kitchen as "Phase I" in the fall of 2005. Susie and I visited approximately a dozen businesses in Reno specializing in imported granite and marble, each with a large warehouse full of stone slabs, almost like meat lockers. Watching homeowners stroll among the future floors and counter-tops, I half-expected someone to exclaim, "Oh, *lovely* slab!"—a perverse twist on the beautiful title of my favorite Jeffers poem. No one ever actually said this, but I carried the phrase in my head throughout the entire process of selecting stone for our remodeling project: "Oh, lovely slab."

With pounding and sawing reverberating in the background, I reread the Jeffers poem in the context of this new reality (new to me, at least) of a flourishing global trade in stone. Any discussion of "Oh, Lovely Rock" should also occur in the context of the excellent articles on Jeffers and geology in the issue of *Jeffers Studies* (volume 8, number 1, dated Spring 2004) that appeared about a year before my renewed attention to the poem: ShaunAnne Tangney discusses the idea of "catastrophic geology," George Hart compares Jeffers's geological work with the writing of Kenneth Rexroth and Gary Snyder, and most excitingly, for my own purposes, Robert Kafka provides a detailed gloss on Jeffers's August 1936 hike up the east fork of Ventana Creek with his son Garth and Garth's friend Lloyd Tevis, the experience that inspired "Oh, Lovely Rock."

Jeffers's poem begins as follows:

> We stayed the night in the pathless gorge of Ventana Creek,
> up the east fork.
> The rock walls and the mountain ridges hung forest on forest
> above our heads, maple and redwood,
> Laurel, oak, madrone, up to the high and slender Santa Lucian
> firs that stare up the cataracts
> Of slide-rock to the star-color precipices. (*Wild God* 163)

As Kafka reveals in his precise written interview with Lloyd Tevis (conducted in the fall of 1997, some sixty-one years following the actual experience), the three hikers began on the Pine Ridge Trail, which traverses the southerly wall of the Big Sur River Canyon, aspiring to climb the Double Cone or the "Double Ventana Cone," and then eventually dropped down into the Ventana Creek gorge and made their way through the low creek waters of late summer. They were prevented from reaching the Double Cone by the steep "cataract of rock" and cumulus clouds forming overhead, perhaps presaging a flash flood. Although they may have encountered other hikers on the initial trail, they were by themselves when they turned north into the "pathless gorge." I find it important, on rereading the poem, to note that the poet and his young companions, in the narrative of this text, have selected such an isolated route for their trip, a place off the beaten path. In order to contemplate "truth" and the "immense beauty" of the planet, it's best to avoid the distraction of other humans—so wrote the poet in March 1951. And yet one of the crucial tropes of this poem is the poet's contemplation of his *sons* (Garth, who was present during the Ventana Creek walk; and Donnan, who was not) and the personified rock of the nearby cliffs—the fact that the speaker is not entirely alone is very important to the meaning of the poem, I think, emphasizing *relationships* rather than solitude.

The poem begins with the phrase "We stayed"—ironic because, like so many of Jeffers's stone works, the poem concludes with a meditation on mutability. It is ironic for us to think of ourselves as staying *anywhere*, even for a brief spell of time. I am struck, too, by the verb used to describe the relationship between various kinds of trees and the "rock walls and mountain ridges"; Jeffers tells us the maple, redwood, laurel, oak, madrone, and—up high—"slender Santa Lucian firs" are *hung* on the rock, a conspicuously precarious state of being. The trees (and later the rock itself) are imbued with a kind of sentience and "stare up the cataracts / Of slide-rock to the star-color precipices." The reference to "slide-rock" contrasts strangely with the humans who *stay* the night, suggesting that even stone is mutable, portable, prone to *slide,* despite the fact that the upper cliffs resemble the seemingly immortal stars.

The lengthy second stanza of the poem reads as follows:

We lay on gravel and kept a
little camp-fire for warmth.
Past midnight only two or three coals glowed red in the cooling darkness;
I laid a clutch of dead bay-leaves
On the ember ends and felted dry sticks across them and lay down again.
The revived flame
Lighted my sleeping son's face and his companion's, and the vertical face
of the great gorge-wall
Across the stream. Light leaves overhead danced in the fire's breath, tree-
trunks were seen: it was the rock wall
That fascinated my eyes and mind. Nothing strange: light-gray diorite with
two or three slanting seams in it,
Smooth-polished by the endless attrition of slides and floods; no fern nor
lichen, pure naked rock . . . as if I were
Seeing rock for the first time. As if I were seeing through the flame-lit
surface into the real and bodily
And living rock. Nothing strange . . . I cannot
Tell you how strange: the silent passion, the deep nobility and childlike
loveliness: this fate going on
Outside our fates. It is here in the mountain like a grave smiling child. I
shall die, and my boys
Will live and die, our world will go on through its rapid agonies of change
and discovery; this age will die,
And wolves have howled in the snow around a new Bethlehem: this rock
will be here, grave, earnest, not passive: the energies
That are its atoms will still be bearing the whole mountain above: and I
many packed centuries ago,
Felt its intense reality with love and wonder, this lonely rock. (163)

This passage begins with the speaker and his companions coming into
physical contact with little pieces of stone (although Garth Jeffers later noted
that his father "always had trouble sleeping on the ground" and probably
spent most of the night in the gorge sitting near the fire and scribbling on a
scrap of paper [Kafka 36]), and the speaker of the poem later *grasps* the rock
wall with his "fascinated . . . eyes and mind" before he is forced to distinguish
between the fleeting human realm that "will go on through its rapid agonies

of change and discovery" and the monumental energy of the stone's seething atoms "bearing the whole mountain above." I suppose most readers will be particularly intrigued, as I am, by the analogies suggested between the children who accompany the poet (actually, as Kafka explains, Garth and Lloyd were in their early twenties at the time of the 1936 hike) and the rock wall that the poet is studying—he refers to the "childlike loveliness" of the rock, he describes the vast geological fate of the stone as a "grave smiling child," and he concludes by using a phrase that requires a readerly double take—we expect Jeffers to repeat the title "lovely rock," but instead the final words of the poem are "this lonely rock," emphasizing not the rock's *beauty* but the poet's perception that it is "living" and that it experiences relationships (and the lack thereof) and corresponding emotions.

■　■　■　While some might argue that Jeffers revels in a kind of stony inhumanism that would rather kill a man than a hawk and that attributes sensitive feelings to a rock wall in a poem that says little about his own boys except that they are mortal and ephemeral, I think something else is actually going on in "Oh, Lovely Rock," and it has everything to do with coming to terms with the emotions caused by loss and death—caused by *change*. Rather than simply pulling back from the inhuman phenomenon of stone and describing it as the ultimate *other,* the essence of the nonhuman, Jeffers delicately humanizes the *lovely* rock, the *living* rock, and the *lonely* rock throughout this poem, adopting it in what is literally a fatherly fashion and reaching with his mind to feel, as he says, "its intense reality with love and wonder." Actually, what he says in the peculiar and astonishing final sentence is: "and I many packed centuries ago / Felt its intense reality with love and wonder, this lonely rock." As he makes the local rock from the wilderness near his home a part of his own family, he also performs an imaginative leap and becomes, perhaps, the entire geological history of this place, experiencing the "intense reality" of this particular rock in the Ventana Creek gorge (the reality of an entire mountain bearing down, *packing* down, from above), rock which is "younger" (more childlike) than the rock that was pushed up from the earth earlier in geological time, subjected to the elements, and ultimately weathered into gravel.

By declaring this affinity for rock, by projecting humanness onto it and by drawing geology into himself, Jeffers seems to reach toward a transcendence of his ephemerality, even as he states explicitly, "I shall die, and my boys / Will live and die." But this transcendence of mortality through association with stone depends on a particular notion of stone that predates contemporary environmental writing and the contemporary stone trade. For Jeffers, stone is still the locus of the local and the locus of a kind of permanence: as he puts it toward the end of "Oh, Lovely Rock," "this rock will be here, grave, earnest, not passive." This rock will *be here*.

In his recent article, Robert Kafka tells of his own visits to the gorge in 1997, 1998, and 1999, finally encountering during the more recent trip "a perfectly vertical rock wall, several hundred feet high . . . with an erosion-smoothed face at the bottom" (45)—perhaps Jeffers's lovely rock. Unless times change dramatically and California rock becomes as cheap as the rock in Mexico, Turkey, Spain, or Brazil and finds itself carved up and spread along the office walls of corporate Tokyo or Beijing, the rock is likely to remain in place. Another thing about Jeffers's lovely rock that Kafka confirmed in an interview with Santa Monica College professor Bill Selby is that it's probably diorite, a type of plutonic rock with large crystals that is not among the granites, marbles, and slates most prized by dealers who imported more than 3 million tons of such stone in 2005 alone—this figure comes from www.stoneworld.com, the Web site of the primary trade journal for dealers in stone slabs.

Jeffers seemed to prize his lovely rock for its fixity and sublimity—its awesome contrast to his own human ephemerality—onto which he tried imaginatively to graft human characteristics (childlike beauty, living energy, loneliness), perhaps as a means of coming to terms with his own mortality. Briefly now, I'd like to compare Jeffers's fascination with stone with a few examples of contemporary environmental writing.

Lest it seem that meditations on mortality are the product of distant eras, irrelevant to the jaded and edgy postmodern perspective, I must confess that I detect a persistent philosophical and psychological strand in contemporary American writing about humans and nature that explores these timeless issues of life and death, brevity and longevity. I find myself thinking, for instance, of

Oregon poet and essayist John Daniel's moving piece of prose, "Some Mortal Speculations," from his 1992 collection *The Trail Home: Nature, Imagination, and the American West,* in which he grapples with his own "discontent with mortality" (197), trying to take solace in the "grandeur in the prospect of evolutionary time" but resisting "abstract consolation" (198) in favor of what he calls "smaller things, things that happen close in front of me, things I can see and turn slowly in memory and see again, in imagination's second light" (199). Writing at the age of forty, some ten years younger than Jeffers was when he crafted "Oh, Lovely Rock," Daniel finds himself "look[ing] carefully at things that live, because everything [he] see[s] is hieroglyphic of what [he] might become" (201).

Another particularly relevant meditation on human mutability is Indiana writer Scott Russell Sanders's "Cloud Crossing," included in his 1987 collection *A Paradise of Bombs.* This essay recounts a 1978 hike up Hardesty Mountain southeast of Eugene, Oregon, when the author was thirty-three years old and carrying his infant son on his back. The essay begins with the sentences, "Clouds are temporary creatures. And so is the Milky Way, for that matter, if you take the long entropic view of things" (49). Later in the narrative, when Jesse reaches out of the backpack and pulls a handful of moss from the rock along the trail, Sanders is compelled to focus more intently on what has been revealed. "Looking more closely at the rockface," he writes,

I see that it is crumbling beneath roots and weather, sloughing away like old skin. The entire mountain is migrating, not so swiftly as the clouds, but just as surely, heading grain by grain to the sea. (53)

In the final line of the essay, as the small child looks out the window of the author's car and shouts "Moon [. . .] moon, moon," the narrator seems to be hinting at the universal human desire to reach beyond ourselves—to grasp our commonality with clouds and mountains, with the moon and stars. But unlike Robinson Jeffers's predominant emphasis on the relative fixity and durability of stone, Sanders seems to appreciate that fact that *all* things, even mountains, mutate and migrate. Mortality loves company, you might say. There is a sense of "calm" in Jesse's backseat "babbling" and in the author's prose (57).

My final example of recent environmental writing on the mutability topos comes from Colorado essayist John Calderazzo's 2004 volume, *Rising Fire: Volcanoes and Our Inner Lives*. The opening lines of Calderazzo's prologue reveal the relevance of this entire project to the focus of my discussion here. He writes: "Rock moves. It moves all the time, everywhere, in big ways and small, through deep time and fast forward, on the surface of the earth and far below it" (v). And the personal motivation for undertaking this series of essays on volcanoes throughout the world and their cultural and psychological significance becomes clear at the end of the prologue when the author tells the story of the time, when he was in his thirties, that a dermatologist discovered a malignant melanoma on his back. He concludes his opening explanation of how he became fascinated with volcanoes by describing the comfort he came to feel while "meditating about long-term geothermal forces, the sliding of continent-sized plates, currents of stone welling up from the depths of the planet over millions of years. Compared to all that," he acknowledges, "my time on the earth was so fleeting. Volcanoes were helping me find solace in the liquid nature of rock, in the impermanent nature of everything, including me" (xvii–xviii). For Calderazzo, it is reassuring to recognize the transience of all things in nature, from the human to the geological, while for other thinkers, such as artist Andy Goldsworthy, it is startling and unsettling (and at the same time beautiful) to perceive and emulate the instability of stone, as he states in the 2004 film *Andy Goldsworthy: Rivers and Tides*: "We set so much by our idea of the stability of stone, and when you find that stone itself is actually fluid and liquid, that really undermines my sense of what is here to stay and what isn't."

Much of what I've been talking about, the use of the poetic and narrative imagination to explore the *relation* between writers and their apparently distant subject matter (rocks, volcanoes, celestial objects, and so forth), demonstrates what philosopher Anna L. Peterson calls "relational selves" in her 2001 book *Being Human: Ethics, Environment, and Our Place in the World*. In contrast with mainstream, Western notions of human objectivity, Peterson argues that "Asian, Native American, and feminist approaches [to objectivity] all portray humanity as shaped and even defined by relations to a host of other beings, including people, animals, plants, and natural processes." She argues that the Western emphasis on "autonomy" (on detached objectivity) "is ideological in a particularly insidious way, reinforcing ecological, political, and economic practices that marginalize and exploit other persons and other species" (205). Although there is nothing explicitly addressing the pressing contemporary social issues of environmental justice and conservation in the examples I've offered here of relational thinking in the work of Edwards, Thoreau, Jeffers, Abbey, Daniel, Sanders, and Calderazzo, I do believe it's fair to suggest that the type of imagination demonstrated in this literature is a prelude to the breaking down of the very detachment—the pretense of *autonomy*, as Peterson puts it—that underlies many of the social and ecological problems we face in the world today. In his 1991 study of Jeffers's shifting voice in "Oh, Lovely Rock," David Copland Morris argues that what we find in the poem is not only a reflection on the poet's relationship with stone, but a testing of the relation between the language of scientific detachment and that of emotional connection: "The language of geology and the language of feeling can both apply," he writes in his description of the poem, "but each alone is too limited" (120). For Morris, what's significant about the language of "Oh, Lovely Rock" (and Jeffers's other writing in the inhumanist vein) is its paradoxical struggle to achieve a balance between appreciation of genuine, autonomous *otherness* and its projection of *feeling* onto that which is other. He concludes: "I submit that knowing away from and beyond ourselves is the necessary precondition for any sane environmental policy, as well as the very state of sanity itself" (121).

In the era of postmodern narrative and criticism, as authors like Edward Abbey certainly intimate, the ability to know the world beyond the mind—or beyond human fabrication—has become troublingly (and comically) complicated. Take Karen Tei Yamashita's 1990 novel, *Through the Arc of the Rain Forest,* in which stone appears as a motif, as a case in point. Yamashita suggests that in this age of high technology and global movement of commodities, we may think we're looking at stone when we're really seeing plastic. At one point, she writes:

The Matacao, scientists observed, had been formed for the most part within the last century, paralleling the development of the more common forms of plastic, polyurethane and Styrofoam. Enormous landfills of nonbiodegradable material buried under virtually every populated part of the Earth had undergone tremendous pressure, pushed ever farther into the lower layers of the Earth's mantle. The liquid deposits of the molten mass had been squeezed through underground veins to virgin areas of the Earth. The Amazon Forest, being one of the last virgin areas on Earth, got plenty. (202)

One of the implications here is that, along the lines of Bill McKibben's 1989 clarion cry in *The End of Nature,* we can no longer (as if we ever could) discern the difference between what's human and what's "away from and beyond ourselves," as David Morris puts it. Ursula Heise, in her study of Yamashita's novel, places the work in the context of multinational commerce, showing how globalization interferes, too, with our efforts to engage with "pristine nature," with something that is real insofar as it originates beyond human construction. Concerning Yamashita's wry presentation of postmodern geology, Heise states:

The new raw material here turns out to be artificial and a by-product of industrial garbage, though it has been transformed by geological processes in such a way that the very terms "natural" and "artificial" seem no longer to apply. Moreover, what looked initially like a pristine rainforest locale violated by the advent of multinationals turns out to have been invaded by globalization long before and in a much more insidious fashion, by global plastic masquerading as local rock. By global plastic that *is* local rock, since the distinction itself has become meaningless. . . . The local bedrock that reveals itself to be at the same time global plastic waste functions as a striking trope for the kind of deterritorialization John Tomlinson analyzes, the penetration of the local by the global that leads to the loosening of ties between culture and geography. But Yamashita takes the idea of deterritorialization one step further than Tomlinson in that she describes specifically the local *natural* environment as global and artificial at the same time. A landscape where digging into the soil leads not to rock or roots but polymer makes implausible any return to nature via the immersion into the local of the kind envisioned by many environmentalist writers. The native soil itself is deterritorialized in Yamashita's vision. ("Local Rock" 135)

The psychological and political value of such *deterritorialization,* when processed (and perhaps exaggerated) through the voice of a literary artist, is that it helps to provoke in audiences a questioning of the effects of losing a sense of what is real and what is artificial, of where things come from, of where things (including ourselves) *belong.* Just as Jeffers in "Oh, Lovely Rock" curiously *deterritorializes* (if I can use the term metaphorically) permanence and transience, by making the human speaker relatively permanent ("and I, many packed centuries ago") and the lovely rock relatively childlike and emotionally delicate ("this lonely rock"), the postmodern writer of globalization intensifies readers' consciousness of relationships, of what belongs where.

Another striking work of postmodern ecocriticism is Lee Rozelle's new book *Ecosublime: Environmental Awe and Terror from New World to Oddworld* (2005), in which he explores the continuing significance—and the curious permutations—of the aesthetic concept of the sublime in twenty-first-century American culture. The sublime is the perspective that underlies much of Jeffers's stone work as well as the writings I've mentioned above by contemporary environmental writers. Albert Gelpi, in his introduction to *The Wild God of the World,* goes so far as to say, "Jeffers speaks of 'the beauty of things' often, but he really means the sublimity of things. He is the poet of the sublime without peer in American letters" (14). Rozelle, in his book, makes the rather postmodern (and, in its own way, optimistic) assertion that "there is no affective difference between the natural sublime and the rhetorical sublime; both have the power to bring the viewer, reader, or player to heightened awareness of real natural environments. Both can promote advocacy. My work," he explains, "thus argues that mountain peaks, ozone holes, books, DVDs, advertisements, and even video games have the potential to spark environmental awe and terror" (3). It takes *particular* kinds of natural experiences to achieve this extraordinary combination of joyous awe and mortal terror—for instance, gazing at an exquisite cliff in Yosemite (as pictured on the cover of Rozelle's book) or in the Ventana Creek gorge (as depicted in "Oh, Lovely Rock"). And the careful depiction of beauty and degradation that occurs so often in environmental literature, even when it accepts the inevitable mortality or change of human beings (and perhaps of all things), evokes in us—in most instances—the response, "Yes, but not yet." Yes—all things are subject to change. But let us hold onto this beauty just a little bit longer.

    ▪ ▪ ▪   In April of 2006, two months after I had offered my preliminary reflections on "Oh, Lovely Rock" in the context of contemporary American ideas about stone and the current movement in environmental literature and ecocriticism as the opening talk at the annual Robinson Jeffers Association Conference (to an audience that consisted of all the great Jeffers scholars, from Robert Brophy and James Karman to Tim Hunt and Robert Zaller), an invitation from Robert Kafka arrived by e-mail: would I like to join a group of scholars on a three-day backpacking trip into the still-pathless gorge of Ventana Creek in order to see, touch, measure, and document the "lovely rock." How could I refuse? And yet *why* did I feel this urge to go to the rock itself?

Years ago, as a graduate student in New England, I found myself reading a study of Charles Olson's *Maximus Poems,* in which the author had traveled to Olson's Gloucester, Massachusetts, in order to retrace the very footsteps of the poet's persona, Maximus, along the weathered pavement of the old city. I thought to myself that I would never be the sort of literary scholar who would devote my life so singlemindedly to the study of another's life and ideas that I would actually desire to be in the place where that writer's ideas erupted into words. Why walk the streets of Dublin with Joyce's Stephen Daedalus? Why peer through the hazy veil of waterfalls in Yosemite with the ghost of John Muir?

And yet, when I had a spare afternoon during my years in Providence, I often found myself driving north to Concord, to bask in the red and golden autumn sunlight at Walden Pond. Later, after moving to Reno, Nevada, it wouldn't take much more than a whisper about granite cliffs and searing blue skies to spur me toward Yosemite, a three-hour drive to the south. After receiving Rob's terse invitation to join the scholarly search for "the rock," I immediately ran the idea by Susie, and within hours we had signed up for the trip some three months hence.

Any good traveler (or travel writer) knows that the journey itself is as important as the journey's destination. As the six of us began our day-long walk from the Pfeiffer Big Sur State Park into the Ventana Wilderness at nine in the morning on August 4, some seventy years to the day after Robinson Jeffers had walked into the same woods, I reminded myself to savor the journey—the strain of the backpack on my shoulders, the mingling smells of oak and pine, the sizzling sweat after hours of walking, and eventually the sharp contrast of hot head and frigid feet when we reached the Big Sur River and waded across, nearing the northward turn up Ventana Creek.

Our party consisted of Jeffers scholar Robert Kafka, his son Gene (who had joined the earlier trips to find the lovely rock as a high-school student and earlier in the summer had graduated from Colby College with majors in physics and English), Tor House docent and Jeffers enthusiast John Courtney, Jeffers's grandson (son of Donnan) Lindsay Jeffers, my wife, Susie Bender, and me. It took us seven hours of steady plodding up the Pine Ridge Trail, down the strenuously steep (and poison-oak filled) trail to the Ventana Campground on the Big Sur River, half a mile west on the Big Sur, and then north up Ventana Creek (I should say *through* the Ventana, for we sloshed upstream in the creek for more than an hour) to reach our campsite at Ladybug Flats, a small rise on the western side of the creek, made breathtaking by the towering cathedral of *sequoia sempervirens* arching over the tarps, where we would sleep for two nights and enjoy our tiny human meals and conversations for a mere fraction of their arboreal lives.

Even during the first day's walk, I found myself riveted by the Jeffersian drama of age and youth, vigor and frailty, displayed by our group. When we lost the trail the first time we ventured down toward the Big Sur River, Susie twisted her ankle under the weight of her heavy backpack, and I could see the face of Rob, our leader, twist with concern for Susie's health and for the fulfillment of our mission to reach the rock. Swept up in the furious desire to make contact with the actual rock that had inspired the poem that had inspired me to reflect for months on the meaning of rock and words about rock, I strapped Susie's heavy pack to the back of my own large pack and hiked for three hours thus laden, unable to imagine myself as anything other than a mortal being, one who would eventually reach my physical limits and collapse. I also began, on the first day of our walk, to notice the relationship between fifty-eight-year-old Rob and Gene, in his early twenties, the father rather pale and somewhat trembling with age and exertion (and commenting on his scrape with death and surgery since the last time he had made this journey to the rock) and the dark-skinned (half-Japanese) son intrepidly leaping off cliffs into the river and leading the way as we hiked upstream through waterfalls and through tangles of fallen sequoias. How appropriate to have a father and son along on this journey, demonstrating the crucial familial relationship that Jeffers himself contemplated as he took notes at night by the lovely rock and, later, as he crafted his poem about the experience.

Despite fatigue and the simple pleasure of lying flat on my back without having to heft a heavy pack against gravity, I slept fitfully that first night, waking often to stare up at the branches of several nearby *sequoia sempervirens*, each hundreds of feet high, silhouetted by the almost-full moon. My brief stay here seemed to be in elegant and tragic contrast to the extended lives in this one place of these ancient trees—I was passing through, intensely conscious of these living beings that belonged here and nowhere else, while they were reaching upward toward the stars, trunks blackened by wildfires and yet green and healthy at heights human visitors could barely glimpse. I watched the glowing moon pass gradually across the sky behind the spray of branches.

Saturday morning, the 5th, we donned lightweight day packs and ventured further up Ventana Creek, determined to find Jeffers's rock. Our entire walk would be on wobbly river rocks today, sometimes through ankle-deep shallows, sometimes through waist-deep pools, and at times through rushing waterfalls. At one point, about two hours out of camp, we encountered a shirtless, brown-skinned man, crouching over small plants he seemed to be cultivating in the sandy soil on the bank of the creek, a pot of food (apparently onions) boiling over a campfire—he refused to look at us, to acknowledge our apologies for interrupting his solitude. Later, as we hiked back downstream past his campsite, he was gone, as were his small array of crops and his tent and fire—all that remained were piles of excrement close to the creek. "Like someone out of a Jeffers narrative," said John Courtney, who'd guided many a visitor to Tor House and knew Jeffers's work by heart.

We began the day's walk at nine, stopped for a half-hour lunch, and by shortly after one in the afternoon found ourselves homing in on our goal. Pausing by a small bluff on the east side of the creek, Rob wondered if this could be the place and poured over his published article about the earlier trips in order to refresh his memory of Lloyd Tevis's description of the actual rock wall and its orientation. We shook our heads, admitted that this must be a "mock rock," and pushed further upstream. Susie, concerned about her ability to walk all the way back to camp on her injured ankle, turned around at this point, just twenty minutes or so before we came upon the lovely rock.

Upon reaching this place, which had been made sacred by the poet's vivification through language and which we had resanctified through our efforts of reenactment, you might think we would have simply paused, dropped our packs, and sat meditatively to gaze at the stone, the trees, and the sparse patches of sky above the narrow canyon, reflecting on the poet's words of geology and mortality and lovely, lively, lonely things. You might have expected us to try "seeing rock for the first time," getting a running start toward such intensity of vision with the aid of the poet's words and then flinging ourselves mindfully toward deeper appreciation than any of us had managed before. Instead, there was a curious haste and pragmatism as we scurried around the gravel bed facing the rock wall. Rob, Gene, and John used a simple surveying contraption to estimate the height of the wall, quickly realizing that the canyon walls were too close together and the string they'd brought too short to determine the exact height, as we'd hoped to do—scientific measurement foiled, we were forced to *estimate* that the wall was between eighty and a hundred feet high. Lindsay walked around and peered at the wall from various perspectives, presumably savoring the fact that he had just, in his mid-fifties, repeated a walk that had been so meaningful to his grandfather seventy years before, at the age of forty-nine. I found myself watching my companions and, feeling distracted, relied on my digital camera to record and preserve the experience—to preserve the rock itself, at least in my memory—until I could reflect upon it later in more tranquility. I touched the rock and thought about its crumbling, fractured features, so unlike the solidity I had imagined from the poem. I touched the mosses and ferns that grew from the rock face and considered how unlike the poet's description of "pure naked rock" the actual rock had become, seventy years (about the length of an average American lifespan in 2006) since the poet's visit in 1936. We all posed for pictures, individually and in a group, the shutters clicking automatically when we set the cameras on timers. Then Rob dramatically read "Oh, Lovely Rock," his voice shaking with emotion. He would never return to this place, he later told us—I wondered if any of us would.

I am recording this narrative approximately a month after the actual trip to Ventana Creek and the lovely rock. My poison oak has healed by now, and my shoulders are no longer sore from the heavy pack I carried during the hike. Susie's injured ankle is a vague memory. We are both looking ahead now to other adventures—my lecture trip to India in a week, her trip to China next month to recruit international students for the university. In such itinerant lives—lives driven by curiosity and commitment and adrenaline—it is sometimes hard to slow down and feel "with love and wonder" the "intense reality" of any place we happen to be, of other people, of trees and dogs and rocks. When we undertake a pilgrimage to Walden Pond or Ventana Creek—or even to the Great Wall of China (or the Three Gorges Dam), as I did in the weeks prior to the hike to the lovely rock—the purpose seems to be to foster this "love and wonder," this intensity of feeling, that we might have difficulty sustaining in our lives day in and day out. It is the nature of human emotion to wax and wane, mostly to wane. So we cultivate special words and special experiences in order to remind ourselves how to care, how to love, how to be more fully alive.

16 | Out of Time

SOGGY AGAIN

The alarm on my wristwatch rang this morning, as usual. Seven o'clock. But today I responded in a different way than I normally do. I stopped the insistent beeping, leaned out of bed, and hid the watch in one of my briefcase pockets, out of sight. Thus began my little experiment in timelessness, an experiment planned ahead and expected to last three days, approximately half of my stay in the green and misty forests of the central Oregon Cascades.

I am visiting the H. J. Andrews Experimental Forest, about fifty miles east of Eugene. These are the woods of my childhood, familiar and foreign in peculiar balance. The bushy greens of tilting pines are a familiar sight that returns me to the years of elementary school, junior high, and high school, before I went away to college. Vivid, impressionable years. Years of comfort, family, and adolescent struggles. In some ways this is my original landscape, my originating landscape. This is the landscape I still see in my dreams at night, although for decades now I've called freeway-strewn California foothills, narrow, buckling New England streets, rural, muggy small-town Texas, and brilliantly brown Sierra peaks "home." For a week now, I'm back in Oregon, back in rainy green, dwarfed again by widow-making firs, soggy again to the bone.

PRERELEVANT

I arrived at "the Andrews" yesterday at midday. Scheduled to meet geologist Fred Swanson and poet-essayist-housebuilder-gardener Charles Goodrich at noon, I pulled into the headquarters parking lot at precisely five seconds after twelve o'clock, fastidiously punctual even for me. We spent the afternoon chatting over lunch in the field-station library. Fred demonstrated a geologist's penchant for story, relating the history of the research performed at this site and going into detail about his own special interest in landslides and other natural catastrophes and how ecological systems respond to such events. I wasn't taking notes, but I tried to retain as much of this information as possible, keying in on particular phrases. Windthrow. Long-term. Temporal mind bending. Prerelevant.

Impressed by the hundreds of experiments that have been conducted at the Andrews since its founding in 1948 and by the idea that the nearly sixteen thousand acres of the forest are full of monitoring devices and research plots, I wondered whether there was a clear plan for each of these studies or whether some of the data was simply being collected in hopes of later determining its relevance, its meaning. Fred explained that it's often the case that scientists gather information that doesn't seem relevant to issues of the day but that later takes on meaning.

That later takes on meaning. How often do we have the luxury of gathering information, storing it, bringing it out again on that "rainy day" when we need answers? Sitting in the Andrews library, a repository of data about the myriad studies of stream flow, biodiversity, and the rotting and regeneration processes of this temperate rain forest, I am straining to hold on to the information flooding into me through Fred's narrative, metaphor-rich language. I want to know this place. I should know this place. This is the place of my youth, and yet I'm a stranger.

I continued to wear my watch throughout the afternoon and evening. Kathy Moore and her husband Frank and their colleague Dawn, the mother of one of my former graduate students, showed up to accompany us to several long-term ecological reflection sites and to dinner. The afternoon was one of companionship and conversation. Time still dominated. "What time is our reservation for dinner?" "I guess it's time for the Corvallisites to hit the road." I returned to my apartment, read myself to sleep, and plotted my escape from time the following morning, promptly at seven.

INSPIRATION, EXPIRATION

My room in the Rainbow Right apartment has a low window with a perfect view of green, green, and more green. There's the pale lime green of lawn, followed by a dense thicket of young Douglas firs with light new growth and darker green inner branches, and then come the tall and ancient trees down closer to Lookout Creek, about thirty of them, each over two hundred feet tall and more than five hundred years old.

Watch or no watch, I'm here to work, so I put on my layers, grab the umbrella, and slosh my way down to Lookout Creek to observation plot number one: a giant fir tree that fell during a big storm in 1996 and now straddles the creek, about a three-minute walk from where I'm staying. Yesterday Fred suggested that this is one of the scenes I might wish to contemplate during my week at the Andrews. No problem, I thought. I can come here and contemplate. Then he said: "You might want to climb out on the fallen tree and sit above the creek while you do your observations." Hmmm—not so sure about that. Then he proposed: "You could also go through the underbrush over to that gravel bar that washed up in the '96 storm." Not much more enticing. I could just see myself trying to clamber over the four-foot diameter of the fallen, moss-covered tree, slipping awkwardly into the miscellany of rocks and branches, and spraining an ankle or worse my first morning in the woods.

When the time came on morning one to do some observations, I headed out into the rain down to the fallen tree and found that my preferred observation method was simply to stand on the tree near the trail. No need to perch myself above the rushing torrent. The view was fine from the log, but the main challenge was balancing the umbrella on my head while holding a small, folded piece of paper in one hand and pen in the other. I tried to make some initial observations, still self-conscious, not yet settled into this new place. It always seems like this when I begin a new project—the stiff self-consciousness. And this time I felt even more awkward than usual. How to conduct "long-term ecological reflections"? A mere human, standing atop a fallen giant that came crashing down in the forest after living about seven times longer than the average person. I felt like a flea standing on a dog. What could I say about this place? It's green, it's cold, it's wet. The rushing creek drowned out my thoughts—almost like the effect of the rhythmic crashing of waves on a seacoast, except here the sound of moving water is even more constant, coupled with the clicking sound of raindrops on my umbrella.

The sun broke through the clouds for a moment, brightening the mossy twigs near my head. I noticed the stillness of the trees, the movement of dripping water. In the creek, the fallen giant was a picture of stillness, massively immobile, while underneath the water rushed. I thought of how many things in the world exist in opposition to each other. This weekend, running with my father in the mountains, he used the word "orthogonal" to describe phenomena that exist in opposition to each other. Stillness and motion. But I did not feel orthogonal to this landscape, just out of synch. Too fast moving, too impatient. Gazing out over the fallen log and the rushing creek, I noticed a small insect rising before my eyes, then dashing away (or being dashed away by the breeze). I could scarcely force myself to see it before it vanished. I was a bug to this landscape. I was a flea on a dog's back, aspiring to perform long-term reflection.

Perhaps a walk in the woods would help to generate some thoughts. Guided by one of the researchers, I drove six miles up a narrow paved road called 1506 that eventually became a gravel road, stopped at the obscure entrance to the Lookout Creek Old Growth Forest Trail, donned my pack, then made my way into the dark, damp depths of temperate rain forest. Unlike the manicured public trails I've always hiked in the past, this trail was magnificently rugged and chaotic. Huge trees lay atop each other like pick-up sticks that will never be picked up. They are subsiding into the earth, as they should. Fallen logs crossed the trail, so it was necessary to creep under them. I found myself especially interested in the shallow roots of uprooted forest giants. So little underground to hold such trees to the dirt. I tried to imagine the steady tilt of tall trees becoming a rush and roar of windfall. I've never actually seen a tree fall in the forest, but here I was on a rainy day when the soil was loose, surrounded by thousands of tilting giants, any one of which could come down with a moment's notice.

Somehow the map didn't make it clear that this Old Growth Trail requires major altitude changes, including movement up from rain into the snow zone of higher elevations. I knew the trail was about three and a half miles long, but to be alone in the woods like this, perhaps the only hiker in this entire forest on a wet day like today, intensified my feeling of isolation. Eventually the physical process of straining uphill on the narrow trail had its desired effect. I stopped thinking so much—stopped thinking about thinking—and started simply breathing. I tried to figure out what I heard as I walked—the gurgles of rainwater, the occasional whooshing of steep streams, distant caws and cackles of birds, and my own breathing—in and out, in and out.

I recalled Richard Nelson's notion that when you're in a place, you bring the place into you by drinking its water, eating what lives there, and breathing in its air. I concentrated on breathing this forest into myself as I hiked.

As my breathing intensified and I began to sweat, I found myself thinking about my dog Silly's last breath. I saw her take it five days earlier when Susie and I brought her to the vet's office to be euthanized. Silly, a fourteen-year-old golden retriever, had reached a point where she could no longer stand up on her own. For about a week I had carried her outside several times a day to relieve herself, but finally she couldn't even stand when I set her down on the grass, and she was so weak she could scarcely lift her head anymore. We made the difficult decision to "put her to sleep." The entire process took only a few minutes—the shaving of a small area on her lower back leg, the insertion of a large syringe full of pink sedative, Silly's instinctive flinch at the prick of the needle, and then her sudden collapse from her prone position on the metal table when her heart stopped and she'd taken her last breath. She was not there anymore, just a hunk of skin and bones.

As I walked through the old-growth forest—ancient living trees, giant snags still standing, deadfall everywhere in the process of fertilizing decay—I found myself more fascinated with my own meager breaths. Nothing momentous about a single tiny person walking and breathing in the woods. But the rhythm of my breathing had, for the moment, joined the other rhythms of this forest—the rhythms of water and air, of movement and stillness, of living and dying. This felt good to me.

I HAD A DREAM

Woke up this morning without an alarm clock, without any clock at all, and I felt myself emerging from a dream. I'm not someone who normally remembers dreams, so the fact that this one stayed with me out of sleep is unusual. I dreamed that I was living in a small, watertight space, surrounded by flowing water. My central concern was staying dry. I couldn't see out of this living space, had no idea what the environment was like. Everything was dark, but there was an abiding sound of flowing water, and my room seemed to shift occasionally, like a strange, semi-sensory-deprivation amusement-park ride.

As I tottered stiffly out of the bedroom, it began to dawn on me that I must have been dreaming about reflection plot number one, the fallen log across Lookout Creek. Beyond the log in the area, I haven't yet been able to visit because of the treacherous footing and thickets of debris in the pile of stones at the torrent's edge. Last night, before going to sleep, I read Fred Swanson's notes on the reflection plots and saw that he called this pile of rocks a "gravel bar." I must have been dreaming about the gravel bar, imagining the effects of incessant nearby water flow. But instead of playing the role of a human observer, standing nearby and gauging the mechanics of flow affecting rocks, I imagined myself to be inside one of the stones. I imagined this three-room apartment for research staff to be a stone at the edge of the creek, temporarily stable but subject to the whims of the physical world. Strangely, this was not a sad or disturbing notion. It felt comfortable not to be in control, but there was nonetheless a strong desire to stay dry.

HIDING THE CLOCK

As I walked into the kitchen the morning of day two to heat some water for coffee, I recognized the absence of regular ticking. The day before, after hiding my watch in my briefcase, I had come into the kitchen to prepare for the day's excursions, but there had been a persistent ticking in the room. During breakfast, I had assumed the ticking was somewhere in my head—sound patterns internalized through years of living by the clock. But as I put on my boots, I glanced at the wall near a poster on the ecology of a Pacific Northwest old-growth forest, and there was a large clock with images of twelve colorful birds, each representing one of the hours. I debated for a moment, then stepped over and removed the clock from the wall and placed it in a kitchen drawer. When I return to time in a few days, I'll hang the clock back on the wall, if I remember. But it seems important to be consistent in removing myself from clock time during this several-day experiment, if I'm to bother with it at all.

You might wonder about the clock in the upper right-hand corner of my computer—how could I avoid looking at that while trying to experience freedom from seconds, minutes, and hours for a few days. Well, that clock said two fifteen A.M. as I gazed at the midmorning scene from my window and wrote this sentence. The irrelevance of such clock time made it easy to ignore the numbers.

TAKEN BY A NOTION TO EXPERIMENT

Free from the constraints of a schedule, I found, as Edward Abbey once put it, that I was taken by a notion to experiment. No, I didn't seek out a rabbit or a small bird to brain with a rock. Nothing that brutal. In the thinning light of late afternoon, I drove down to Road 1501 and over to the clear-cut on private land that Fred suggested I visit occasionally during my stay at the Andrews. This morning, thwarted by snow when I tried to drive up Road 1508 to the Blue River Face cut and burn, I drove down in the direction of 1501, but not far enough. This forested country feels quite disorienting to me—vistas concealed by dense masses of trees, only roads providing narrow strips of visibility.

Buoyed by good feelings after an afternoon run, I hopped in the car and tried again, and this time I made it down to the gravel road that passes through the lower portion of clear-cut 1501. I didn't know the name of this place, so that's what I called it in my notes: "clear-cut 1501."

The cut is close to Highway 126, and the traffic was audible as I sat at the base of the treeless landscape and considered what to do. I heard airplane engines above the clouds, a jay of some sort chittering invisibly in the trees beyond the clear-cut. Misty clouds wafted among moss-covered alders beginning to grow on the distant edge of the twenty-acre barren hillside. This was really a quintessential clear-cut, it occurred to me. Almost nothing remains—minimal debris, scattered stumps in various stages of decay, and some small fir seedlings no more than a few years old.

A fresh rain shower was coming in as I got out of the car, but it blew through in a few minutes. When the waning sun pushed through the clouds for a moment, I was stricken with a notion to experiment by taking a walk around the contours of the clear-cut—a circumambulation of sorts. Normally writers and New Age folks do this at sacred places, such as Mount Tamalpais in Marin County—the walk around the base of Mount Tam is called a "circumtam." My friends Gary Snyder and David Robertson sometimes escort groups of university students and true believers on such hikes, pausing now and then to read poetry and take pictures. Today I was by myself, and I had no poetry to read. And this was probably not a sacred landscape, although it was clearly a *scarred* one. What does one call a walk around a clear-cut? I asked myself, as I began to claw my way up the steep and rugged hillside at the eastern edge of the cut. Well, I guess you could call it a "circumcision"!

I don't know how long it took me to hike up and down, then up and down again, following the undulations of the land around the perimeter of the cut. I don't know whether I was breaking some property laws by walking this land, owned by a private person rather than the government. As I began coming down the upper part of the western side of the cut, a white-haired man pulled up in his SUV behind my small green Nissan in the distance, letting his dog out of the car to roam around. I felt furtive and guilty and made my way into the shelter of still-standing trees at the edge of the clear-cut, not wanting to be reported to the landowner if my transgression, my circumcision, were noticed. Here at the forest's edge, I found fallen, rotting logs to be soft paths down the steep slope, a striking contrast to the thickets of slash and blackberry vines that made the going tough on the logged-over hill.

I have never spent so much time at a clear-cut before. Typically, I am flying over them in planes or hurrying past in a car. Once, while visiting Bob Pyle in southwestern Washington, I asked him to take me to see some of the gaping clear-cuts near his home—but we merely stood at the edge and shook our heads. Today, watchless and temporarily out of time, with nothing to do but run and walk through the woods or sit inside listening to rain fall and grading papers, I felt strangely free to commune with the clear-cut, to gaze at it and crunch my way around its edges. It did not feel like a good place. Up close, it looked like a kind of junkyard, a forty-degree hillside littered with debris. The only signs of animals I noticed, apart from distant birdcalls, were deer turds here and there . . . and shotgun shells down by the road.

When Abbey killed the rabbit with a stone and then crowed about it in *Desert Solitaire,* he said his experiment made him feel more deeply enmeshed in the world, part of the tangle of predator and prey. My experiment made me feel strangely truant, a kind of truancy I cannot overcome. Lured by the freedom from time, I indulged myself with a walk where the woods once stood. I did not heal anything with this circumambulation, this circumcision. Back at the apartment, I plucked a sliver from my finger. I washed a pair of dirty socks in the bathroom sink. But I could not wash the feeling of that place, "clear-cut 1501," from my mind. I wondered if another walk in the deep, dark woods would help.

TILTS AND THRESHOLDS

The first things you notice when walking into an apartment here at the Andrews Forest are the safety items sitting on the counter: a heavy-duty radio and a hard hat. The first item seems reasonable enough, considering the remoteness of the locations people visit out here to collect climate data, water samples, and demographic information on spotted owls and other species, sometimes in iffy weather and at night. The hard hat seems more dubious, as the chances of rockfall are limited and the effects of tree fall so catastrophic as to nullify the value of a plastic hat. I quickly decided I'd carry the radio with me on all of my excursions this week, but I'd leave the hard hat on the kitchen counter.

This morning, day three, I decided to visit the Lookout Creek Old Growth

Trail again before stopping at one of my favorite reflection sites, the Log Decomp site. I didn't know how high I'd get when driving up to the Old Growth trailhead, as it had been snowing heavily at the higher elevations for the past three days. I made it about six miles up Road 1506 to its isolated intersection with 350, but my city car couldn't get any further and it seemed risky to try. I could hear the car's bottom scraping against the snow in the middle of the road, and the tires were slipping on truck tracks now increasingly filled with slush. With about three inches of snow on the road and the depth increasing as I made my way up Lookout Ridge, I decided not to enter the deep forest for a three- or four-mile trudge on the steep trail to the exit point higher up on 1506. I pulled back from that challenging walk and decided instead to explore the road a ways, where I could at least be sure not to get lost.

Today I had intended, like two days ago, to examine the threshold between the snowy and clear sections of the trail, to contemplate the transitional margin between the two kinds of walking. On Monday, following the dips and rises of the steep trail, I found myself shifting back and forth between snow and no-snow, savoring the threshold, the relative security of the clear trail and the riskiness of the ever-deepening snow at higher elevations. Today there was only snow, deeper and deeper snow, as I walked up the road. Had I been wearing my cross-country skis, this would have been a pleasure jaunt—in my skidding boots, the walk felt more like a trudge. About a quarter-mile up the road from where I abandoned my car, I noticed heavy tracks in the snow, apparently moving up the road. The tracks were hours old and partly filled with recent snow. Mountain lion? Lynx? Perhaps an elk? I didn't feel directly threatened by such tracks, but there was something vaguely ominous about them, about knowing I had unseen companions with me on this snowy walk.

In addition to considering thresholds of snow and no-snow, I had intended this morning to contemplate the tilts of trees and land. This is not a simple, perpendicular landscape, with flat ground and up-tending vegetation. Soon after arriving here, one notices that most of the land is sloped, many of the trees (especially those two hundred feet or taller) tilted. To my mind, tilts imply danger—the danger of mud slides, rockfall, or the cataclysmic upheaval of timber. On the Old Growth Trail itself, I was captivated by the many fallen giants, uncut, rotting in the dark forest depths, roots uplifted, sometimes still caked with mud and still grasping boulders. Interesting how at the base of a tilting snag, there often seems to be no tilt at all. Tree after tree seems sturdily upright, but a glance at the sky—or from a distance—shows major tilt . . . and risk.

Walking on the snowy road, the air almost windless and misty, I felt little threat from the tilting trees. The presence of wind would make this a very different kind of place, each tree suddenly posing a significant danger. There was no overt and urgent danger during my walk this morning, nor was there a pressing need to turn back and resume another task back at the apartment. Watchless, I had no idea how early or late it was. I had indicated on the sign-out sheet back at headquarters that I expected to return by "early afternoon." There was plenty of time.

Still, after a mile or so of snowy hiking, I decided to turn around. It seemed to me that enough was enough. I wasn't tired, wasn't bored. It was beautiful and peaceful in the deep woods on a snowy morning. The faint itching of a possible blister on the top of a toe on my right foot caused some concern. The large footprints in the snow, just parallel to my own clunky boot prints, caused slight uneasiness and curiosity. I wondered, too, if my little car would make it down the curvy, snow-covered road, bordered by steep drop-offs into rushing creeks with no guardrails. I decided I had reached the edge of my risk-benefit threshold. The risk of becoming mired in the snow now outweighed the benefit of peaceful exercise. The recognition of limits did not come with a momentous sigh of recognition, just a pause, a pivot, and a continuation of the walk, now downhill.

I wonder if our society, too, will come to a recognition of limits someday, not through cataclysm, but merely through pause, pivot, and continued motion in a new direction.

LOG DECOMP

It sounds like a kind of tepid punch line. So, what did you do on your spring break? I sat in the woods and watched logs rot.

This is what I've actually done this week. It's been one of my favorite experiences at the Andrews. One advantage of the Log Decomp site just up from the intersection of Roads 1506 and 1508 is that it's low enough to be free of snow when the higher-elevation sites are icy and inaccessible to people driving cars like mine. I haven't been able to reach one reflection site, the Blue River Face cut and burn all week—too much snow. But today I stopped by to watch the logs rot for the fourth time, the third time by myself.

There's something special about this place. It's more peaceful than anywhere else I've visited at the Andrews—mossier and quieter (at least when the owls who live nearby aren't hooting). This is where Mark Harmon and his colleagues are conducting the 200-year decomposition study, now in its twentieth year—I'm intrigued by the choice of 200 years for the duration of the study, launched less than a decade after the 1976 bicentennial of the United States, as if there might be something magical about such a time span, which represents 40 percent of the current lifetime of the trees still standing in this area. There is something peculiarly anthropocentric—no, Americano-centric—about the choice of a 200-year "long-term ecological research" project, beginning in 1985. Why not 250 years? Why not 500?

At the actual decomp study site, a number of mossy logs have been placed hither and thither, some with white buckets attached, devices used to study gaseous releases from decomposing wood—the scientists are monitoring, among other things, how much carbon is stored in dead wood, a phenomenon linked to global warming. In all six of the log-decomp study sites at the Andrews, there are some 530 logs, formally decaying under the scrutiny of scientists. The logs at this particular site lie amid towering Douglas firs, western hemlocks, and mossy-bearded Pacific yews. En route to the decomp, I now have a habit of bending to smell the red, fleshy tissues of the huge logs that fell across the trail and have been sawed apart to maintain trail access—they have a ripe, mintlike smell, it seems to me. The tissues of wood look like filets of salmon, except more jagged, like something a hungry bear might have left behind.

When I visit "Log Decomp," I tend to keep walking to a ferny glade around the corner. A dip in the path has filled with clear water from days of rain, and the ferns, mosses, wildflowers, and russet maple leaves look like creatures in a seaside tide pool. There being no tide here, these must be "trail pools." A herpetologist would probably detect signs of rough-skinned salamanders here, but I see only plant life. The only motion is caused by fast- or slow-falling droplets of water, either actual rain or just residual wetness sliding off branches above.

Today I walked further than usual, all the way to the end of the trail spur. The canopy thinned and more light came in. I noticed many silent, shaggy yews. This is a quiet place. No rushing water and, for today, no branches sighing in wind. Some drops of water, and everywhere around me the silence of decay and the silence of mossy growth. Even as I passed through the enormous tree trunks that were sawed through to keep the trail open, that violence seemed forgettable, the sawing itself distant and unimportant. Like so much violence in the human realm, morality subsides as fiber erodes.

CONTINENTAL DRIFT

Last night I dreamed again of the gravel bar and cross-stream logs not far from the forest headquarters and my apartment. I wake up each morning and tramp down the wet trail to my observation place—this has quickly become a routine, and today, my fourth in the woods, is no different.

Each day I find myself becoming bolder, more comfortable in this place. Some of this may be due to the fact that the rain has let up, and with it the rush of Lookout Creek seems to have subsided, become quieter and less threatening. Perhaps this is merely an illusion—I'm not a measurer of stream flows—but this is how it seems, how it *sounds,* to me.

Yesterday, wearing running sweats and Teva sandals, I stepped through a side channel of the creek and went out onto the gravel bar deposited by the February 1996 flood. There I found a boulder covered with pale green moss and sat for a while, reflecting and taking notes. The first thing that occurred to me was that the island of small rocks, newly leafing alders, and young firs and hemlocks seemed "permanent." I wrote the word "continental" on my piece of notepaper. Everything on the island appeared, from my vantage, mossy, fixed, old. I recalled Fred's brief lecture about the place four days earlier, his mention of the flood less than a decade ago that created this new island—at the time, the information was "prerelevant" to me, unrelated to anything I knew I should be thinking about. Today, after several days of visiting this place and looking at it from different angles, the solidity of the stones, mud, logs, and new growth here felt startlingly contradictory to the actual newness of this landscape in the context of geological time. The gravel bar was an infant, yet to me it felt permanent.

At the same time, there is a vibrant sense of upheaval here, as if the entire sweep of water, hillsides, and trees is a sort of waterfall, frozen in form during the brief moment when I'm here to witness it. My friend John Felstiner is fond of describing waterfalls as "flux taking form"—he's referring to the "paradoxical dynamic" in Western nature poetry of the past two centuries, and in nature itself, by which "raw energy can show design." The Lookout Creek gravel bar also strikes me as "flux taking form," as I can see the future of this place written in the not-flooding creek and in the many tilting skyscrapers, pausing now en route back to earth. Just because we don't see actual change, our eyes being as temporary as the rest of our being, doesn't mean change isn't happening right before our eyes. This gravel bar, it occurs to me, is a rare clearing in the forest, a viewpoint—strangely like a clear-cut, but without the debris of tree limbs, the steepness, the stumpage and with many more rocks, mossy with new life. A kingfisher zipped past as I sat on my wet boulder, following the flow of the creek. An airplane groaned overhead, unseen above the clouds, its sound competing with the rush of water—and then there was only the water.

On day four, I took a different angle on this scene, following my increasing comfort here and stepping carefully out to the middle of the fallen log, then sitting cross-legged to write in the middle of Lookout Creek. Here I noticed not only yesterday's gravel bar upstream of the fallen log, but another large gravel bar downstream, this one without alders and small evergreens, just a graceful curve of stones, like a Goldsworthy sculpture.

In contrast to the solidity and apparent—if illusory—permanence of the two gravel bars and the log on which I sat above the moving water, there were two LBJs (little brown jobbies) flitting near the edge of the creek. I tried to watch them for several minutes, but found it difficult, agitating. Their jerky movements seemed nervous, the purposes of their jumps from perch to perch unclear. Their ephemerality was exaggerated by juxtaposition with so many unmoving rocks and trees, but I knew that even trees fell and rotted, and even rocks drifted when the stream flooded. Sitting there on the temporarily sturdy log above fast-moving water gave me a pronounced sense of the continuum of fixity and change: everything I am able to know is, within one time frame or another, both stable and mutable.

Last night, when dreaming about the gravel bar, I remembered a disturbing passage from the book I've been reading lately, John Perkins's *Confessions of an Economic Hit Man,* a memoir about his role in destabilizing economies and political regimes in developing nations, at the behest of corporations and the U.S. government. Perkins notes that

For every $100 of crude taken out of the Ecuadorian rain forests, the oil companies receive $75. Of the remaining $25, three-quarters must go to paying off the foreign debt. Most of the remainder covers military and other governmental expenses—which leaves about $2.50 for health, education, and programs aimed at helping the poor. . . . Thus, out of every $100 worth of oil torn from the Amazon, less than $3.00 goes to the people who need the money most, those whose lives have been so adversely impacted by the dams, the drilling, and the pipelines, and who are dying from lack of edible food and potable water.

Because of this brutal inequity, Perkins concludes, "All of those people—millions in Ecuador, billions around the world—are potential terrorists. Not because they believe in communism or anarchism or are intrinsically evil, but simply because they are desperate" (xx).

It occurs to me that America's catastrophic impact on the rest of the world is akin to the occasional flooding of Lookout Creek. Our corporate culture, supported by the government, is changing the world's cultural landscape. What the corporate and governmental leaders fail to understand, however, is that when such changes occur, the agent of change, the flood itself, cannot remain unchanged. Not only is our nation's violent mistreatment of other cultures prompting violent reactions, but there is a profound corruption, a kind of rot, at the heart of our apparently stable society. Morris Berman establishes an ominous parallel between contemporary America and the late Roman Empire in his recent book, *The Twilight of American Culture*. In the ecstasy of exerting today's power, we perilously ignore the lessons of fixity and change that become clear to us after a few days walking in the woods, reflecting upon gravel bars and fallen logs. Remember, even continents drift.

TRANSITION TO CLOCK TIME

I had intended to spend today, day four, on my own again, walking any trails I could find without too much remaining snow. But as I pulled out of the parking lot at headquarters, I noticed John Moreau ahead of me in a pale green Forest Service SUV, pulling the snow cat on a trailer. At the turnoff to Road 1506, the main route to my reflection sites, John pulled up ahead of me and came walking back. "I'm headed up to Carpenter Mountain today to check some met stations in the snow cat—got room for two." In an instant, my plans for a quiet stroll at the log decomp site were scratched. I recalled a photo from my apartment, showing a giant vehicle in a snowstorm with glowing headlights and tread like a tank, the caption reading, "'John Moreau Collecting a Precipitation Sample for Water Chemistry Analysis,' H. J. Andrews, Watershed 7, January 1990." Seemed like an opportunity to learn something new.

I parked my car down by the cement bridge, not far from the log decomp site I'd be visiting later, and jumped in with John for the ride up to the snow. We left the jeep at the junction of 1506 and 350, not far from the Old Growth trailhead where I'd hiked earlier in the week. It took only a moment to learn that riding in a snow cat is essentially the opposite of a peaceful woodsy experience. The grinding roar of the engine comes from right in between the two seats in the cab, and the powerful tank treads do indeed get you up the mountain, but with the cost of a kidney-pulverizing shake. And the entire purpose of our journey into snow country was to collect meteorological data and check three of the forest's major climate stations. This was to be a reimmersion into clock time and scientific measurements.

At the first station, as John went through a calibration checklist and changed the paper in a meter of some sort, I noticed the time, 11:40, on his wristwatch sans band, which he placed on the work counter. It was the first time I'd looked at a watch in nearly four days. Fifteen minutes later we climbed back into the snow cat and continued our errand, pausing occasionally to take readings from snow poles on the road or placed back in the forest: 1.3 feet, 1.9 feet, 2.2 feet. We noticed animal tracks on the road ahead of the tractor and tried to identify them: elk, deer, rabbit, perhaps bobcat or coyote. The vicious tread of the machine swallowed up most of the tracks, leaving a snowy washboard pattern in our wake.

Higher up the mountain, we had to leave the snow cat and hike a hundred meters through deep snow to the met station. I walked in John's snowshoe tracks, but my boots still sunk another six or eight inches into the snow. Hard going, this transition back into clock time and scientific measurements, this hike into deep slush. The met station, John explained to me, measures ground temperature, ground moisture, wind speed and direction, air temperature, precipitation height and weight, among other things—all of this collected in an electronic data recorder inside the small building up at the station and also sent back to headquarters via radio telemetry. "It's eight degrees Celsius," he reported, explaining the snowmelt raining down from trees all around us.

John used a large core-sample pole to take five snow readings, and I helped record the data on a sheet of paper—depth 23.5, sample length 20.0, weight 19.5, and so forth. After lunch in brilliant sunlight, gazing out at Mount Washington, Belknap Crater, and the Three Sisters, we rattled back down to the jeep in the snow cat, and John offered to drive me up to the Blue River Face cut-and-burn site, which I'd been unable to visit so far this week, since my little Nissan couldn't handle the snowy road. "Let me return the snow cat to headquarters first. I'll meet you at Log Decomp Number 3 in forty-five minutes," he promised. Although I still wasn't wearing my own watch, I felt myself being enveloped again by clock time and numbers. The timeless decomp site I'd been visiting all week now had a name: "Number 3." And instead of having as much time as my mind needed to engage with this place, I now had an appointment to hitch a ride up to another reflection site in forty-five minutes.

For the better part of an hour, I walked among the old growth and rotting logs at the decomp site, enjoying the extraordinary quiet following the skull-shattering roar of the snow cat. I marveled at the former "trail pools," which had already absorbed all of the shin-deep water from the day before. I looked at the distinct glow of sunlight passing through mossy beards on yew trees. When John pulled up, I was waiting near the road, holding a handful of epiphytic moss in my hand, counting the individual strands—twenty-five, twenty-six. How easy it had been to return to a numerical frame of mind.

Up at the Blue River Face, where scientists are experimenting with alternatives to clear-cutting—leaving some of the big trees, burning slash to regenerate the natural forest—I sat on a blackened stump among a sea of small rhododendron plants, counting Douglas fir seedlings and trying to estimate the distance between each of them. About fifteen feet. I climbed into John's jeep and noticed the time was 4:21. Back at headquarters, I went inside to erase my outing details from the sign-out board and noticed that when John had driven down to return the snow cat, he had changed my ETA from "early afternoon" to "18:00."

I had known this would happen again eventually, this return to clock time, but when I woke up this morning, I resisted the temptation to put on my watch again and return smoothly to my urban, professional, clock-checking identity. Tomorrow I would spend the day walking again in the usual places: gravel bars, log decomp, and possibly the clear-cut, if not the cut/burn, wearing my watch again, just to see how that affects the experience, if at all. How awkward it had been at first, pulling away from time and numbers—how strangely rapid and natural this return to measurements.

HANGING THE CLOCK

This morning, day five, I woke at early dawn and went to the kitchen to rehang the clock I'd removed from the wall three days ago. For the past few days, I've kept the clock in a kitchen drawer, hiding it from me and myself from it. I've known all along it was in there, ticking steadily, keeping track of time. Perhaps it has not really been time I've tried to avoid this week, so much as the monitoring of time. A person who lives somewhat inordinately by clock time, uses the wristwatch as a whip, I figured this week in the woods might be a rare chance—a week with few appointments, perhaps none at all—to experience a somewhat different state of mind.

Of course, I've known all along how the week would end. The plot of this experiment was mapped out from the beginning: hide the clock early on, hang it up again at the finish. And despite the flexibility of my daily schedule here at the Andrews, I've clearly had things to accomplish, or at least to attempt—visits to particular sites, taking notes, massaging notes into reflections, reading books, grading papers. And each day, before heading into the woods, I've dutifully marked the sign-out board in forest headquarters, indicating where I'd be going and when I'd return: midday, early afternoon, before dark. I wonder if I've behaved any differently than usual without the clock on the wall of the apartment, a watch on my wrist while hiking and observing. To some extent, any differences in behavior were predetermined by the decision to experiment with the avoidance of timekeeping devices. I hid my wristwatch because I *intended* to avoid making decisions this week according to a strict schedule, and thus I *did* act more patiently and flexibly than usual, or so it seemed to me at week's end.

Although I've certainly not suspended the temporal frames that structure much of my life, and the lives of so many others in this society, I probably have managed, in a small way, to moderate the press of time on my daily behavior this week. I've always known I'd be hanging out here for about six days, with a big appointment at the end: a 5:00 rendezvous at Hovland Hall, OSU's Philosophy Department, at the end of the experience. Then a drive home to Reno the following day, return to the office the day after, and class again the day after that. The entire experience of a clockless week has been artificial and circumscribed—you might even say it's been "scripted."

I find myself comparing the relative orderliness of my life, with or without clocks, with the story line of nature. It seems to me that there are certain predictable, or *scripted,* processes in nature, too. Rules that must be followed. "Water moves downhill" is an obvious one. Everywhere in the Andrews, at least this time of year, you can see this plot occurring: each trail I've walked has presented tiny mountainside rivulets carrying water to larger runoffs, then to creeks, and finally into rivers. Yesterday, up on the high slopes of Carpenter

Mountain, the downward movement of water was conspicuous—it almost seemed to be raining on a brightly sunny day, as showers of melting snow fell from every branch of every tree. No avoiding this process, the tug of gravity, except through the evaporative force of heat upon fallen water. Other inevitable processes also govern this place and the objects and beings in it: photosynthesis, plant growth, animals eating and evacuating the waste. Things around here may not operate strictly by clock-driven schedules, but there is order nonetheless.

I guess the main purpose of my clock-hiding gimmick has been to test the attachment of my own mind to temporal measurements. I have a few small personal habits—checking the keys in my pocket, pushing the hair away from my forehead. But perhaps my most persistent habit, or tick, is feeling for my wristwatch and checking the time. This has become almost unconscious in my normal life, but it means, it seems to me now, that I'm always compartmentalizing my activities, finishing one task and moving on to the next. This is how I get things done, I suppose. But after a week here in the woods without my watch, I begin to wonder whether "getting things done" is the same as living.

OUT OF "OUT OF TIME"

The phrase "out of time" sounds like a threat, doesn't it? Perhaps a line from a tough-guy movie: "Buddy, you're out of time and out of luck."

That's not really how I've meant it in my title for these reflections. What I had in mind was an assertion of freedom: what would it be like to step out of time for several days and act as if there were simply day and night, rain and shine, no other minute parceling out of hours, minutes, and seconds?

The Andrews Forest, located not far from the woods of my childhood an hour's drive west of here, also seemed like a unique setting in which to pursue this experiment. Perhaps in a small way it *would* be possible for me to suspend time or scroll it backwards, spending part of the week simply wandering in forests like I did as a child and adolescent in Eugene, near Edgewood School or on the slopes of Spencer Butte, south of the city. A chance for some "temporal mindbending," to use one of Fred Swanson's phrases.

It had been my plan to spend Saturday morning, April 2, the day of my departure, taking a more specific step backward in time and driving up Highway 126 a few miles to Paradise Campground, where I would run on the extraordinary McKenzie River Trail, one of Oregon's most magical forest pathways. I last ran here about thirty years ago—1975 or 1976, I believe. My father drove us here on a cloudless summer day—the two of us, my younger brother Steve, and my friend Bill McChesney. That was a time of innocence and fitness, bold plans and playful energy. Bill and I ran all the way to a reservoir filled with snowmelt and then leaped again and again into the icy water until Bill complained that his "brain was freezing" and decided to stop. A few years later he became a U.S. Olympian unable to compete in the boycotted Moscow games, then a salesman of high-school graduation trinkets, and then the victim of a car accident on a rainy coastal highway. Steve is now a busy Portland surgeon, my father and I itinerant researchers and lecturers. I wander far and wide around the planet, meeting with colleagues and seeking beautiful places to run—sun-flooded beaches in Australia, wooded campuses in India, elegant city parks in Taipei, the slopes of Mount Blanc in France. Tomorrow, stepping back in time, I would run again on the soft pine needles of the McKenzie River Trail, through the dark passageways of the forest of my youth.

But upon returning to headquarters after my morning circuit of the reflection sites, there was an e-mail from my mother, expressing concern about incoming snow in the Cascades and proposing that I drive down to Eugene that evening to have dinner with them and spend the night.

Had I already said my good-byes to the Andrews Forest reflection sites? I recalled the trip to the vet with Silly last week, and how, when the vet asked if we'd like another minute by ourselves with our dear old dog after she was dead, Susie said, "We've already said our good-byes."

I could stay in these forests for months, perhaps longer, extending and deepening my observations, but for now, five days of visits to the gravel bars and the log-decomp site and a few stops at the 1501 clear-cut and the Blue River Face cut/burn, four days without wearing a watch and one final day back in clock time, have prompted plenty of reflections. I feel I've said my good-byes here.

But I cannot leave without running the MRT again, after three decades. It's raining again today, mostly drizzling but sometimes pounding down. The trails are truly soggy. I've made a promise to myself, though—in some ways, this trail run is the central purpose of my stay here in the McKenzie River drainage.

■   ■   ■   Thirty minutes out, thirty minutes back. Thirty years out, thirty years back. I've got my watch on again, so keeping track of time is no sweat. Thirty minutes out, thirty years back. Temporal mindbending. This morning, driving down Road 1506 after visiting the decomposing logs for what turned out to be the final time, I pulled over to the side of the road and made a note: "Change is a physical phenomenon—time is psychological." For some reason, it seemed important that I write this down.

Dressed in rain gear and my gray New Balance running shoes, I drive twenty minutes east to Paradise Campground, just as I had planned to do tomorrow. Highway 126 had little traffic, and the campground is empty. I find the trail-head sign and pull my little green car to a stop.

When I lean against the "McKenzie River Trail" sign to stretch my Achilles tendons, the gray and fraying sign wobbles and nearly falls over. I recall this as a fresh, new sign for a dazzling new trail system. Wooden signs seem to rot in the woods just as experimental logs do.

Moving east on the trail, I quickly find my rhythm, breathing smoothly, feeling my shoes squish the soggy trail, slapping in the mud, sinking into moist pine needles. Faster and faster I run, sometimes skirting the full river, other times turning with the trail into dense old-growth glades. Memories flood my mind—thoughts of the past week in the Andrews, thoughts of my last run on this trail thirty years ago with father, brother, and friend, inside my teenage self. Faster, faster. No one else on trail. Shimmering leaves of Oregon grape, glowing moss-beards on hemlock and yew. Dancing across patches of what I call "feather moss," clambering over fallen logs. Faster, faster. I remember a recent e-mail announcing my junior-high coach's eightieth birthday—Coach Andrews would be shouting at me now, "Is that all you got in you, son? Come on, Tiger!" I goose the accelerator and sprint uphill, trying not to sprain an ankle on tree roots, careful not to slip on rain-slickened muck. Flashes of light on shimmering leaves, dark tree bodies, the rushing river flashes silver where the woods recede. Rushing, breathing, moving, running, thinking. I cannot see, cannot see myself. Only my young hands, my dancing feet. I am flying through the woods, breathing, breathing. I cannot think my name, cannot speak it.

Red cedar, pungent branches on trail. Multifaceted, giant cedar trunks, splaying out like fig trees. Giant trees, red cedars. Thinking of our family house in Sunriver, named "Red Cedar" because of street name. Red cedar, shining branches, like ferns. Flashes of leaves, serrated, Oregon grape. Puddles on trail. Breathing, breathing.

I think of my friend, father, brother, running just behind me. Breathing, breathing. The forest opens to embrace us, to enclose us. Sense of being together, squinting back tears. Pushing harder, harder. "Come on, Tiger, is that all you got in you?" Glancing back, no one is with me. Where is my friend? Alone, moving through the forest.

No pen, no paper, just a breathing, running mind, absorbing, remembering. Bright leaves push the light back, dimly glowing leaves take it in. Reflection, absorption. Supposed, supposed to be reflecting, making sense of this experience. Not my way. My mind a mossy thinker, taking, taking in, not glinting out.

Thirty years out, thirty minutes back, breathing, breathing the forest in. A week of images, thirty years of memories, sixty minutes of rushing sounds, sights, smells, sixty minutes of wobbling, squishing feet on soft forest trail.

■ ■ ■ Later, driving back to the Andrews, sweaty hands on steering wheel, it occurs to me that I may not be terribly good at long-term ecological reflection. What I do is "long-term ecological absorption." The impressions I've gathered during this past week in the Oregon woods will surely remain with me, move me, sustain me. Perhaps in thirty years, I'll return to this forest and consider what changes have occurred with the Lookout Creek gravel bars, the fallen logs, the decomp sites, the cuts, clear and otherwise. It's three P.M. now, about time to begin driving to Eugene. For now, my out-of-time experience is over—I am out of "Out of Time."

17 | Even Better than the Real Thing

Like many of my colleagues, I have long been a devotee of "the real thing." As I've discussed in my essay on Jeffers's "lovely rock" and the traditional importance of "the real" in environmental literature and ecocriticism, the very concept of essential reality and the possibility of feeling as if we can grasp some wisp of the thing itself is what lures many of us time and again into the dark forest of words, following bread crumbs of ideas that evanesce even as we write them down.

At the risk of trivializing what I take to be a rather serious topic—the essential focus of this collection of essays, the efforts of a scholar both to enjoy the beauties of literature, community, and the natural world and to respond appropriately to occasions that call for social/political engagement—I wish to tell the story of how my appreciation for "the real thing" took a surprising twist in the wake of a lecture trip to the other side of the world.

En route to present versions of my Jeffers/stone talk at the first conferences of the Organisation for the Study of Literature and the Environment and the Indian branch of the Association for the Study of Literature and Environment—and to talk with the leaders of these rival scholarly groups about the possibility of coexisting in mutually supportive ways—I arrived at the airport in Chennai, India, just before midnight in September 2006, rested for four hours at a nearby hotel, and then took a taxi back to the airport through the still-dark streets to catch an early flight up to New Delhi. In Delhi I found a taxi driver standing among the throngs at the airport with my name on a handwritten sign, and we alternately inched and sprinted our way through the chaotic traffic of India's capital city toward the Hauz Khas neighborhood and the offices of Navdanya, where I had a one o'clock appointment to interview Dr. Vandana Shiva for an hour about her strategies for communicating quantitative information to technical and lay audiences. The *Numbers & Nerves* project, launched years ago (and outlined in chapter 14, "Seeking a Discourse of Environmental Sensitivity in a World of Data"), had just been funded by a substantial grant from the Hewlett Foundation, and part of it would be devoted to sponsoring interviews on this issue with leading social and environmental thinkers throughout the world. While sitting in the Navdanya offices waiting for Vandana to arrive, I reread two of her books, *Staying Alive: Women, Ecology and Development* and *Water Wars: Privatization, Pollution, and Profit,* and I paid the young man clipping newspaper articles in the office for copies of several pamphlets and in-house publications, including *Seeds of Suicide: The Ecological and Human Costs of Seed Monopolies & Globalisation of Agriculture, Intellectual Property Rights and Patents, Building Water Democracy: People's Victory Against Coca-Cola in Plachimada,* and the Polaris Institute's *Coke Water Wars.*

Late in the morning, hoping to wash away my jet lag, I went out for a stroll along the dirt and gravel streets of Delhi, stopping to take photos of browsing cows and Coca-Cola ads painted on building walls around the corner from Navdanya. My morning reading had freshly reminded me of the oppressive impacts of the corporate water wars on local communities in this country, and I found it ironic that the arch nemesis of this activist organization was marketing its products so prominently in the Hauz Khas district. At least, I thought to myself, there are no billboards crowing about the contributions of Monsanto to Indian peasants.

Shortly before one o'clock, Vandana's assistant, Priya, walked me over to a small café a few blocks from the office, where Navdanya offers healthy soups and sandwiches made with organic, local grains and vegetables and a variety of interesting teas and fruit juices. A laminated green and brown poster hung on the café's wall, declaring in English and Hindi: "This is Coke Pepsi Free Zone." Promptly at one, Vandana walked in, friendly and businesslike, and found me waiting for my lunch to arrive. She impressed me during the interview with her careful approach to "counterexpertise" and the use of story to communicate scientific ideas and numerical information to general audiences and with her passionate devotion to the plight of peasants and local people, caught in the sweep of globalization. During the next five days of my stay in India, I self-consciously avoided buying cans of Coke at the university canteen during the ASLE-I conference in Pondicherry, and when I purchased some water to carry with me during the meetings, I noticed in reading the fine print on the label that the Aquafina water was actually bottled by Pepsi. Even when sensitized to social and environmental concerns associated with globalization, it's not easy to live in a way that meshes with one's awareness. What would it be like to go through life obsessing over the small print? And yet what alternative do we have if we wish to be socially engaged, socially responsible?

■ ■ ■ After returning to Reno from India, I weaned myself from soft drinks and bottled water. This seems like an easy sacrifice, but all it accomplishes is partial peace of mind for the abstainer—it doesn't make the slightest dent in the multi-billion-dollar profits (or the worrisome activities) of the companies being boycotted. So after two months of private abstention, I pulled myself away from piles of student papers and prepared the following letter to the CEO of Coca-Cola:

18 November 2006

Mr. E. Neville Isdell,
Chairman, Board of Directors and CEO
The Coca-Cola Company
P.O. Box 1734
Atlanta, GA 30301

Dear Mr. Isdell:

I write to you as a longtime fan of your company's best-known product—Classic Coke. I grew up enjoying this drink and have, until very recently, remained an enthusiastic consumer of various Coca-Cola products.

However, during a recent lecture trip to India, I became aware of the impact Coca-Cola and its rival companies—chiefly, Pepsi and Parle Bisleri—are having upon Indian society through the privatization of water and the pollution of water resources in places like Kerala, Uttar Pradesh, Tamil Nadu, and Himachal Pradesh. I'm sure you are well aware of what your company is doing in India and throughout the world, and I feel ashamed that I've become aware of these water issues only recently. I do applaud the concept of bringing clean water to parts of the world—Latin America, South Asia, and Africa—that have suffered historically from a scarcity of potable water. However, I was deeply concerned during my trip earlier this fall to learn that thousands of subsistence farmers and other local residents in India have, in recent years, lost their access to the water that their communities have traditionally used for farming, livestock, and daily consumption. No doubt, the Indian government has facilitated the privatization of this water by Coca-Cola and other corporations (for the production of soft drinks and bottled water in India), but while this access to local water supplies has enabled your company to open the Indian market to your products, there have been dramatic and terrible consequences for the most vulnerable Indian citizens. From what I've read since my return to the U.S., similar tradeoffs have occurred elsewhere in the world as a result of the corporate control of water resources.

I suppose the reason I'm writing to you at this time is simply to let you know that even some of your company's most loyal customers are concerned about Coca-Cola's participation in the privatization and contamination of water resources throughout the world. In my case, I have decided as a result of this knowledge no longer to purchase or consume products of Coca-Cola or other corporations that I know to be involved in this practice. You may think this is a rather trivial complaint—that of a single Coke drinker. However, I happen to spend much of my time traveling around the world lecturing to audiences of teachers and scholars in my branch of literary studies—I would estimate that I reach combined audiences of several thousand influential people in an average year, and each of these listeners (not to mention readers of my articles for academic and popular audiences) is likely to encounter hundreds of students and colleagues in a year. Even though my lecture topics tend not to have much to do with soft drinks, I have found ways to work comments about my disenchantment with Coca-Cola and other soft drink (and bottled water) corporations into many of my lectures and plan to continue doing so indefinitely, until I learn that a new era of corporate responsibility has arrived. I have read Coca-Cola's *Corporate Responsibility Review,* and it contains nice-sounding language about the company's responsibility for environmental stewardship and toward the communities where it does business, but, as I realized during my visit to India, these slogans do not yet match on-the-ground reality.

What I ask is that you and your colleagues at Coca-Cola consider making an active effort to think beyond the economic bottom line when it comes to using precious water resources in regions of the world where there are many people who cannot easily afford to buy bottled water or to purchase water for irrigation. Speaking for myself, I would be willing to pay more for your soft drinks and your bottled water if I knew that your company was seriously trying to help people—farmers in India, for instance—maintain access to their local water resources. Many people in the world do not have enough money to buy bottled water—many scarcely participate in the commercial economy—so it makes little sense to bring clean bottled water to the hinterlands of Africa and India, where few can afford to buy the product. In truth, it sounds rather like extortion.

I believe that Coca-Cola is a reputable and important company, and I hope, ultimately, to be able to return as a loyal consumer of your products. However, until I receive some evidence that you are working to respond appropriately to the concerns that people throughout the world are currently voicing about the privatization of water, I'm afraid I will have to boycott all of your products—and I will encourage others to do so as well.

Sincerely,

Scott Slovic

Professor of Literature and Environment

It's possible that this letter will have little effect, but it's possible, too, that something in my words will strike a chord in the offices of the corporate giant. Perhaps the example of this letter will inspire my students to write letters to Coca-Cola or to other companies or government leaders, expressing their own social concerns, close to home or far away. When it comes to engagement, often the most useful thing writers, scholars, and teachers can do is to speak up at meetings or craft letters and e-mails to decision makers.

Approximately a month after I sent my letter to Mr. Isdell, I did receive a detailed and defensive response from someone at Coca-Cola North America, a semi-anonymous person called "William." Here's what he wrote:

December 20, 2006

Mr. Scott Slovic
University of Nevada
Dept. of English
Reno, NV 89557

Dear Mr. Slovic:

Thank you for contacting The Coca-Cola Company. Your letter to Neville Isdell was shared with me for response. We appreciate the opportunity to respond to your concerns about our operations in India.

The reality is that we are not the largest user of water in India—in fact the beverage industry accounts for less than one half of one percent of water use in India—but we are among the most visible.

Our Company makes significant investments in building plants and training workers and it makes no sense to then drain the community of the most important resource that we need to produce our products. We share an interest in water stewardship with our consumers, our share owners and all the communities where we do business.

We have an obligation as a responsible community partner to use water in our own operations as efficiently as possible and to work with communities to steward this precious natural resource.

The facts demonstrate that we are not the cause of groundwater depletion in local communities. In April 2005, the High Court of Kerala determined, on the basis of a year-long scientific study, that the primary cause of the water shortage in the Plachimada area was due to reduced rainfall during the last several years, and that The Coca-Cola Company has the right to withdraw and use water from the local aquifer for our operations. Although the Plachimada plant has been closed since March 2004, we continue to supply drinking water to the local community.

Mehdiganj is neither a water scarce area nor a drought prone area. The monsoon has been regular during the last few years and the average rainfall in the area is 950 mm/year. The allegations that our plant has depleted the water there are not substantiated by official records.

The Coca-Cola Company has reduced our water use ratios in India by 34 percent between 1999 and 2005. We have installed 220 rainwater harvesting structures spread across 17 states, including locations at schools and farms. At our plants, the collected water is used for plant functions and for recharging aquifers. Today, a substantial amount of the groundwater we use in our operations is renewed and returned to groundwater systems.

To further address concerns that we have depleted local water resources in India, we committed to an independent third-party assessment of The Coca-Cola Company's current water resources management practices. In mid-September, The Energy and Resource Institute (TERI), an India-based nonprofit research organization, began this assessment.

TERI is working with an independent steering committee that will oversee the study and provided strategic direction to the assessment process. TERI has told us that they expect to complete the assessment in the first quarter of 2007.

Our Company has pledged full cooperation with TERI and its steering committee in completing this assessment and addressing its findings.

Although The Coca-Cola Company has its own environmental management systems, which includes regular audits of every plant within our global system, we welcome this additional assessment to provide an independent perspective on how we can improve our water resource management practices and policies. We know that we can always improve our performance, and we're committed to doing so.

As always, we appreciate the opportunity to respond to your concerns and share our position with you.

Sincerely,

William

Industry and Consumer Affairs

The Coca-Cola Company

The detailed letter from William gave the appearance of a "final word" from Coke to me, an authoritative defense of the company's record on water use in India, but it seemed to me that the function of a concerned citizen is not to fire a single salvo toward a potential (or actual) offender, but to keep watching. This is true, I feel, in any context, any situation. To write a single time is better than never writing at all, but to write back and say, "I'm still interested, still watching," is even better. At the same time, I did not want to make a pest of myself or come across as a crackpot.

So I wrote a second time to The Coca-Cola Company:

8 January 2007

Industry and Consumer Affairs

The Coca-Cola Company

P.O. Box 1734

Atlanta, GA 30301

To Whom It May Concern:

I sent a letter to Neville Isdell last month, expressing my concern about The Coca-Cola Company's water resources management practices in India and in other developing nations. Today I received a very helpful response from someone named William (no last name provided) out of your Industry and Consumer Affairs office (see enclosed).

I appreciate William's detailed response, and I would be very interested to know more about the results of the "independent third-party assessment" that is currently being conducted by The Energy and Resources Institute (TERI), based in New Delhi. If this assessment will result in any sort of public document, I would very much like to see a copy of the document or receive information about how to access the report online.

As I mentioned in my previous letter, I have access to audiences throughout the world who come to hear my presentations on environmental literature and American culture (including American corporate and consumer practices). If the TERI assessment indicates that The Coca-Cola Company has indeed made significant improvements in its management of water resources in India, I would be happy to share this information with my readers and listeners, many of whom are primarily familiar, at this point, with media and activist reports of problems caused by corporate water use.

Thanks in advance for your response to this request. Also, if William is based in your office, I would like to thank him for his recent letter.

Sincerely,

Scott Slovic

Professor of Literature and Environment

On March 6 I received an e-mail from "Tom" at Coke's Industry and Consumer Affairs office. He wrote:

Thank you for contacting The Coca-Cola Company again, Mr. Slovic. We appreciate your concern.

The information you are requesting is available on our Company website. You may wish to view the press release regarding the safety of our brands in India at the following web address:

http://www.thecoca-colacompany.com/presscenter/nr_20060811P_csl.india.report.html

We hope this information is helpful. Please contact us again should you have additional comment or questions.

Tom

Industry and Consumer Affairs

The Coca-Cola Company

I immediately checked the Web site mentioned in this message, of course, and found a press release dated August 11, 2006, that declared Coca-Cola products in India to be free of pesticides, to be "pure." But this is not what I had written about in either my first or second letters to the company. I had expressed particular concern about the depletion (and privatization) of water resources needed by rural people, people who cannot easily afford to buy their drinking water, let alone water for farming or livestock. The e-mail from Tom completely missed the point of my inquiries to the company. Busy with academic responsibilities and somewhat dismayed by the polite obtuseness of the e-mail I had received from the company in March 2007, I turned away from this correspondence for some months, but I continued my private boycott of Coca-Cola products and I continued to express my concerns about the company and similar companies during my lecture trips throughout the United States and abroad.

In the fall of 2007, while preparing the final manuscript of this book, I searched the Coca-Cola Web site for an update about the TERI assessment, but all I could find was an April 2006 press release stating the company's intention to enlist TERI to conduct an assessment of Coca-Cola's water-management practices in India. To my knowledge the study has not yet been completed. I have received no information about the results, despite my request.

What I've learned from my communications with The Coca-Cola Company is that the process of paying attention and speaking out is ongoing. There will be no simple, quick, reassuring response from the corporate giant. But in addition to—or instead of—shelling out our cash for corporate products and keeping silent about any misgivings we might have, it seems necessary for us, as engaged citizens (and this includes those of us who perform the academic work called ecocriticism), to interact with the corporate and political world in other ways. I believe it is essential for us to use whatever skills we have as writers and public speakers to let the multinationals and government officials know we're paying attention and we care what's going on.

I was sincere, by the way, when I wrote to "William" that I would be glad to publicize Coca-Cola's good deeds as I learn about them, not only its infractions. I take no pleasure in issuing only warnings and critiques.

■　■　■　Ask a stranger on the street in this country what "the real thing" refers to, and he or she will probably recognize this as a line from a commercial: "Coke—it's the real thing." Who can lay prior claim to this line, the soft-drink industry or artists, philosophers, and devotees of nature? Does it matter?

Much of my work, coextensive with my personal life, has been devoted to savoring ("La vida tiene sabor"!) the world's cultural and natural beauty and working to the best of my abilities, and within my limits of time and energy, to support this beauty and meaning. There are times, though, when it just doesn't feel right to enjoy a sip of Coke or a walk in the mountains, when it makes more sense to attend a bicycle advocacy and education group meeting or fire off a letter of concern to a corporation. Sometimes—to quote the U2 song (which does not refer to Coca-Cola)—we need to realize that certain actions are "even better than the real thing."

Appreciation and action overlap at times, but these moments of consonance are intermittent. To live a responsible life means constantly to tweak the balance between art (or scholarship) and activism. But to ask whether activism compromises one's intellectual life, as Alison Hawthorne Deming beautifully explains in *Writing the Sacred into the Real,* is like asking, "Does culture compromise nature? Does love compromise solitude? Does eating compromise prayer? Does the mountain compromise the sky? All of these," she says, "are relationships of complementarity, correspondence, call-and-response, the mutualistic whole of existence" (67).

I guess this is what I've been trying to say in the pages of this essay collection: that ecocritics—and other socially committed literary scholars—must perpetually seek appropriate ways to balance their aesthetic and emotional attachments and their politics. The balance constantly shifts, and the balance necessarily differs from one person to the next. To pursue this balance, though, is what I mean by "responsibility."

Acknowledgments

"Going Away to Think: Travel, Home, and the Academic Life" is reprinted by permission from *Placing the Academy: Essays on Landscape and Identity*, edited by Jennifer Sinor and Rona Kaufman and published by Utah State University Press in 2007.

"Ecocriticism: Storytelling, Values, Communication, Contact" was presented at the October 1994 meeting of the Western Literature Association in Salt Lake City, Utah. An early version is available on the Web site of the Association for the Study of Literature and Environment (www.asle.umn.edu).

"Seeking the Language of Solid Ground: Reflections on Ecocriticism and Narrative" originally appeared in *Fourth Genre* 1, no. 2 (Fall 1999).

An earlier version of "'Be Prepared for the Worst': Love, Anticipated Loss, and Environmental Valuation" was presented at the 1997 Western Literature Association Conference in Albuquerque, New Mexico, and was revised for publication in *Western American Literature* 35, no. 3 (Fall 2000).

"Mother Nature Sends a Pink Slip," is reprinted by permission from *Selu: Seeking the Corn-Mother's Wisdom*, by Marilou Awiakta. Copyright 1993, Fulcrum Publishing, Golden, Colorado (www.fulcrumbooks.com). All rights reserved.

An earlier version of "Authenticity, Occupancy, and Credibility: Rick Bass and the Rhetoric of Protecting Place" appeared in *True West: Authenticity and the American West,* edited by William R. Handley and Nathaniel Lewis and published by the University of Nebraska Press in 2004. Reprinted by permission.

A brief version of "Ecocriticism on and after September 11" was presented at Hiroshima University in Japan on 7 May 2002. The lecture was published (in Japanese) in the book *New Landscape of America: Toward a New Ecocritical Vision,* edited by Shoko Itoh, Mitsu Yoshida, and Yuri Yokota and published by Nanundou Press in 2003.

"Gated Mountains" was first published in *Wild Nevada: Testimonies on Behalf of the Desert,* edited by Roberta Moore and Scott Slovic and published by the University of Nevada Press in 2005. Reprinted by permission.

A briefer version of "Animals and Humans: In Appreciation of Randy Malamud's *Poetic Animals and Animal Souls*" was published in *South Atlantic Review* (Winter 2007).

An earlier version of "Chimeric Opinions" appeared in the September/October 2005 issue of *Orion* magazine (www.orionmagazine.org).

"The Story of Climate Change: Science, Narrative, and Social Action" was first presented as a sermon to the Unitarian Universalist Fellowship of Northern Nevada on 30 January 2005. An abbreviated version of this essay appeared in the spring 2005 issue of *The Okinawan Journal of American Studies,* University of the Ryukyus, Japan.

"There's Something about Your Voice I Cannot Hear: Environmental Literature, Public Policy, and Ecocriticism" first appeared in slightly different form in the 2004 (64/2) environmental issue of *Southerly* (Department of English, University of Sydney, Australia).

"Seeking a Discourse of Environmental Sensitivity in a World of Data: The Divide between Literature and Science" was first presented at The Earth 2000/La Tierra Año 2000, a symposium of scientists and writers sponsored by UNESCO and International PEN, Mexico City, Mexico, January 2000. A different version of this essay appeared in *Tamkang Review* (Spring–Summer 2002).

An earlier version of "Oh, Lovely Slab: Robinson Jeffers, Stone Work, and the Locus of the Real" was presented as the keynote lecture at the February 2006 Robinson Jeffers Association Conference in Big Sur, California, and later as the keynote lecture at the September 2006 conference of ASLE-India in Pondicherry, India. This essay appeared in the OSLE-India volume *Essays in Ecocriticism,* edited by Nirmal Selvamony, Nirmaldasan, and Rayson K. Alex and published in New Delhi by Sarup & Sons in 2007.

Poems by Robinson Jeffers are reprinted from *The Collected Poetry of Robinson Jeffers,* edited by Tim Hunt. Copyright © 1987 by the Jeffers Literary Properties for Orca and 1938, 1966 by Donnan and Garth Jeffers for "Oh Lovely Rock." All rights reserved. Used with the permission of Stanford University Press, www.sup.org.

A previous version of "Out of Time" appeared in the environmental special issue of *Flyway* (Winter 2005).

I am most grateful to Professor Wei Qingqi for his careful work on the Chinese translation of *Going Away to Think.*

Works Cited

Abbey, Edward. *Desert Solitaire: A Season in the Wilderness*. 1968. Reprint, New York: Ballantine, 1971.

Ackerman, Diane. *A Natural History of the Senses*. New York: Random House, 1990.

Adamson, Joni. *American Indian Literature, Environmental Justice, and Ecocriticism: The Middle Place*. Tucson: U of Arizona P, 2001.

Adamson, Joni, Mei Mei Evans, and Rachel Stein, eds. *The Environmental Justice Reader: Politics, Poetics, and Pedagogy*. Tucson: U of Arizona P, 2002.

Anaya, Rudolfo. *Bless Me, Ultima*. 1971. Reprint, New York: Warner, 1994.

Anzaldúa, Gloria. *Borderlands/La Frontera: The New Mestiza*. San Francisco: Spinsters/Aunt Lute, 1987.

Aridjis, Homero. "Grey Whale" and "Love Poem in Mexico City." In *Eyes to See Otherwise/Ojos, de otro mirar: Selected Poems*, edited by Betty Ferber and George McWhirter, 207, 201. New York: New Directions, 2001.

Armbruster, Karla, and Kathleen R. Wallace, eds. *Beyond Nature Writing: Expanding the Boundaries of Ecocriticism*. Charlottesville: UP of Virginia, 2001.

AtKisson, Alan. *Believing Cassandra: An Optimist Looks at a Pessimist's World*. White River Junction, VT: Chelsea Green, 1999.

Awiakta, Marilou. *Selu: Seeking the Corn-Mother's Wisdom*. Golden, CO: Fulcrum, 1993.

Bailey, Ronald. *Eco-Scam: The False Prophets of Ecological Apocalypse*. New York: St. Martin's, 1993.

Barry, Peter. "Ecocriticism." In *Beginning Theory: An Introduction to Literary and Cultural Theory*, 248–71. 2nd ed. Manchester, UK: U of Manchester P, 2002.

Bass, Rick. "Bear Spray Stories." Unpublished essay presented at Fire & Grit. Shepherdstown, WV, June 1999.

———. *The Book of Yaak*. Boston: Houghton Mifflin, 1996.

———. *Brown Dog of the Yaak: Essays on Art and Activism*. Minneapolis: Milkweed, 1999.

———. "The Community of Glaciers." Unpublished essay presented at Fire & Grit. Shepherdstown, WV, June 1999.

———. *The Deer Pasture.* New York: Norton, 1985.

———. *Fiber.* Athens: U of Georgia P, 1998.

———. Note to author, 22 August 2002.

———. *The Watch: Stories.* New York: Norton, 1989.

———. *Wild to the Heart.* New York: Norton, 1987.

———. "On Willow Creek." In *Heart of the Land,* edited by Joseph Barbato and Lisa Weinerman, 7–24. New York: Pantheon, 1995.

———. *Winter: Notes from Montana.* Boston: Houghton Mifflin, 1991.

Bazell, Robert. "Need a Liver? Raise a Sheep: Organ Growing in Animals Raises Ethical Concerns." *MSNBC NEWS* (25 April 2005). http://msnbc.msn.com/id/7631877/.

Bellow, Saul. *Henderson the Rain King.* New York: Viking, 1959.

Berman, Morris. *The Twilight of American Culture.* New York: Norton, 2000.

Berry, Wendell. "Stay Home." *Collected Poems 1957–1982,199.* San Francisco: North Point, 1985.

———. "Word and Flesh." 1989. In *What Are People For?* 197–203. San Francisco: North Point, 1990.

Birkerts, Sven. "American Nostalgias." *The Writer's Chronicle: A Publication of the Associated Writing Programs* (February 1999): 27–34, 36–37.

Blake, William. "I want! I want!" *The Illuminated Blake.* Annotated by David V. Erdman. Garden City, NY: Anchor/Doubleday, 1974.

Branch, Michael P., Rochelle Johnson, Daniel Patterson, and Scott Slovic, eds. *Reading the Earth: New Directions in the Study of Literature and the Environment.* Moscow: U of Idaho P, 1998.

Branch, Michael P., and Scott Slovic, eds. *The ISLE Reader: Ecocriticism, 1993–2003.* Athens: U of Georgia P, 2003.

Brinkmeyer, Robert H., Jr. *Remapping Southern Literature: Contemporary Southern Writers and the West.* Athens: U of Georgia P, 2000.

Brophy, Robert. "Robinson Jeffers: Poet of Carmel-Sur." In *Robinson Jeffers: Dimensions of a Poet,* edited by Robert Brophy, 1–18. New York: Fordham UP, 1995.

Buell, Lawrence. *The Environmental Imagination: Thoreau, Nature Writing, and the Formation of American Culture.* Cambridge, MA: Harvard UP, 1995.

———. *The Future of Environmental Criticism: Environmental Crisis and Literary Imagination.* Malden, MA: Blackwell, 2005.

———. *Writing for an Endangered World: Literature, Culture and Environment in the United States and Beyond.* Cambridge, MA: Harvard UP, 2001.

Calderazzo, John. *Rising Fire: Volcanoes and Our Inner Lives.* Guilford, CT: Lyons, 2004.

Christianson, Gale. *Greenhouse: The 200-Year Story of Global Warming.* 1999. Reprint, New York: Penguin, 2000.

Cohen, Michael P. "Blues in the Green: Ecocriticism under Critique." *Environmental History* 9, no. 1 (January 2004): 9–36.

Coke Water Wars. Ottawa, Ontario, Canada: Polaris Institute, 2003.

Crichton, Michael. *State of Fear*. New York: HarperCollins, 2004.

Cronon, William. "The Trouble with Wilderness; or, Getting Back to the Wrong Nature." In *Uncommon Ground: Toward Reinventing Nature*, 69–90. New York: Norton, 1996.

Crosby, Alfred W. *The Measure of Reality: Quantification and Western Society, 1250–1600*. New York: Cambridge UP, 1997.

Daly, Herman E. "The Steady-State Economy: Toward a Political Economy of Biophysical Equilibrium and Moral Growth." In *Valuing the Earth: Economics, Ecology, Ethics*, edited by Herman E. Daly and Kenneth N. Townsend, 325–63. Cambridge: MIT P, 1993.

Daniel, John. "Ourselves." In *Common Ground*, 62. Lewiston, ID: Confluence, 1988.

———. "Some Mortal Speculations." In *The Trail Home: Nature, Imagination, and the American West*, 193–202. 1992. New York: Pantheon, 1994.

Davis, Fred. *Yearning for Yesterday: A Sociology of Nostalgia*. New York: Free Press, 1979.

DeLoughrey, Elizabeth M., Renée K. Gosson, and George B. Handley, eds. *Caribbean Literature and the Environment: Between Nature and Culture*. Charlottesville: U of Virginia P, 2005.

DeMenocal, Peter. "After Tomorrow: The Peril of Ignoring Global Warming." *Orion* (January/February 2005): 16–23.

Deming, Alison Hawthorne. *Temporary Homelands: Essays on Nature, Spirit and Place*. 1994. Reprint, New York: Picador USA, 1996.

———. *Writing the Sacred into the Real*. Minneapolis: Milkweed, 2000.

Deming, Alison Hawthorne, and Lauret Savoy, eds. *The Colors of Nature: Culture, Identity, and the Natural World*. Minneapolis: Milkweed, 2002.

Deming, Alison Hawthorne, Richard Nelson, and Scott Russell Sanders. "Letter to *Orion* Readers." *Orion* (Autumn 1995): 5.

Dickey, James. *Deliverance*. 1970. Reprint, New York: Delta, 1994.

Dillard, Annie. *For the Time Being*. New York: Knopf, 1999.

———. "Living Like Weasels." In *Teaching a Stone to Talk*, 11–16. New York: Harper & Row, 1982.

Dodge, Jim. "Living by Life: Some Bioregional Theory and Practice." 1990. In *Literature and the Environment: Writings on Nature and Culture*, edited by Lorraine Anderson, John P. O'Grady, and Scott Slovic, 230–38. New York: Addison Wesley Longman, 1999.

Duncan, David James. *The River Why*. 1983. Reprint, New York: Bantam, 1984.

Easterbrook, Gregg. *A Moment on the Earth: The Coming Age of Environmental Optimism*. 1995. Reprint, New York: Penguin, 1996.

Edwards, Jonathan. *Images or Shadows of Divine Things*. 1948, ed. Perry Miller. Guilford, CT: Greenwood, 1977.

Efron, Edith. *The Apocalyptics: How Environmental Politics Controls What We Know About Cancer*. New York: Simon & Schuster, 1984.

Ehrlich, Paul. *The Population Bomb: Population Control or Race to Oblivion?*. New York: Ballantine, 1968.

Ehrlich, Paul R., and Anne H. Ehrlich. *Betrayal of Science and Reason: How Anti-Environmental Rhetoric Threatens Our Future.* Washington, DC: Island, 1996.

Elder, John. "Climbing the Crests." *ADE Bulletin* 117 (Fall 1997): 27–30.

———. *Imagining the Earth: Poetry and the Vision of Nature.* 1985. Athens: U of Georgia P, 1996.

———. *Pilgrimage to Vallombrosa: From Vermont to Italy in the Footsteps of George Perkins Marsh.* Charlottesville: U of Virginia P, 2006.

———. *Reading the Mountains of Home.* Cambridge, MA: Harvard UP, 1998.

———, ed. *American Nature Writers.* Vols. 1 and 2. New York: Scribner's, 1996.

Emmerich, Roland, dir. *The Day after Tomorrow.* Performances by Dennis Quaid and Jake Gyllenhaal. Los Angeles: Fox, 2004. Film.

Estok, Simon. "An Introduction to Shakespeare and Ecocriticism: The Special Cluster." *ISLE* 12, no. 2 (Summer 2005): 109–17.

———. "A Report Card on Ecocriticism." *Journal of the Australasian Universities Language and Literature Association* 96 (November 2001): 220–38.

Fritzell, Peter. *Nature Writing and America: Essays upon a Cultural Type.* Ames: Iowa State UP, 1990.

Fukuoka, Masanobu. *The One-Straw Revolution: An Introduction to Natural Farming.* 1975. Preface by Wendell Berry. Translated by Chris Pearce, Tsune Kurosawa, and Larry Korn. Emmaus, PA: Rodale, 1978.

Gaines, Susan M. *Carbon Dreams.* Berkeley: Creative Arts, 2001.

Garrard, Grey. *Ecocriticism.* New York: Routledge, 2004.

Gelbspan, Ross. *The Heat Is On: The Climate Crisis, the Cover-up, the Prescription.* Reading, MA: Perseus, 1997.

Gelpi, Albert. Introduction to *The Wild God of the World: An Anthology of Robinson Jeffers.* Stanford: Stanford UP, 2003.

Gessner, David. "The Punctured Pastoral." In *Sick of Nature,* 170–80. Hanover, NH: Dartmouth College P, 2004.

Gomides, Camilo. "Putting a New Definition of Ecocriticism to the Test: The Case of *The Burning Season,* a Film (Mal)Adaptation." *ISLE* 13, no. 1 (Winter 2006): 13–23.

Gore, Al. *An Inconvenient Truth: The Planetary Emergency of Global Warming and What We Can Do About It.* Emmaus, PA: Rodale, 2006.

Graulich, Melody. "Speaking across Boundaries and Sharing the Loss of a Child." *Private Voices, Public Lives: Women Speak on the Literary Life,* edited by Nancy Owen Nelson, 163–82. Denton: U of North Texas P, 1995.

Gregory, Robin, Sarah Lichtenstein, and Paul Slovic. "Valuing Environmental Resources: A Constructive Approach." *Journal of Risk and Uncertainty* 7 (1993): 177–97.

Guggenheim, Davis, dir. *An Inconvenient Truth.* Los Angeles: Paramount Classics, 2006. Film.

Hamilton, Joan. "The Danger Ahead." *Stanford Magazine* 34, no. 5 (September/October 2005): 48–55.

Hans, James S. *The Value(s) of Literature.* Albany, NY: SUNY P, 1990.

Hanson, Susan. "Homeland Security: Safe at Home in the World." In *Icons of Loss and Grace: Moments from the Natural World,* 136–44. Lubbock: Texas Tech UP, 2004.

Hardin, Garrett. *Filters against Folly: How to Survive Despite Economists, Ecologists, and the Merely Eloquent.* New York: Penguin, 1986.

Harrington, Henry, and John Tallmadge, eds. *Reading under the Sign of Nature.* Salt Lake City: U of Utah P, 2000.

Hass, Robert. "Listening and Making." In *Twentieth Century Pleasures: Prose on Poetry,* 107–33. New York: Ecco, 1984.

Heise, Ursula K. "The Hitchhiker's Guide to Ecocriticism." *PMLA* 121, no. 2 (March 2006): 503–16.

———. "Local Rock and Global Plastic: World Ecology and the Experience of Place." *Comparative Literature Studies* 41, no. 1 (2004): 126–52.

Hemingway, Ernest. "The End of Something." In *In Our Time,* 31–35. New York: Scribner, 1970.

Hoch, David, and Will Carrington Heath. "Tracking the ADC: Ranchers' Boon, Taxpayers' Burden, Wildlife's Bane." *Animal Law* 3 (1997): 163–87.

Hurston, Zora Neale. *Their Eyes Were Watching God.* 1937. Reprint, New York: Harper & Row, 1990.

Ixquic: Revista hispánica internacional de análistic y creación 2 (August 2000). Special Issue on Spanish and Latin American Ecocriticism, Department of Hispanic Studies, Monash University, Melbourne, Australia.

Iyer, Pico. *The Global Soul: Jet Lag, Shopping Malls, and the Search for Home.* 2000. New York: Vintage, 2001.

Jacobs, Jane. *The Nature of Economies.* New York: Modern Library/Random House, 2000.

Janovy, John, Jr. *10 Minute Ecologist: 20 Answered Questions for Busy People Facing Environmental Issues.* New York: St. Martin's, 1997.

Jeffers, Robinson. *The Wild God of the World: An Anthology of Robinson Jeffers,* ed. Albert Gelpi. Stanford: Stanford UP, 2003.

Jeffers Studies 8, no 1 (Spring 2004).

Kafka, Robert. "Jeffers's 1936 Ventana Creek Hike: A Miscellany." *Jeffers Studies* 8, no. 1 (Spring 2004): 31–50.

Karman, James. *Robinson Jeffers: Poet of California.* Brownsville, OR: Story Line Press, 1995.

———, ed. and intro. *Stones of the Sur.* Stanford: Stanford UP, 2001.

Kerridge, Richard, and Neil Sammells, eds. *Writing the Environment: Ecocriticism and Literature.* New York: St. Martin's, 1998.

Kingsolver, Barbara. *Small Wonder.* New York: HarperCollins, 2002.

Kittredge, William. *Owning It All.* Saint Paul, MN: Graywolf, 1987.

Kolbert, Elizabeth. *Field Notes from a Catastrophe: Man, Nature, and Climate Change.* New York: Bloomsbury, 2006.

Kowalewski, Michael. *Reading the West: New Essays on the Literature of the American West.* New York: Cambridge UP, 1996.

Landman, Janet. *Regret: The Persistence of the Possible.* New York: Oxford UP, 1993.

Landow, George P. *Elegant Jeremiahs: The Sage from Carlyle to Mailer.* Ithaca, NY: Cornell UP, 1986.

Leopold, Aldo. *A Sand County Almanac.* 1949. Reprint, New York: Ballantine, 1966.

Lewis, Corey Lee. *Reading the Trail: Exploring the Literature and Natural History of the California Crest.* Reno: U of Nevada P, 2005.

Lifton, Robert Jay. *Death in Life: Survivors of Hiroshima.* New York: Random House, 1967.

Lifton, Robert Jay, and Greg Mitchell. "The Age of Numbing." *Technology Review* (August/September 1995): 58–59.

Lippard, Lucy. *The Lure of the Local: Senses of Place in a Multicentered Society.* New York: New Press, 1997.

Lopez, Barry. *About This Life: Journeys on the Threshold of Memory.* New York: Knopf, 1998.

———. *Alan Magee: Inlets.* Portland, ME: Joan Whitney Payson Gallery of Art, Westbrook College, 1990.

———. Contribution to "Natural History: An Annotated Booklist." *Antaeus* 57 (Autumn 1986): 295–97.

———. *Field Notes: The Grace Note of the Canyon Wren.* New York: Avon, 1994.

———. "Occupancy." *Orion* (Spring 1995): n.p.

———. *Resistance.* New York: Knopf, 2004.

Love, Glen A. *Practical Ecocriticism: Literature, Biology, and the Environment.* Charlottesville: U of Virginia P, 2003.

———. "Revaluing Nature: Toward an Ecological Literary Criticism." *Western American Literature* (November 1991): 201–13.

Lynas, Mark. *High Tide: The Truth about Our Climate Crisis.* New York: Picador, 2003.

Malamud, Randy. *Poetic Animals and Animal Souls.* New York: Palgrave Macmillan, 2003.

Malthus, Thomas A. *An Essay on the Principles of Population.* 1798. New York: Penguin Classics, 1983.

Marshall, Ian. *Peak Experiences: Walking Meditations on Literature, Nature, and Need.* Charlottesville: U of Virginia P, 2003.

———. *Story Line: Exploring the Literature of the Appalachian Trail.* Charlottesville: U of Virginia P, 1998.

Masumoto, David Mas. *Four Seasons in Five Senses: Things Worth Savoring.* New York: Norton, 2003.

Mazel, David. *A Century of Early Ecocriticism.* Athens: U of Georgia P, 2001.

McKibben, Bill. *The Age of Missing Information.* New York: Random House, 1992.

———. *The Comforting Whirlwind: God, Job, and the Scale of Creation.* Grand Rapids, MI: William B. Eerdmans, 1994.

———. *The End of Nature.* 1989. Reprint, New York: Anchor/Doubleday, 1999.

———. "Global Warming, Genetic Engineering and Other Questions of Human Scale." Lecture presented at the Nevada Museum of Art, Reno, 12 March 2004.

———. *Maybe One: A Personal and Environmental Argument for Single-Child Families.* New York: Simon & Schuster, 1998.

———. "Year One of the Next Earth." In *In Katrina's Wake: Portraits of Loss from an Unnatural Disaster*, 9–15. New York: Princeton Architectural P, 2006.

McPhee, John. *Annals of the Former World*. New York: Farrar Straus Giroux, 1999.

Meadows, Donella H., Dennis L. Meadows, and Jorgen Randers. *Beyond Limits: Confronting Global Collapse, Envisioning a Sustainable Future*. White River Junction, VT.: Chelsea Green, 1993.

Middleton, Harry. *The Earth Is Enough: Growing Up in a World of Trout and Old Men*. New York: Simon & Schuster, 1989.

Mitchell, John Hanson. *Trespassing: An Inquiry into the Private Ownership of Land*. Reading, MA: Perseus, 1998.

Moore, Kathleen Dean. *Riverwalking: Reflections on Moving Water*. New York: Lyons P, 1995.

Morris, David Copland. "Reading Robinson Jeffers: Formalism, Poststructuralism, and the Inhumanist Turn." *Centennial Essays for Robinson Jeffers*, edited by Robert Zaller, 107–22. Wilmington: U of Delaware P, 1991.

Moyers, Bill. "On Receiving Harvard Med's Global Environment Citizen Award." 1 December 2004. http://www.truthout.org/article/bill-moyers-on-receiving-harvard-meds-global -environment-citizen-award.

Murphy, Patrick D. *Farther Afield in the Study of Nature-Oriented Literature*. Charlottesville: U of Virginia P, 2000.

———, ed. *The Literature of Nature: An International Sourcebook*. Chicago and London: Fitzroy Dearborn, 1998.

Nabhan, Gary Paul. *Coming Home to Eat: The Pleasures and Politics of Local Foods*. New York: Norton, 2002.

Nelson, Richard. *The Island Within*. New York: Vintage, 1989.

Nichols, John. *The Last Beautiful Days of Autumn*. New York: Holt, 1982.

Noda, Ken-ichi, and Scott Slovic, eds. *Environmental Approaches to American Literature: Toward the World of Nature*. Kyoto, Japan: Minerva, 1996.

Ornstein, Robert, and Paul Ehrlich. *New World New Mind: Moving Toward Conscious Evolution*. New York: Doubleday, 1989.

Payne, Daniel G. *Voices in the Wilderness: American Nature Writing and Environmental Politics*. Hanover, NH, and London: UP of New England, 1996.

Paz, Octavio. "Wind, Water, Stone." In *A Tree Within*, 25. Translated by Eliot Weinberger. New York: New Directions, 1988.

Peacock, Doug. *Grizzly Years: In Search of the American Wilderness*. New York: Zebra, 1990.

Perkins, John. *Confessions of an Economic Hit Man*. San Francisco: Berrett-Koehler, 2004.

Peterson, Anna L. *Being Human: Ethics, Environment, and Our Place in the World*. Berkeley: U of California P, 2001.

Peterson, Brenda. *Animal Heart*. San Francisco: Sierra Club Books, 2004.

Peterson, Roger Tory. Foreword to *Handbook for Butterfly Watchers*, by Robert Michael Pyle. 1984. Reprint, Boston: Houghton Mifflin, 1992.

Philippon, Daniel J. *Conserving Words: How American Nature Writers Shaped the Environmental Movement.* Athens: U of Georgia P, 2004.

Phillips, Dana. *The Truth of Ecology: Nature, Culture, and Literature in America.* New York: Oxford UP, 2003.

Pope, Carl. "Getting It Right." *Sierra* (January/February 2000): 40–47, 117.

Pyle, Robert Michael. *The Thunder Tree: Lessons from an Urban Wildland.* Boston: Houghton Mifflin, 1993.

———. *Walking the High Ridge: Life as Field Trip.* Minneapolis: Milkweed, 2000.

Quammen, David. E-mail to author, 28 May 1998.

———. *The Song of the Dodo: Island Biogeography in an Age of Extinction.* New York: Scribner, 1996.

Ray, Janisse. *Ecology of a Cracker Childhood.* Minneapolis: Milkweed, 1999.

Reed, T. V. "Toward an Environmental Justice Ecocriticism." In *The Environmental Justice Reader,* edited by Joni Adamson, Mei Mei Evans, and Rachel Stein, 145–62. Tucson: U of Arizona P, 2002.

Reidelsheimer, Thomas, dir. *Andy Goldsworthy: Rivers and Tides.* New York: New Video Group, 2004.

Rigby, Kate. "Ecocriticism." *Introducing Criticism at the 21st Century,* edited by Julian Wolfreys, 151–78. Edinburgh: Edinburgh UP, 2002.

Rogers, Pattiann. *Eating Bread and Honey.* Minneapolis: Milkweed, 1997.

Rolls, Eric. *A Celebration of the Senses.* 1984. Reprint, Brisbane, Australia: U of Queensland P, 1998.

Roorda, Randall. "Message from the President." *ASLE News* (Fall 2001): 1–2.

Rosaldo, Renato. *Culture and Truth: The Remaking of Social Analysis.* Boston: Beacon, 1989.

Rosendale, Steven, ed. *The Greening of Literary Scholarship: Literature, Theory, and the Environment.* Iowa City: U of Iowa P, 2002.

Ross, Andrew. *Strange Weather: Culture, Science and Technology in the Age of Limits.* New York: Verso, 1991.

Roy, Arundhati. *Power Politics.* Cambridge, MA: South End P, 2002.

Rozelle, Lee. *Ecosublime: Environmental Awe and Terror from New World to Oddworld.* Tuscaloosa: U of Alabama P, 2005.

Rueckert, William. "Literature and Ecology: An Experiment in Ecocriticism." 1978. In *The Ecocriticism Reader: Landmarks of Literary Ecology,* edited by Cheryll Glotfelty and Harold Fromm, 105–23. Athens: U of Georgia P, 1996.

Ryden, Kent. *Mapping the Invisible Landscape.* Iowa City: U of Iowa P, 1993.

Sanders, Scott Russell. *Terrarium.* 1985. Bloomington: Indiana up, 1995.

———. "Cloud Crossing." In *A Paradise of Bombs,* 49–57. 1987. Reprint, New York: Simon & Schuster, 1988.

———. "Speaking a Word for Nature." 1987. Reprint. In *Secrets of the Universe: Scenes from the Journey Home,* 205–27. Boston: Beacon, 1991.

——. "Speaking a Word for Nature." In *The Ecocriticism Reader*, edited by Cheryll Glotfelty and Harold Fromm, 182–95. Athens: U of Georgia P, 1996.

——. "Telling the Holy." In *Staying Put: Making a Home in a Restless World*, 143–69. Boston: Beacon, 1993.

Satterfield, Terre, and Scott Slovic, eds. *What's Nature Worth? Narrative Expressions of Environmental Values*. Salt Lake City: U of Utah P, 2004.

Satterfield, Theresa [Terre]. "Distinguishing Values from Valuation in a Policy-Relevant Manner." Proposal to the National Science Foundation, 28 February 1996.

Scherer, Glenn. "The Godly Must Be Crazy: Christian-right Views Are Swaying Politicians and Threatening the Environment." *Grist Magazine*, 27 October 2004. 21 December 2007, http://www.grist.org/news/maindish/2004/10/27/scherer-christian/.

Schneider, Stephen H. *Laboratory Earth: The Planetary Gamble We Can't Afford to Lose*. New York: HarperCollins, 1996.

Shiva, Vandana. *Building Water Democracy: People's Victory Against Coca-Cola in Plachimada*. New Delhi: Research Foundation for Science, Technology and Ecology, 2004.

——. *Staying Alive: Women, Ecology and Development*. London: Zed, 1989.

——. *Water Wars: Privatization, Pollution, and Profit*. Cambridge, MA: South End, 2002.

Shiva, Vandana, and Shalini Bhutani. *An Activist's Handbook on Intellectual Property Rights and Patents*. New Delhi: Research Foundation for Science, Technology and Ecology, 2001.

Silko, Leslie Marmon. *Ceremony*. New York: Penguin, 1977.

Slovic, Scott. "Beneath the Smooth Skin of X: Locality and Distance as Topoi of Environmental Literature." *Proceedings from UNR Symposium on Japanese and American Environmental Literature*, 186–99. Tokyo: Japanese Ministry of Education, 2002.

——. "Ecocriticism: Storytelling, Values, Communication, Contact." Paper delivered at the Western Literature Association Conference, Salt Lake City, 5–8 October 1994.

——. "'The eye commanded a vast space of country': Alexander von Humboldt's Comparative Method of Landscape Description." *Publication of the Society for Literature and Science* (May 1990): 4–10.

——. "Giving Expression to Nature: Voices of Environmental Literature." *Environment* (March 1999): 6–11, 25–32.

——. "A Paint Brush in One Hand and a Bucket of Water in the Other: Nature Writing and the Politics of Wilderness." 1994. Reprint, *The Literary Art and Activism of Rick Bass*, edited by O. Alan Weltzien, 11–29. Salt Lake City: U of Utah P, 2001.

——. *Seeking Awareness in American Nature Writing: Henry Thoreau, Annie Dillard, Edward Abbey, Wendell Berry, Barry Lopez*. Salt Lake City: U of Utah P, 1992.

Snyder, Gary. "The News Hour with Jim Lehrer." PBS video, 22 April 1996.

Solnit, Rebecca. *Hope in the Dark: Untold Histories, Wild Possibilities*. New York: Nation Books, 2004.

——. "Yucca Mountain: No Way to Contain the Waste." *San Francisco Chronicle*, 4 August 2002.

Speth, James Gustave. *Red Sky at Morning: America and the Crisis of the Global Environment*. New Haven: Yale UP, 2004.

Stegner, Wallace. *Angle of Repose*. Garden City, NY: Doubleday, 1971.

———. "Coda: Wilderness Letter." *The Sound of Mountain Water*, 145–53. 1969. Reprint, New York: Dutton, 1980.

Steinbeck, John. *The Grapes of Wrath*. 1939. Reprint, New York: Chelsea House, 1988.

Stevens, Wallace. "Sunday Morning." In *The Norton Anthology of Modern Poetry*, 2nd ed., edited by Richard Ellmann and Robert O'Clair, 281–84. New York: Norton, 1988.

Tallmadge, John. *The Cincinnati Arch: Learning from Nature in the City*. Athens: U of Georgia P, 2004.

———. *Meeting the Tree of Life: A Teacher's Path*. Salt Lake City: U of Utah P, 1997.

Tamkang Review 34, nos. 3–4 (Spring–Summer 2004). Special Issue on Ecological Discourse, edited by Jim Tarter. Published by the English Department, Tamkang University, Tamsui, Taipei, Taiwan.

Tannen, Deborah. *The Argument Culture: Stopping America's War of Words*. New York: Ballantine, 1998.

Thomashow, Mitchell. *Bringing the Biosphere Home: Learning to Perceive Global Environmental Change*. Cambridge, MA: MIT P, 2002.

Thoreau, Henry David. *The Journal of Henry D. Thoreau*, edited by Bradford Torrey and Francis H. Allen. Vol. 4. Boston: Houghton Mifflin, 1906.

———. *Walden*. 1854. Reprint, Princeton: Princeton UP, 1971.

Upgren, Arthur, and Jurgen Stock. *Weather: How It Works and Why It Matters*. Cambridge, MA: Perseus, 2000.

Weltzien, O. Alan. *The Literary Art and Activism of Rick Bass*. Salt Lake City: U of Utah P, 2001.

White, E. B. "I arise in the morning torn. . . ." *Yoga International* 87 (January 2006): 15.

———. "A Slight Sound at Evening." In *Essays of E. B. White*, 234–42. 1977. Reprint, New York, Harper Colophon, 1979.

White, Richard. "'Are You an Environmentalist or Do You Work for a Living?': Work and Nature." *Uncommon Ground: Toward Reinventing Nature*, edited by William Cronon, 171–85. New York: Norton, 1995.

Wiesel, Elie. "Peace Isn't Possible in Evil's Face: Rational People Must Intervene Against the Likes of Hussein." *Los Angeles Times*, 11 March 2003.

Wilkinson, Charles. *The Eagle Bird: Mapping a New West*. New York: Pantheon, 1992.

Williams, Terry Tempest. "Bloodlines." *Testimony: Writers of the West Speak on Behalf of Utah Wilderness*. 1995. Reprint, edited by Stephen Trimble and Terry Tempest Williams, 50–52. Minneapolis: Milkweed, 1996.

———. "A Man of Questions: A Tribute to Wallace Stegner, April 1, 1996." *Journal of Land, Resources, & Environmental Law* 17, no. 1 (1997): 1–7.

———. Note to author, 19 May 1998.

———. *Refuge: An Unnatural History of Family & Place*. New York: Pantheon, 1991.

———. *An Unspoken Hunger*. New York: Pantheon, 1994.

Wilson, Edward O. *Biophilia.* Cambridge: Harvard UP, 1984.

Winton, Tim. *Dirt Music.* Sydney: Picador/Pan Macmillan Australia, 2001.

Worster, Donald. *Dust Bowl: The Southern Plains in the 1930s.* New York: Oxford UP, 1979.

———. *Nature's Economy: A History of Ecological Ideas.* 1977. Reprint, Cambridge: Cambridge UP, 1985.

———. *The Wealth of Nature: Environmental History and the Ecological Imagination.* New York: Oxford UP, 1993.

Yamashita, Karen Tei. *Through the Arc of the Rain Forest.* St. Paul, MN: Coffee House, 1990.

Yeats, William Butler. "The Second Coming." *Selected Poems and Two Plays of William Butler Yeats,* edited by M. L. Rosenthal. New York: Collier, 1962.

Zepeda, Ofelia. "It Is Going to Rain." *Jewed 'I-Hoi/Earth Movements.* Tucson: Kore, 1997.

Zwinger, Ann. "What's a Nice Girl like Me Doing in a Place like This?" In *The Nearsighted Naturalist,* 281–90. Tucson: U of Arizona P, 1998.

Index